SHORT WALKS
IN LAKELAND

The River Rothay between Grasmere and Rydal Water (Walk 5)

SHORT WALKS IN LAKELAND

Book 1:
SOUTH LAKELAND

by

Aileen and Brian Evans

CICERONE PRESS
MILNTHORPE, CUMBRIA

ISBN 1 85284 144 3
First published 1994, Revised reprint 1997
© Aileen Evans and Brian Evans 1994
A catalogue record for this book is available from the British Library

This book is dedicated to
Albert and Betty Riding
true lovers of the fells and woodlands
whose joy in simple natural things spreads to those
privileged to know them

ACKNOWLEDGEMENTS

Our book would have been less accurate without the help of our chief check walkers, Maurice and Marjorie Tedd, whose comments and criticism proved invaluable. Others who helped include Raif and Alison Evans, Gladys Sellers and Anne Pilkington. Our meetings with the following footpath officers were most useful; Dave Thomas and Peter Rogers of the Lake District National Park, George Flynn of South Lakeland District Council and Keith Crocker of Cumbria County Council. We are especially grateful to Mr S.J.Power and David Wilkinson of the National Trust for their co-operation in establishing the permissive footpath to Low Park-a-Moor.

Other Cicerone Guide books by the same authors
SHORT WALKS IN LAKELAND Book 2: NORTH LAKELAND
SHORT WALKS IN LAKELAND Book 3: WEST LAKELAND (*in preparation*)
SCRAMBLES IN THE LAKE DISTRICT R. *Brian Evans*
MORE SCRAMBLES IN THE LAKE DISTRICT R. *Brian Evans*
WALKS IN THE SILVERDALE/ARNSIDE AREA R. *Brian Evans*
THE JURA: WALKING THE HIGH ROUTE and WINTER SKI TRAVERSES
    R.*Brian Evans* with *Kev Reynolds*
THE ISLE OF MAN COASTAL PATH *Aileen Evans*

Front cover: Looking across Grasmere from the ascent of Loughrigg

CONTENTS

ADVICE TO READERS

Readers are advised that whilst every effort is taken by the authors to ensure the accuracy of this guidebook, changes can occur which may affect the contents. A book of this nature with detailed descriptions and detailed maps is more prone to change than a more general guide. New fences and stiles appear, waymarking alters, there may be new buildings or eradication of old buildings. It is advisable to check locally on transport, accommodation, shops etc. but even rights-of-way can be altered, paths can be eradicated by landslip, forest clearances or changes of ownership. The publisher would welcome notes of any such changes.

The Goose Bield (Walk 16)

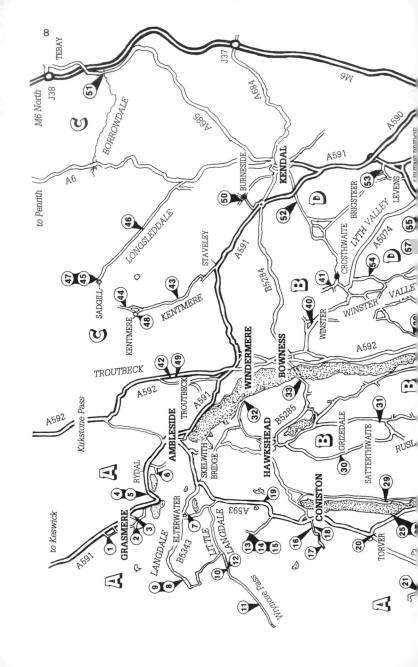

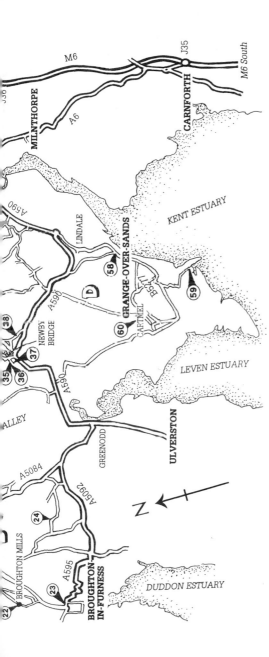

LOCATION OF THE WALKS

Ⓐ - THE CENTRAL FELLS No's 1 - 22

Ⓑ - AROUND CONISTON WATER & WINDERMERE No's 23 - 41

Ⓒ - THE EASTERN FELLS & DALES No's 42 - 52

Ⓓ - THE LIMESTONE FRINGE No's 53 - 60

PREFACE

This guidebook covers South Lakeland from Grasmere to the Kent Estuary; from the Coniston Fells to Kendal. It is an area rich in variety. There are rugged mountains of hard volcanic rocks where sparkling tarns mirror shapely peaks; the softer scenery of the Silurian rocks which create rounded hills now clothed in trees, edging the lakes of Windermere and Coniston Water; and the hills of grey limestone which run from Kendal to the coast. Here you walk on close cropped turf or through delightful woods, with airy views of distant fells and shimmering sea.

The walks are mostly short, yet enough to fill pleasantly a good half day, ideal for day visitors or family walkers. Some longer walks included could be split. It is not a high fell-walking guide, although several of the most popular summits are included. Priority is given to the lower fells, which our experience shows to be as rewarding as their higher brethren.

We have aimed to present a combination of comprehensive coverage, detailed route description and easy-to-follow maps in an interesting way. If you work your way through the walks you will, like us, retain many rich memories of some of England's most scenic countryside.

We hope you enjoy the walks as much as we have

Aileen and Brian Evans
Preston 1993

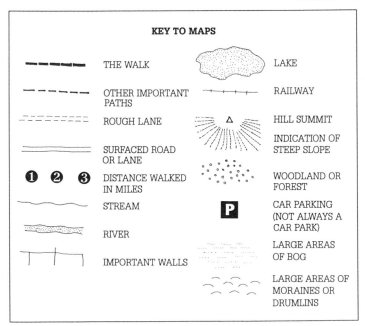

KEY TO MAPS

▬▬▬▬	THE WALK		LAKE
─ ─ ─ ─	OTHER IMPORTANT PATHS	─┼─┼─┼─	RAILWAY
‑ ‑ ‑ ‑ ‑	ROUGH LANE	Δ	HILL SUMMIT INDICATION OF STEEP SLOPE
══════	SURFACED ROAD OR LANE		WOODLAND OR FOREST
❶ ❷ ❸	DISTANCE WALKED IN MILES	**P**	CAR PARKING (NOT ALWAYS A CAR PARK)
	STREAM		
	RIVER		LARGE AREAS OF BOG
	IMPORTANT WALLS		LARGE AREAS OF MORAINES OR DRUMLINS

INTRODUCTION

The book is split into four sections: The Central Fells; Around Coniston Water and Windermere; The Eastern Dales and Fells; and The Limestone Fringe. Each has its distinctive character and appeal. Many of the walks are well used, particularly in summer, but other walks seek quieter places.

Maps

To locate your chosen walk, there is a complete map on pages 8 & 9 which pinpoints the start of the walks and shows approach roads. The individual maps show each walk in detail and should be clear enough for you to follow the route. It is helpful to have the relevant Ordnance Survey map which shows more of the surrounding area; these are specified in the route introductions with the following codes:

OL6	=	OS Outdoor Leisure No 6
		The English Lakes South Eastern Area 1:25,000
OL7	=	OS Outdoor Leisure No 7
		The English Lakes South Western Area 1:25,000
PF626	=	OS Pathfinder Sheet 626
		Broughton-in-Furness & Newby Bridge 1:25,000
PF627	=	OS Pathfinder Sheet 627 Milnthorpe 1:25,000
PF636	=	OS Pathfinder Sheet 636 Grange-over-Sands 1:25,000

Footwear and Clothing

Lightweight boots with a cleated rubber sole are the best footwear for almost all the walks, as there are usually some wet patches or rough ground to contend with. A wide range is available and as almost all the walks are on tracks or paths, there is no need to choose the most expensive boots. Comfort is the chief priority. In a dry spell in summer, trainers are quite adequate for many of the walks, although make sure the soles still retain good tread - care is needed on steep slopes.

Clothing needs to be sensible - bear in mind that even on a warm summer day it can be cold and windy on the fells. In winter snow and ice may render the high fells dangerous. The high fells can be wintry until May. Every year unprepared walkers die of exposure in unexpected bad weather. There are plenty of low level woodland walks in this book which are ideal for a day when conditions on the higher fells are dangerous or unpleasant.

The Lake District is notoriously wet and a wise walker never sets out without a waterproof / windproof, a jumper or pile jacket, warm trousers - not shorts. A small daysack completes the gear, with a torch for short winter days, a compass (you need to practise how to use one!) some spare food and drink.

A recommended book which tells you all you need to know about walking in the hills is *The Hillwalker's Manual* by Bill Birkett (Cicerone).

Access

Almost all the walks are on rights-of-way or permissive paths, or over fell country with open access and a long history of use. On the higher fells many of the paths are stony and worn. These have had a considerable amount of repair work done on them in recent years, with great success.

Please keep to paths instead of walking a parallel route which leads to ever greater erosion. However, the majority of walks described in this book are on paths which are pleasant underfoot. Where the paths go through farmland it is necessary to keep strictly to the path and these are usually waymarked, often with tiny yellow arrows. Away from the rough fells and forests, some of the paths cross pasture with grazing animals. Normally they do not bother walkers, although cows may be alarmingly interested in your dog, particularly if it is black and white. Occasionally they may have a bull with them - if in doubt as to your safety skirt the field to avoid problems.

Ornamental ironwork is a disappearing feature. This gate latch in Yewdale has been replaced by a modern gate.

Dogs should be under control at all times and on a lead when necessary.

Parking

The walks start where possible from recognised car parks or places where parked cars can be tucked well out of the way of other road users. Please park sensibly. Remember that the Lake District is no different from most other places in Britain and Western Europe with regard to thieving from parked cars. Take everything of value with you and leave doors locked and windows closed.

Directional instructions

Left and right are abbreviated to L and R in the text.

CHAPTER 1

The Central Fells

This is the area of rough fell country around Grasmere, Great and Little Langdale, the Coniston Fells and their southerly extension towards the coast.

Whilst this book is not specifically a hillwalking guide, it would be incomplete without including some of the popular summits. Precedence is given to the smaller hills which have all the character of their higher neighbours but without their eroded paths or long tiring ascents. The walks seek interesting places - tarns, woodlands, streams or relics of long gone industry. Often the paths used for our walks are ancient ways, once used by drovers, quarrymen and miners.

This is the area which attracts many visitors to the hills, for to most people it is the 'real' Lakeland. You will rarely be alone on the popular walks, although we do include several for the lover of solitude.

Where feasible the walks start from convenient parking places, away from the busy villages or towns, although this is not always possible. In summer, the car parks around Grasmere and Ambleside become very crowded. In Central Lakeland it is the policy of the National Park to charge a fee at their busiest car parks.

Most of the walks in this section encounter some wet patches and rough paths, so boots are strongly advised. Note that even the lower fells can be confusing in mist and remember to take enough warm clothing to combat cold and windy conditions on the heights.

Swaledale ewe

WALK 1: Helm Crag & Greenburn

SUMMARY: Helm Crag, with its distinctive summit rocks, the Lion and the Lamb, is a magnet for all who visit Grasmere. It can be ascended easily in a very short walk from the village, but the route described is a more varied and interesting way. It visits the quiet valley of Greenburn with its distinctive glacial combe, then climbs to the Gibson Knott ridge by an ancient barely discernible pony track and finally the exhilarating hill crest culminating in the arresting viewpoint of Helm Crag. Return via Lancrigg Woods.

HOW TO GET THERE AND PARKING: From the A591 Ambleside to Grasmere road, 1½ miles north of Grasmere take the turning to Town Head. Park on the grass verge just before Raise Beck Bridge.

Distance:	5¼ miles 8½km
Grade:	Strenuous
Terrain:	Medium fell and valley walk
Summits:	Helm Crag - 1306ft (398m) Gibson Knott
Map:	OL7

THE WALK: Cross the bridge and turn R up the 'Private Driveway'. As the way climbs, Town Head appears as a picturesque group of buildings backed by the flanks of Great Rigg, Fairfield and Seat Sandal. Pass a group of cottages and enter the National Trust Greenburn boundary by the left hand gate. Now facing into the valley the Green Burn is white with falls and cascades. Go along the path beside the wall, then through a gate where the path continues with unrestricted views of the tumbling burn.

[N.B. The footbridge left gives access to a very steep direct path up Helm Crag, via a gap in a wall, a stone stile, a ladder stile, the col of Bracken Hause* then turn L to the summit.]

Carry on through the next gate between walls and on up the valley. An iron wheel on a leat hints at a farm water supply. The path still climbs and it is worth pausing for the classic view of 'The Lion and the Lamb'. *The old path is well preserved as it rounds a spur of rocks, it stands a tribute to the builders of these fine Lakeland pony tracks.* Cross the water leat and pass a small dam with a reminder not to pollute the drinking water. The path bends to touch a broken wall. Cross a small stream. The path now appears to fork but it is just a dual carriageway · choose your lane and carry on up the valley.

On reaching Greenburn Bottom you are sure to be impressed by the atmosphere of this lonely glacial corrie, its flat floor occupied by a plant-rich bog held captive by drumlins - rounded heaps of glacial moraine.

Turn L and cross the outlet stream using a wobbly boulder hop. The path continues making a rising traverse up the left (south-west) side of the valley. Pass a sheepfold, built by utilising huge boulders as cornerstones. Cross a side stream and continue to ascend below a two-buttress outcrop. The path levels at a green platform with a cairn. (Directly opposite across the valley is silhouetted a prominent stone on Blakerigg Crag.) Turn L up the hillside. The path is meagre and disappears as it reaches a wet area. Keep left of the rushes and straight up to a tiny cairn. (A rock resembling a begging dog shows on the skyline above.) The path soon becomes obvious again and bends right as the old pony track is encountered on a rising traverse once more. Pass boulders and under a crag with scree. Keep on the path which rises more steeply now to a sharp bend left and a final pull up to a cairn.

Here we leave the old pony track, which wends its way right to the head of Wythburn and over to Borrowdale.

Greenburn Bottom

Looking back along the ridge from Helm Crag

Here we leave the old pony track, which wends its way right to the head of Wythburn and over to Borrowdale.

Carry straight on to the next large cairn at the junction with the ridge top path and a face-on view across Far Easedale to Deer Bield Crag, Easedale and Wetherlam on the far horizon.

At the large cairn turn L along the ridge top path. This path is well trodden and runs along the NE side of Far Easedale over hummocky Gibson Knott to Bracken Hause, the col before Helm Crag. It has ups and downs with windings here and there but is easy to follow and allows you to enjoy the superb views it offers.

At the junction of cross paths on the broad open col of Bracken Hause keep straight on. (The path right (SW) goes to Far Easdale and Grasmere. The path left (NE) drops steeply into Greenburn*.)

Keep straight on where huge cairns indicate the unmistakable path up Helm Crag to the summit. There is a short easy rock step on nearing the top and the crowning rock protrudes from a grassy platform.

WARNING: The Greenburn side of the summit falls away in overhanging crags.

After admiring the extensive view continue along the path to the

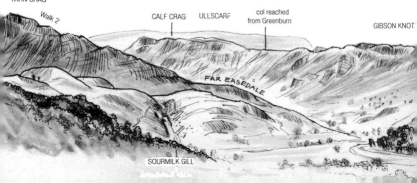

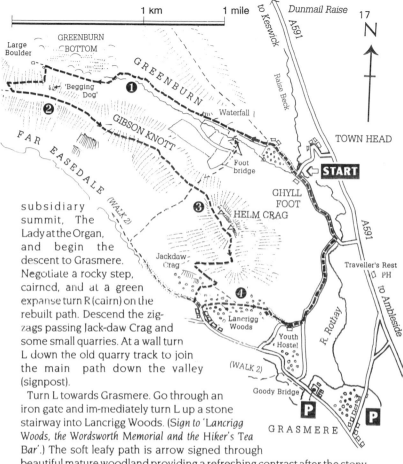

1 km — 1 mile

to Keswick — *Dunmail Raise* — A591

N

GREENBURN BOTTOM

Large Boulder

GREENBURN

GIBSON KNOTT

'Begging Dog'

❶

❷

FAR EASEDALE (WALK 2)

Waterfall

Raise Beck

TOWN HEAD

Foot bridge

⬅ START

GHYLL FOOT

HELM CRAG

❸

A591

Jackdaw Crag

❹

Traveller's Rest PH

to Ambleside

Lancrigg Woods

R. Rothay

Youth Hostel

(WALK 2)

Goody Bridge

P   P

GRASMERE

subsidiary summit, The Lady at the Organ, and begin the descent to Grasmere. Negotiate a rocky step, cairned, and at a green expanse turn R (cairn) on the rebuilt path. Descend the zig-zags passing Jack-daw Crag and some small quarries. At a wall turn L down the old quarry track to join the main path down the valley (signpost).

Turn L towards Grasmere. Go through an iron gate and im-mediately turn L up a stone stairway into Lancrigg Woods. (Sign to 'Lancrigg Woods, the Wordsworth Memorial and the Hiker's Tea Bar'.) The soft leafy path is arrow signed through beautiful mature woodland providing a refreshing contrast after the stony descent. We find it aptly named The Poet's Walk at the next building. Carry on to Lancrigg Hotel and The Hiker's Tea Bar which we can recommend.

HELM CRAG

At the next junction turn L again, past the Youth Hostel to a surfaced lane. Turn L and carry on for 1 mile past Underhelm Farm, Keep L at the junction by Low Mill Bridge and continue to the cottages at Ghyll Foot. Turn R over the bridge to the start.

WALK 2: Easedale Tarn, Codale Tarn and Tarn Crag

SUMMARY: Easedale Tarn set in its drumlin spattered hollow, is perhaps the most popular short walk from Grasmere. This walk extends further up the valley to skirt the rocky peak of Belles Knott and visit placid Codale Tarn on its remote upland shelf. Return is over the ridge of Tarn Crag, a fine viewpoint. Rough and wet in parts - boots recommended.

HOW TO GET THERE AND PARKING: There are three car parks in Grasmere village, the two described being the most convenient for this walk in order of preference.

1). About half a mile along the road to Goody Bridge and Easedale from the village a small car park is on the right. This convenient car park fills up at weekends in summer with walkers making for the high fells.

2). On the Keswick road from the village is a large official car park. On leaving the car park cross the road and just before the Rothay Bridge take

Distance:	6¼ miles 10km
Grade:	Strenuous
Terrain:	Medium fell and valley
Summit:	Tarn Crag - 1801ft (560m)
Maps:	OL6/7

the footpath to Butterlip Howe. This pleasant shady path rises over a low ridge and descends to join the Easedale road where you turn right soon passing car park 1.

Upper Easedale from the outlet of Easedale Tarn

TARN CRAG

BELLES KNOTT

CODALE TARN (behind)

THE WALK: Continue on a roadside path to Goody Bridge and turn L on the path signed Easedale Tarn. The footpath goes over a wooden bridge, a stone-slab bridge then through an iron gate and Easedale is spread before you. As *you progress across the meadows you will realise why visitors to Grasmere are*

Belles Knott

drawn, in never decreasing numbers, on a pilgrimage to Easedale Tarn. The flanks of Silver How on the left and Helm Crag on the right channel the eye to the cascades of Sourmilk Gill, pouring as if from an unknown source, yet replenished by Easedale Tarn hidden in its upland hollow.

The path continues between a wall and the stream into the heart of the valley. Go through a gate into the open pasture and cross to a bridge. Bear L, signed to Easedale Tarn, and continue to a gate with holly trees standing like sentries. The path now begins to rise and you are face to face with the lovely cascades. Go through the intake gate. *This section of path was once a real penance but it is now smoothed, bridged and drained allowing all to enjoy the intimacy of the tumbling water in the gill and not on the path.*

When level with the top of the waterfalls the angle eases as the path crosses a reedy basin. The main path is cairned and begins to rise once more and suddenly the tarn is spread before you. *After the heat of the climb there is always a cooling breeze (or howling gale) induced by the valley at this spot and a few stones by the big boulder is all that is left of a former Victorian tearoom shelter. The island boulder however has its resident blackheaded gull to oversee the disposal of titbits left by hungry walkers.*

SHORT RETURN: Cross the tarn outlet stream and turn R. A small path descends the north side of the stream and turns away over a slight shoulder, where the main route from Tarn Crag rejoins before descending to the bridge at Stythwaite Steps in Far Easedale.

TO CONTINUE THE ROUTE: Do not cross the outlet but take the path on the L (south) of the tarn. The cirque of mountains is higher and in dull weather their grim slopes can imbue a feeling of foreboding when reflected in the deep waters, but the path is easy to follow as it threads its way along the moor and past the show of water lilies and cotton grass at the tarn's end. The rock cone of Belles Knott is now prominent ahead right with the

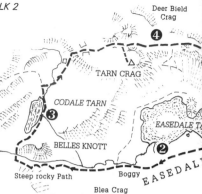

dark crags of Blea Rigg to the left.
The path is narrow and occasional
stone-hops over spongy morasses
interrupt the pace. Height is
continually gained and you may be
entertained by the sight of
scramblers puzzling their way up
the crags of Belles Knott. Now the
climb becomes steeper and
impressive rock scenery is to either
side. On gaining the brow the angle
eases revealing the triangular bulk
of Sergeant Man ahead.

The path forks. Turn R and cross the stream. (The path to the L goes over
to Langdale via Stickle Tarn.) Our path now works its way round the back
of Belles Knott where Codale Tarn awaits. A true mountain tarn, it is
tranquil and unfrequented. Circle its grassy shore on the R (east) by a small
path crossing the outlet stream on the way. It would be sad to leave
without spending a few moments by the water, reaping the reward the
climb has earned. The path leaves by a big boulder on the right. Cross a
small peaty stream to a flat area of rushes. A path to Sergeant Man bends
left by a crag and a rowan, this is not our way. Bend R to cross the peaty
stream again and follow it upstream keeping on its right in the direction of
an old walled sheepfold. On the facing hillside is a narrow but distinct path.

Go up this path which zigzags up a slight spur passing a billberry scree
slope to gain the Tarn Crag ridge. Turn R at the path junction and stroll
easily along enjoying the broad sweep of the sky supported on a colonnade
of peaks. A good path now passes rocky outcrops, peat hags and the
private grassy haunts of lone sheep. Stop beyond an evil looking bog-hole
just before the path begins a descent through a rock gateway. Turn R on
the trace of a path which passes a small pool whence the cairn on the
summit of Tarn Crag will guide you to its satisfying viewpoint.

Return to the rock gateway to continue the descent. Note the line of the
path as it makes its way down the ridge. On reaching a grassy saddle take
care not to deviate R to Easedale Tarn but keep on the now undulating
ridge path. Look out for a sharp bend L taking care as the path drops
steeply to avoid the crags ahead. Keep to the path, cairn, which steepens
then becomes a green trod through bracken. Do not be seduced by
attractive sheep trods to either side but keep ahead to meet the major
path (short return).

Turn L into Far Easedale. There are now yellow arrow waymarks and a

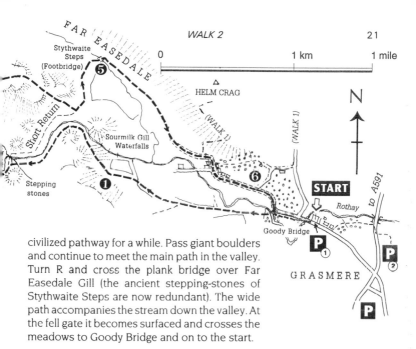

civilized pathway for a while. Pass giant boulders and continue to meet the main path in the valley. Turn R and cross the plank bridge over Far Easedale Gill (the ancient stepping-stones of Stythwaite Steps are now redundant). The wide path accompanies the stream down the valley. At the fell gate it becomes surfaced and crosses the meadows to Goody Bridge and on to the start.

Herdwick Sheep

This hardy breed of sheep is well suited to the rigours of the weather encountered in the central fells of the Lake District. It is said that the Herdwick has its roots in Spain and arrived in the Lake District after a shipwreck on the Cumberland coast at the time of the Armada. More probably, the breed was already long established in the area. The sturdy short legged white faced Herdwick is a familiar sight, together with the black faced, grey muzzled Swaledale.

Most of the ewes spend the whole year on the fell, apart from mating late in the year and lambing in April when they are gathered into the fields close to the farm. The sheep are dipped to control pests, however your dog may pick up sheep ticks from the bracken as it walks past. The tick nips into the dog's skin and sucks its blood until it resembles a tiny grape. The best way to remove the tick without leaving its nippers behind is to swab it with insect repellent or methylated spirits then extract it firmly with fine tweezers.

WALK 3: Silver How

SUMMARY: A popular ascent from Grasmere, Silver How is a fine grandstand from which to enjoy the view over Grasmere vale and lakes. Having reached the summit it seems a pity to go down straight away, so the route describes a gentle stroll along the broad grassy ridge which stretches westwards, past tarns and knolls to the grassy dome of Swinescar Pike. An interesting descent through giant juniper to the well kept parkland around Allan Bank is enhanced by the views over Helm Crag and Easedale.

The route recommended includes surprisingly pleasant riverside paths to start and finish.

Distance:	5 miles 8km
Grade:	Moderate. Medium fell walk. Good paths
Summits:	Silver How - 1296ft (395m)
	Swinescar Pike - 1344ft (410m)
Map:	OL7

HOW TO GET THERE AND PARKING: There are 4 car parks in Grasmere. This walk can be done from any of these, but the parking for cars only on the B5287 leading north out of

The view west from Silver How

PIKE O'
BLISCO

CRINKLE CRAGS

THE BAND

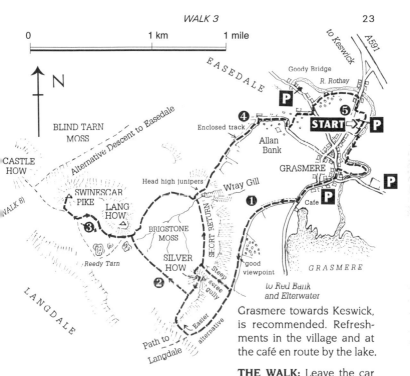

Grasmere towards Keswick, is recommended. Refreshments in the village and at the café en route by the lake.

THE WALK: Leave the car park by the footbridge over the River Rothay which leads onto the riverside walk. This attractive footpath has been specially constructed allowing the disabled to enjoy this pleasant way into the village.

At the village street turn L for 50 yards passing the churchyard where a constant stream of international pilgrims pays homage at William Wordsworth's grave. Turn R into Red Bank Road and pass the Tourist Information Office, a telephone box and a car park. *Ahead are the slopes of*

Silver How and to the right across the fields stands the ochre building of Allan Bank, the third of Wordsworth's homes (1808-1813) in Grasmere. He disliked the house saying it was 'a temple of abomination with smoking chimneys which couldn't heat the rooms'.

When level with the cafe at the end of Grasmere (the mere) turn R on a footpath to Langdale. An old walled pathway rises boldly to the fell gate, (yellow waymark arrows) then crosses a field passing a set of smooth glaciated rock slabs to an exit gate. Keep the wall on your left and go through a kissing gate in the cross wall. Cross a stream - in wet weather a series of pretty miniature cascades - and continue along the line of the wall. Pass a cairn then take a halt at a level grassy area for a view of the Grasmere valley in all its splendour. At the next cairn (somewhat flattened) the wall bends away to the left. Turn R and take the steep and rather daunting red path. (A longer but less tiring way continues ahead to a col. From here turn R for the summit ridge of Silver How.) The upward grind is mocked by the refreshing sounds of water trickling unseen below the scree but the large cairn on the col above is soon reached with its view over a boggy basin to Sergeant Man and the head of Easedale. Bear L on a small path which zigzags up a short distance to the summit of Silver How where the circular panorama is magnificent.

SHORT RETURN: Re-trace your steps to the large cairn on the col then turn L and down. The path bends right around the eastern edge of the boggy basin of Brigstone Moss. Cross the stream which flows into Wray Gill and on joining the other return routes turn R*.

SILVER HOW TO LANG HOW TARN

Before you leave the summit examine the way ahead. From the cairn go along the summit platform for 10 yards to an elongated shallow pool. Turn R, go down into a depression then right again on a slight cross path. You should be facing the Langdale Pikes (W). The path becomes more prominent as it keeps fairly level and above the west side of the boggy basin for quarter of a mile and sports the occasional cairn. Suddenly the tarn appears where a growth of bog bean makes an attractive foreground for a photograph so typically Lakeland. Cross the outlet stream and follow the shore to a path junction and tarn cairn.

TO RETURN: Turn R**
TO CONTINUE: Turn L

TARN TO SWINESCAR PIKE

The continuing walk is an easy quarter of a mile and very rewarding. Turn L at the tarn and follow the path as it passes between the

HELVELLYN DOLLYWAGGON PIKE SEAT SANDAL
NETHERMOST PIKE

hump of Lang How and the larger overgrown tarn at the head of Robin Gill. This elevated broad ridge between Easedale and Langdale possesses the atmosphere of the mountains. The path is well cairned and the modest summit of Swinescar Pike, its cairn resembling a broken tooth, is visible. The path skirts the Pike on its left. Turn R from the path and walk the final few feet up the grass to the summit.

Return by the same route to the tarn cairn. Here join return**.

A clear path descends to the level of the Brigstone Moss, and passes along its north-western side. A small cairn confirms the direction seemingly straight over the edge into thin air.

HERE JOIN SHORT RETURN*: Keep on and arrive at the head of Wray Gill. The wooded ravine contains a cascading gill which is worth leaving the path to peep into. Work your way down the gillside path which soon bends left (cairns) between head-high juniper bushes to join another stream. Enter a walled - and once paved - path at a kissing gate and carry on to a second kissing gate by a barn. Go ahead to a surfaced lane then turn R to Grasmere. There are lovely views of the valley and Allan Bank, seen on the outward route, is on the right. Turn L on a grass track towards a white house, and on getting nearer stay in the field along the fenceside to gain the road by an iron gate and retro sign to Score Crag. Turn L along the road for 50 yards then turn R on the public footpath just before the houses. This path now leads over Butharlyp Howe, a delightful wooded knoll by the River Rothay. At the road turn R, cross over the road and onto the riverside path. Follow it to the start.

Mammilated topography

The plateau between Silver How and Swinescar Pike is what the geographers call a 'mammilated topography'. During the Ice Age when glaciers carved out the Lakeland valleys the ice sheet covered the Silver How plateau, smoothing it into rounded hillocks and hollows, whilst the higher more rugged slopes of Castle How and Blea Rigg further along the ridge remained free of ice and its smoothing effect.

Looking over Grasmere village to the fells beyond

FAIRFIELD   STONE ARTHUR   GREAT RIGG   HART CRAG   BUTTER CRAG   DOVE CRAG   ALCOCK TARN   HERON PIKE

WALK 4: Alcock Tarn & Grasmere

SUMMARY: A strenuous short walk which climbs the steep fellside of Butter Crag by a delightful path through woods, to placid little Alcock Tarn. Views across the Vale of Grasmere are idyllic. A steep descent into Grasmere is followed by a visit to Wordsworth's Dove Cottage and a final stroll through the woods at the end of Grasmere lake. The walk is described from White Moss where the parking is less likely to be full than in Grasmere. A very popular walk.

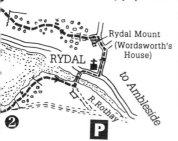

Distance:	4¼ miles 6¾km
Grade:	Strenuous
Terrain:	Medium fell walk
	Good paths but steep in parts
Summits:	1214ft (370m)
Map:	OL7

HOW TO GET THERE AND PARKING: A591 north of Ambleside (3 miles) to White Moss Common. There are parking areas on both sides of the road. The walk begins from the east side opposite the toilets.

THE WALK: Set off on a broad track from the public footpath signpost by 'The Coach House' gate. It is immediately attractive and climbs beside a stream with a small waterfall. Fork L and follow the stream as you climb a wooded hillside. Cross the stream easily at a rock slab with a pool and continue up the opposite bank. Leave the little vale and veer L crossing more open ground. Views, curtailed by the wooded valley, begin to appear as height is gained. Climb a bracken slope then pass by twin hawthorns to a gate in a wall. *A plaque in a rock just before the gate tells of* W.H.Hills *a lover of the fells.* Turn L on the surfaced lane for 50 yards to a junction.

[A tiny log bridge L and the ensuing path - wet in parts - leads to the fine summit viewpoint of White Moss Common. Return the same way.]

Continue along the lane past a pond (which must be a botanist's paradise) and Heugh Folds. The lane descends - look for a seat by a track on the R, with a pristine view of Grasmere and Silver How. Turn R along the track, public footpath sign to Alcock Tarn. At Wood Close and National Trust sign Bracken Fell turn L through the gate. A wide path rises gently through a mature woodland to another gate in an iron fence. The fellside is very steep and rocky but the path climbs considerably in sweeping zigzags. There are seats, placed at intervals, which insist you sample their rewarding vistas. Pass a small pond R and an iron gate R. The road can be seen rising to Dunmail Raise. And what a bird's eye view of Grasmere village, set about with velvet water meadows.

Go through a gate with NT sign Alcock Tarn. Pass a stand of larches and rocky Grey Crag looms ahead. The path bends L over a little stone-arched bridge and traverses below the crag, then curves back to the summit and the climb is done (*see panorama*). Turn L to a gap in the wall and on over smooth green turf from which the tarn appears most unexpectedly. Stroll along the water's edge to the far end (*ignore the gate* L), to a stile/gate in the wall. Pass a boggy area and a massive cairn (of encouragement for those toiling up our descent route). A little path of set stones indicates the direction of the descent. Keep on the cairned path which steepens considerably, dropping into the side of Greenhead Gill. The steep path demands your close attention until you meet the forest corner and turn L.

View from path up to Alcock Tarn

The bridge crossing the Gill is the aqueduct built in 1892 *which carries the water main from Thirlmere to Manchester.* Pass a seat and keep by the wall to the streamside but do not cross here. Turn L by the wall then cross by a lower footbridge, then L through a gate to join a lane. Walk quarter of a mile to the road. (Return sign public footpath to Greenhead Gill and Alcock Tarn.) Turn L and at the triangle bear R to the main road (A591) at the Swan Hotel - bus stop - telephone box.

Turn L along the main road in the direction of Ambleside. At the neat stone church of Our Lady of the Wayside cross the busy road to use the pavement on the other side. Go through a gate R onto a path. After the steep, earthy descent the flat valley floor, with its lush green meadows, is a welcome contrast. Go through another gate and keep by the R-hand wall/fence. Proceed through a kissing gate opposite a stand of fir. Cross the field slightly rightwards to the next kissing gate, in duplicate. Looking up to the east there is a good view of Grey Crag and our route. *An odd bare swathe running straight up the fellside is worn by Grasmere Sports runners in the Fell Race.*

Keep in the same direction to a gap between some trees and a more distinct track which leads to a kissing gate by the River Rothay. Keep ahead then bend R past the old school and Workmen's Reading Room, and the new school to the village - bus stop, telephone, toilets etc. Turn L on the B5287 for 300 yards to the main road. Cross the A591 and go along the minor road to pass Dove Cottage - *Wordsworth Museum* .

Keep ahead where a narrow lane forks off R and climb steeply to a double road junction. Pass a pond and fork R signed to Ambleside. Go over the rise and look on the L for a gate marked with two white spots. Go through and here the character changes once more. Walk along the narrow footpath through a woodland with young oak saplings until joining the road again. Pass a garage, then look for an iron gate with white indicator spots on the R. The path leads down through an oak wood, sweet with bluebells in the spring, to the main road. Cross to gain the pavement and turn L. The road is not too unpleasant as the waters of Grasmere lap the wall and the reflections of Silver How draw your eyes across the

ER HOW
BOWFELL HARRISON STICKLE PAVEY ARK SERGEANT MAN HIGH RAISE TARN CRAG ULLSCARF HELM CRAG

EASEDALE
ALLEN BANK
GRASMERE VILLAGE

shining surface. After 150 yards look for a white arrow R and steps into a lovely beech wood. Follow the path over wooden bridges to the lake outlet. Keep on the L bank of the river on a clear path through the wood, and a field to the picnic area with toilets adjacent to the car parking areas and the start.

Grindstone at Dove Cottage

Dunmail Raise

This important pass from Ambleside to Keswick was named after Dunmail, the last Norse king of Cumbria who was defeated in battle at the pass in AD 945 against Edmund of England. Some say the pile of stones around which the modern road reverently splits, is Dunmail's grave, and others that he lived on to marry a Cheshire princess and was killed in France by the Saracens on a pilgrimage to Rome.

Dove Cottage

Dove Cottage is now Wordsworth's shrine. He did his best work there. Now it is a Wordsworth museum and bookshop specialising in Lakeland books. It was formerly a pub, The Dove and Olive Branch, on the turnpike.

Gramere Sports

Grasmere Sports is a renowned gathering held on the third Thursday in August. Traditional are the wrestling, hound trailing and fell race.

Grasmere

Grasmere takes it name from 'Grismere' - the lake of the pigs. Pigs were kept in the forest, but as the forest dwindled sheep became more important.

Grasmere and Helm Crag

Greenhead Gill

Greenhead Gill has some old copper mine levels exploited in the sixteenth century by German miners.

WALK 5: Around Rydal Water

Sketch map on page 26

Sketch map on page 26

Distance:	3½ miles 5½km
Grade:	Easy
Terrain:	Valley walk on good paths
Map:	OL7

SUMMARY: The short, easy walk around lovely Rydal Water is one of the most popular in the Lakes, on good paths with idyllic views over Wordsworth's country - a beautiful mix of richly-hued fellside, woods and the ever-placid lake, only marred by the drone of traffic on the busy road. You will meet many people old and young on this walk, in all kinds of footwear. A longer walk is easily acheived by combining walks 4 and 5.

HOW TO GET THERE AND PARKING: Park at one of the large car parks on White Moss Common situated between Rydal Water and Grasmere on

the A 591 Ambleside to Keswick road. The route is described from the left-hand car park when approaching from Ambleside.

THE WALK: Leave the car park by the gate near the information board. The popular broad path passes the Wetland Conservation Area (toilets to the right by the road wall). Cross a tiny bridge over a small stream and on through an area of grassland by the River Rothay. Year-long, whatever the weather, this beautiful vale draws its admirers. A footbridge spans the river (beyond is a yellow arrowed waymarked route rising steeply up the hillside) however, our route does not cross the bridge but keeps upstream on the right bank. Go through a kissing gate, cross the field and exit at another kissing gate. Take the onward rising path through the oakwood ignoring the path branching right. Mount the rise then descend to a footbridge at the outflow of Grasmere. Cross the river and turn right along the causeway. Go a little way along the lakeshore. Here is a splendid view across the water to the surrounding fells. *While the adults gaze the youngsters can dam a little stream, build on the beach, skim pebbles on the water or clamber on the causeway; it is a spot for all to enjoy.*

Turn back to the causeway and take the path slanting up the bracken slopes. (The Loughrigg Terrace path can be seen traversing the fellside at a higher level on the right.) The path gradually rises to run by a wall and joins the waymarked path from the first river bridge. At the junction go ahead between the seat and the fence on a narrow traversing path to a second seat and on to join the Terrace path. Below on the left lies Rydal Water, brimful of reflections, with Heron Pike beyond. Keep in the same direction of travel but now on the Loughrigg Terrace path and cross several small streams trickling from the craggy slopes above. The path rises to a bench seat with a worthy view then beyond suddenly ends on a flat dressing floor surrounded by tall larches. In the crag on the right is Loughrigg Cave, a disused quarry now taken over by a family of yellow wagtails. You may see them if you approach quietly but will not if you call up the resident echo. **WARNING:** The water in the pool is deep.

Descend on the quarry track between the larches. Pass two more quarries. *If you are tempted to scramble into the easy-looking one be warned. It is easy to climb in but awkward to get out.* Keep on, crossing a stream, then choose a path to descend steeply left to gain the one by the waterside. Go through an iron kissing gate and enter Rydal Woods. Stroll along the waterside through Wordsworth country to leave the woodland at a gate. Keep ahead and cross the emerging river's footbridge. At the A591 turn R for 100 yards, cross, then turn L to Rydal Mount.

On the left is St Mary's church and the renowned Dora's field (planted with daffodils by Wordsworth for his daughter). The road rises past Rydal

The summit of Silver How, with Fairfield behind (Walk 3)
The new generation of Lakeland paths - this one winds up Loughrigg (Walk 6)

Elterwater forms a perfect foreground to the Langdale Pikes (Walk 7)
Tiny upland tarns are common on the fells (Walk 6)

Hall to Rydal Mount, the home of William Wordsworth from 1813 to 1850.

Rydal Mount: Mar - Oct.   9-30 to 5-00
                            Nov - Feb.   10-00 to 4-00
                            Closed Tuesdays in winter

Keep up the steep road then turn L on the Public Bridleway to Grasmere. The gate leads into an enclosed way, once the old road. Go through a gate and along the gently rising way through the woodland. Gates and gaps in the wall act as frames for views south across the lake to Loughrigg Fell but stay your enthusiasm as this can be enjoyed uninterrupted a little further on.

Until 1824 when Rydal church was built coffins were taken along this road for burial at Grasmere church. Look out for the Coffin Stone used to give the bearers a respite. This stretch became known as the 'Coffin Trail'. The old roads kept above the valley base to avoid swamps. Horse-drawn coaches were the main form of transport until the advent of steam-powered motor buses around 1905.

The way runs under Nab Scar. Keep on the level upper path and along past a wall retaining a tiny dam. (A short-cut return can be made by turning L after the next gate.) Continue on the bridle path past Brockstone where the track becomes surfaced.

[From this point a ten-minute expedition to the summit of White Moss Common, an excellent viewpoint, can be made. We say expedition because a multitude of paths and trods, with wet patches, criss-cross the slopes. Return by the same way.]

Turn L on a track which leads steeply down crossing a stream to the road opposite the toilets and parking.

Still in use the Coffin Stone serves as backrest to a welcome seat

WALK 6: Loughrigg

SUMMARY: A fell walk in miniature which captures the spirit of Lakeland, with extensive views over wooded valleys where lakes reflect the surrounding richly hued fellsides. The summit is reached by a stiff climb to reveal an intricate plateau of hummocks and hollows, some of which hold attractive tarns. There is a network of confusing paths, so save this walk for a clear day. If you like company then this walk will suit you, for the Grasmere area is one of the busiest in Lakeland.

HOW TO GET THERE AND PARKING: About 1 mile north of Ambleside on the A591 Keswick road, turn L at Pelter Bridge on a minor lane. Immediately over the bridge turn R and in 100 yards there is a small car park on the left.

Distance:	4¹⁄₄ miles 6³⁄₄km
Grade:	Moderate
Terrain:	Medium Fell walk
Summits:	1099ft (335m)
Map:	OL7

THE WALK: Turn L up the winding road and immediately gain height towards the level of Loughrigg Terrace. On passing the last cottage the road becomes an unsurfaced quarry track towards the old Loughrigg Quarries, the largest of which has been elevated in status and is often known as Loughrigg Cave or Rydal Cave. After the next gate keep on the upper path where opportune seats invite appreciation of the beautiful view over Rydal Water. Carry on along the path which leads to the quarries.

(If you fancy scrambling into the first one note that, like a lobster pot, it is easier to get in than to get out. It is best to postpone your interest for 100yds until you reach the great cave where you can greet the resident echo before going inside to be impressed.)

This cave is a good objective with very young children where they can dam the tiny emerging stream, feed the incumbent robin and play on the dressing floor under your watchful eye, but be warned the shallow water becomes very deep near the left-hand cave wall. **Note that quarried caves have collapsed recently**

To continue turn R at the edge of the dressing floor. Keep L on the upper path which is the Terrace running almost level across the fellside (seat) and above a plantation. On passing the plantation keep high on the L fork. Over the brow the vale of Grasmere backed by Silver How comes into sight. Join the wider path rising up from the right and continue along the terrace. *However many times you walk this well-loved path you will never see the gentle vale clothed in the same hue.*

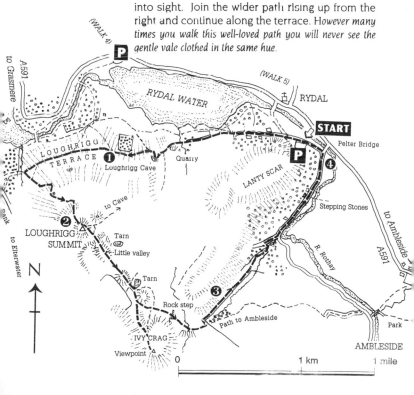

On approaching the wood at the end of the terrace we turn L up the steep newly-repaired path. *Before doing this you may like to cross the stream and go to the gate at Deer Bolts Wood. The wall ahead is of unusual construction, its protruding through stones being pierced to hold an extension fence above, presumably once a deer fence.*

The Langdale Pikes from Loughrigg

Climb up the steep path to a large cairn where the U-shaped pass of Dunmail Raise and Far Easedale now stretch north of Grasmere village. Pass a small rock bar to a grassy shelf. Keep L on the broad swathe to the large cairn on the first summit. From here you can enjoy a wonderful mountain panorama at ease whilst those who have dashed up the direct path recover their composure. The path to the summit triangulation point is clear ahead. *As you walk along consider Loughrigg itself - once a single peak it was shorn by glacial ice into mammilated topography, the array of humps and tarn-filled hollows we see today.*

Set off from the summit, ahead is a flat area with cairns. Head for the left-hand cairn (towards Windermere), drop steeply into a scree-sided shallow valley, or trough. Continue down the line of the trough, cairns, along a well-walked path. Presently a wall comes into sight on the right. Keep ahead on the main path, over the next rise is a minute tarn in a gap. (Off to the left is a larger tarn which is worth visiting.) Keep on to face the next hillock with two pools linked by a stream at its feet (the narrow yet prominent path over its left shoulder ends in soggy ground). Turn R to join a bigger path and circle left round the hillock for 100yds to a cairn .*

DIVERSION TO IVY CRAG - Recommended ¼mile

Fork R on a green path passing a cairn. From the path, which keeps to the high ground, you can look west to Loughrigg Tarn and over lower Langdale to the Coniston Fells beyond. Straight ahead is the little cairn on Ivy Crag, with its generous view of Windermere and offering a glimpse of Coniston Water too on a clear day.

Return to the cairn* or in 50yds descend and short-cut R to join the path lower down.

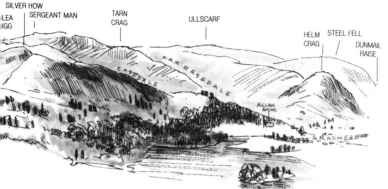

SILVER HOW
LEA
IGG
SERGEANT MAN
TARN CRAG
ULLSCARF
HELM CRAG
STEEL FELL
DUNMAIL RAISE
FAR EASEDALE
EASEDALE
ALLAN BANK
GRASMERE

TO CONTINUE

From the cairn* go downhill to a boggy shelf (join shortcut from Ivy Crag), and continue on the cairned path. Take care at a steep band of rock and carry on to cross a stream. Keep straight on over the next brow. On approaching the intake walls turn L on a small path which skirts the wall-held bog. (The main path, to Ambleside, goes through the gate and by a plantation.) Bend R holding to the line of the wall. It is refreshing to be off the beaten track as this quiet little path steals between the wall and the foot of a holly-decked rocky knoll. Make your way down Fox Ghyll through arches of rhododendrons to the gurgles of the stream. Cross a slab bridge and up steps to an iron kissing gate. Continue along a leaf-mould path to the road and River Rothay. Turn L along the road to the stepping stones where a merry interlude to the far bank and back will cheer the last bit of road walk. Just before Pelter Bridge turn L to the car park.

Stepping stones over the River Rothay

Wetherlam from Elterwater

WALK 7: Elterwater, Little Langdale & Great Langdale

SUMMARY: A varied walk with several alternatives. Elterwater to Skelwith Force is classic Lakeland with a backdrop of fine fells across a reed-edged lake. Colwith Force is more retiring, hidden amongst attractive woods. The return to Elterwater can be extended by a quiet woodland and riverside walk, or for those with energy to spare there is a strenuous fell finish along an airy balcony path with splendid views. The walk is so good that it is worth doing again for the alternatives you missed the first time! Boots recommended for the fell finish.

Distance:	8 miles 12³/₄km or 9¹/₄ miles 15km
Grade:	Easy by the riverside path. Valley walk
	Strenuous by the fell finish. Valley and low fell
Summit:	951ft (1290m)
Map:	OL7

HOW TO GET THERE & PARKING: Start at the public car park in Elterwater village.

THE WALK: From the car park take the path signed 'to Skelwith Bridge'. It is a well made footpath which follows the bank of Great Langdale Beck downstream. *Inevitably this superbly beautiful and easily accessible stretch of the Cumbria Way is very popular, but the path is wide enough for all to share and the music of the hurrying water muffles the tramp of many feet.*

Soon Elterwater is in sight and at a footbridge over a stream the path becomes less formal and bends away from the river. Cross another bridge and follow the path through a bluebell wood. Go through a kissing gate in

Colwith Force

a wall into open lakeside parkland. *The water now slides out of Elterwater as the River Brathay and makes its lazy way onward; an ideal spot from which to paint, photograph or just admire the classic view up Langdale.* Walk on across the short turf keeping left of a rocky knoll to a gate in the wall ahead. Both the path and the River Brathay now change character. The path narrows and there is a metal platform on the right from which to contemplate the river as it frets in its gorge and plunges over Skelwith Force. Continue along the wallside path to the factory of the Kirkstone Green Slate Quarries. Go straight through its interesting yard. Just beyond is the craft gallery and cafe. *An up-to-date weather forecast is usually pinned to the cafe door.* Keep by the river past cottages to the road bridge.

CAUTION: The next short stretch of busy road has blind corners and no pavements.

Turn R over the bridge then right again up the Coniston road. Take the second public footpath, on the right, signed to Colwith Bridge.

Go through a gate to the left of the private road onto a narrow path which enters light woodland and winds uphill and over a brow. At the junction with a track keep R along it to pass a cottage. There is an attractive corner where the water from a little spring merges into a 'Percy Thrower' garden. Climb the stile by the spring and cross a field with woodland on the left to a track. Pass by the towbars of a small caravan site which must possess one of the finest mobile views in the Lake

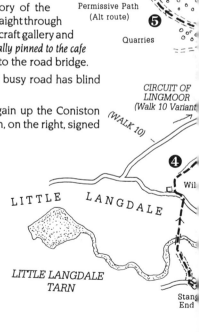

Slate Fences   Harry Place

FELL FINISH

CIRCUIT OF LINGMOOR
(Walk 10 Variant)

GREAT

Needle

6

Oak Howe

THE RIVERSIDE PATH

LANGDALE

LINGMOOR FELL

Baysbrown

Permissive Path
(Alt route)

5

Quarries

Balcony Pa...

CIRCUIT OF LINGMOOR
(Walk 10 Variant)

(WALK 10)

4

Wil...

LITTLE   LANGDALE

LITTLE LANGDALE TARN

Stang End

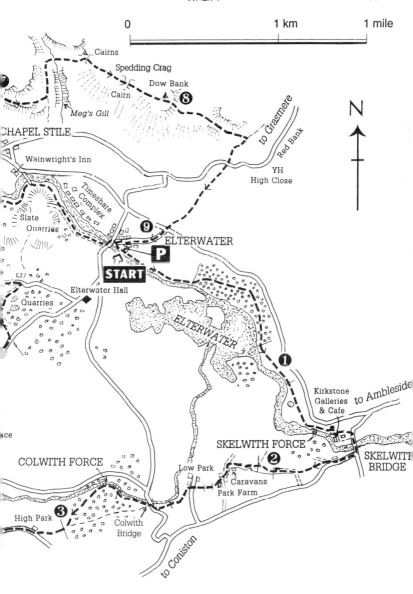

0   1 km   1 mile

Cairns
Spedding Crag
Dow Bank **8**
Cairn
Meg's Gill

CHAPEL STILE
Wainwright's Inn
Timeshare Complex
Slate Quarries
9
ELTERWATER
Quarries
Elterwater Hall
P
START
Elterwater Hall

to Grasmere
Red Bank
YH High Close

N

ELTERWATER

1
Kirkstone Galleries & Cafe
to Ambleside

ce
COLWITH FORCE
Low Park
SKELWITH FORCE
2
Caravans
Park Farm
SKELWITH BRIDGE

High Park **3**
Colwith Bridge
to Coniston

District for to the right the gently wooded lowlands of Great Langdale contrast with the bleak felltops of the Langdale Pikes. The track bears left and becomes gravelled through the yard of Park Farm. As you pass the building on the left notice the stonemason's alphabet built into its wall. Look now for the arrowed path between the outbuildings leading to a stile in the wall ahead.

The small path is easily followed over stiles and becomes enclosed before crossing a surfaced lane. Go through a rusty kissing gate opposite and across a pasture, the open aspect giving views over Little Langdale to Wetherlam and Crinkle Crags. Do not climb the next stile with gay abandon, it is on the very edge of a sheer bank with the river far below. Go down the steep path (care needed if at all wet) to a stile by the waterside, cross the field to a step stile and the road (sign to Skelwith Bridge).

(Short return by road to Elterwater village for the weary 1 1/4 miles.)

Turn R along the road for 50 yards. On the left before the river bridge take a footpath (public footpath sign) with steps up the wall into the woodland. The major path goes straight on but we turn immediately R on the permissive path to Colwith Force. The path is narrow and makes its rooty way upstream. Soon the roar of Colwith Force can be heard then the falls seen as the Little Langdale Beck plunges in a fine cascade and twin torrents.

There are good opportunities for taking photographs as the gorge is wide and the curve of its walls amenable but children and dogs should be kept under strict control.

Make your way upstream on any of the paths you fancy until they plait together to cross a tiny stream and broken fence by an old wall. The path now leaves the river and rises through a larch wood, bending left under a mighty beech. Continue up the rising path to join the public footpath keeping right to a gate which opens onto the fell pasture (Key signpost to Colwith Force if walking in the opposite direction). Turn R along the wallside, blue arrow, to another gate on the right. Follow the direction arrows through the High Park farmstead to the road. Turn R along the road.

(Our route does not take the next path right which goes down to the river, but if you want to test your nerve there are stepping-stones which are sometimes dry. Go up the field on the opposite side of the river to the road and turn L to join the route by Wilson Place.)

Go ahead on the narrow road enjoying the scenery. *The thin ribbon of road winding up Little Langdale to Wrynose Pass was one of the principal routes of ancient times from coastal Ravenglass to Ambleside.* The next farm is Stang End. Bend R (arrow to Millgarth) and through a gate right by a cottage into a green walled lane. This leads through a picturesque landscape to a gateway. Cross the field ahead to a substantial wooden footbridge over the river and up the field ahead to reach the road by a white house. Turn L on the narrow road for a few yards then R up the lane past Wilson Place Farm. Footpath sign. A gate gives access to the fell ahead. Keep straight on up the track staying by the fence to reach a step stile then a slit stile. Now bear L on a white stony path by gorse bushes. Just before reaching the flat saddle near the end of Lingmoor Fell take a break to look south. *The silent spoil heaps of Tilberthwaite stand testimony to the time when quarrying was in its heyday some 200 years ago.*

Join the bridle road from Little Langdale to Elterwater at a gate. Turn R towards Elterwater. (Follow this road for a short return to Elterwater.)

To continue our route after a gateway on the bridle path, fork L on an old path which cuts up through woodland. The pathway has an abandoned air and winds over a crest between mossy walls and descends past a new plantation and old quarry workings in the woods to cross a wider track. Turn L on the surfaced road by a house.

(Turn R on the road for short return to Elterwater.)

This is a lovely way to walk up Langdale. The road winds through Baysbrown Wood where trickling water alternates with birdsong, although all too soon the woodland ends and the farm at Baysbrown is reached. *This was the earliest settlement in Upper Langdale.* Keep straight on above the buildings, over the cattle-grid and along the track. Fork L (signs) on a rising quarry track and enter Hag Wood. Branch R from the quarry track, small bridleway sign. Slow down and look through gaps in the trees to the skyline ahead, for from here is a rare appearance of the square-topped profile of Oak Howe Needle (somewhat blunt from this angle).

The woodland ends and by the sides of the track bare rocks scored by passing glaciers provide a perch from which to survey the route onwards across the flat floor of Great Langdale and the ascent of Spedding Crag. Keep along the wallside past a high-walled sheepfold and a gate. The way underfoot now becomes stony and descends, curving rightwards to Oak Howe Farm. The farmhouse sits on a peninsula of rock thrust out into the space of the valley and host to fine mature pines. Here we say *"bonne route"* to the Cumbria Way as it turns off left and we pass in front of the house and walk down the track to the bridge over the Great Langdale Beck.

RIVERSIDE RETURN TO ELTERWATER

Follow the track through the meadows by the river and at a bridge keep straight on into light woodland along a permissive footpath (yellow waymarks). This is a delightful stretch where the river chuckles its way over mossy stones. Cross a small sidestream by the slate quarry spoils and join a better path. Across a footbridge is the Wainwright's Inn, once 'The Langdales'. If you're not gasping for a drink continue on the south side of the stream to join a quarry road. *Across the stream you can admire the Langdale timeshare complex built on the site of the old gunpowder factory. It has turned an eyesore into a pleasant collection of timber and stone chalets - one of the country's better timeshare efforts.* Stroll along the lane to reach the bridge at Elterwater. Now you can have your drink at the Britannia across the green!

FELL FINISH

If you have energy left to continue on the final part of the route you will not regret the effort, it will be an elating experience. Go over the R.W. 'Bill' Bailey memorial bridge and maintain direction through three fields, the path through the third passing by a thorn and slate hedge. At the road (footpath sign) turn R past Harry Place Farm. *This sunny south facing flank of Langdale has several sixteenth- to seventeenth-century 'statesmen's' farms.See page* 267. Look for the next footpath sign pointing steeply uphill on the left. Go up to the gate in the intake fence, then follow the wall using faint traces of a zigzag path to ease the climb. By the time the wall corner is reached the views are becoming splendid. Turn R and take the more gently rising path first along the intake wall, but presently the path leaves the wallside and veers left to a skyline shelf with a craggy knoll, where you can have the chocolate-bar-stop you have promised yourself, and feast your eyes on the head of Langdale and its circlet of mountain splendour.

Pass the craggy knoll and continue on the upward-slanting path across the hillside. Cross a stream then make your way up and over the grassy promontory of Thrang Crag. Descend briefly to cross a stream then by a second stream look carefully for a small cairn indicating the path ahead which traverses up and across the craggy hillside - it looks somewhat

exciting. Check your bootlaces and keep your eyes on the narrow path and not on the unfolding gleam of Windermere and the distant Bowland Hills. Keep on past scree slopes and the next rise reveals deeply cut Meg's Gill barring the way. Cairns now accompany the path. Climb steeply to the point where Meg's Gill can be crossed. A lonely group of shrubs poised on the lip of a waterfall and the thread of a path continuing right show the crossing place. The angle is now more gentle. Turn R over the gill and along the exposed but sound traversing path from which you can admire the cascades. When the traversing path evaporates, go straight up the turf to a small neat cairn then on to a larger untidy one on the crest of the ridge.

Turn R - south-east - along the comfortable ridge-top path which is well supplied with cairns and has, in marked contrast to the rest of the walk, a mountain atmosphere and views to match. It is now downhill all the way so freewheel along and admire Grasmere and Rydal Water backed by the grand mass of the Fairfield fells.

Keep on to the end of the ridge until above Elterwater village where a grandstand appraisal of most of the route can be made. The path now becomes steep and stony and slants down to the Red Bank road. Cross the road and choose one of the many paths across the common. Cross the main Langdale road and walk on into Elterwater village and the start.

Elterwater

'Elptarvatn' - swan's lake. Whooper swans from Scandinavia are sometimes seen here in winter, along with merganser. The lake is shallow and is gradually being filled with silt. Above Chapel Stile the flat valley floor is an old lake bed completely silted up.

Kirkstone Galleries

Tea rooms, art gallery, craft shop and slate showrooms on the site of a 17th-century corn mill. The path from the top of Skelwith Force follows the line of the old mill leat. Specimens of polished sawn slate show the attractive patterns formed by the ripples in the beds. Lakeland slate is used as a decorative and hard-wearing facing in many buildings world-wide. The howitzer cannon on the gallery forecourt was used to test gunpowder made in the nearby gunpowder factory.

The Langdale Timeshare Complex

Langdale Timeshare Complex is an admirable example of how such schemes can benefit an area. It is built on what was the derelict site of the old gunpowder factory (1824-1918). Little remains of the South Lakeland gunpowder factory sites as Board of Trade regulations required careful destruction of the works so that no explosive remained. Chapel Stile and Elterwater villages developed due to quarrying and the gunpowder factory.

WALK 8:

Langdale - Blea Rigg & Stickle Tarn

Stickle Tarn with Pavey Ark

SUMMARY: This walk escapes the crowds by starting along the climbers' path to White Gill and Scout Crag, continuing above the intake wall on little-walked tracks (dense seasonal bracken) to reach an old smooth green pony track which zigzags up the steep hillside. Views up the valley are splendid.

Once the ridge is gained you will encounter fell walkers again, over the knobbly summit of Blea Rigg where the dark crags of Pavey Ark dominate the background. A grassy descent to Stickle Tarn is followed by the steep rough track by Stickle Gill, where relief is found when the paved track is gained. Boots recommended. The ridge could be very confusing in mist.

HOW TO GET THERE AND PARKING: Park at the National Trust site at New Dungeon Gill, Langdale (refreshments, toilets).

Distance:	4³/₄ miles 7¹/₂km
Grade:	Strenuous
Terrain:	Medium fell walk
Summit::	Blea Rigg - 830ft (558m)
Maps:	OL6/7

THE WALK: Start on the path to Stickle Gill (Mill Gill) for 20 yards. Turn R through a gap in the wall into a field then L under a holly arch and over a bridge. Cross a stone slab bridge over a side stream, and follow up the bank on a newly laid path

HARRISON STICKLE   PAVEY ARK   BLEA RIGG   SERGEANT MAN

Blea Rigg from the ridgetop path

(sign Path to White Gill). A kissing gate right gives access to the open fell. Go along the path above the intake wall and here the walk's fine views begin. Pass a larch plantation and the bottom of White Gill. *This popular climbing crag can be seen high on its right with the climb 'Do Knot' in profile.* Cross the dry gill and keep along the intake wall. *Above is Scout Crag - a popular playground for rock climbers with 'L' plates.* The path now descends a little then rises again to be obstructed by a small crag. TAKE CARE. Where the path appears to end at an edge, turn uphill for 30 feet to make a crossing behind a holly tree (as the sheep do). Work your way down to the wall again and follow the path when the wall swings away. Rise up to a collection of boulders meeting with the wall again. Go steeply uphill then traverse again. Cross Scale Gill - a good place for a rest with a view - continue on the wallside path crossing a gill with pretty little waterfalls, to a ladder stile (to right, Right of way path to road). Turn L on the old pony track to Easedale (cairned) which rises diagonally up the hill to a lone holly tree. Set up a steady headbent plod, as views enlarge, to a streamside ash, then bend L up to a zigzag and past a pathless area of rushes to the wide ridge. Here we join the ridge path from Silver How.

Turn L towards Little Castle How. Pass a ruin and stone shelter. The path is well walked and well cairned and rises to the knolls of Little Castle How. Descend to a col and ascend the other side to Great Castle How. In front looms shapeless Blea Rigg with the flat-topped summit of Harrison Stickle behind. Descend to cross a depression, pass a small tarn. Continue up a little gangway, on and over the shoulder of Blea Rigg. Cairns are now less frequent but the path is well defined along the broad summit ridge. The going is more or less level. Pass peat hags and a small tarn and fenced area to the left. Bend round a rock hump and begin the descent, the path is on beaten grass at first but now passes the odd cairn. Take a dog-leg round a boggy area and arrive by beautiful Stickle Tarn. Keep along the tarnside path, enjoying the reflection of Pavey Ark's screes and crags, to the dam.

At the dam cross the outlet stream and turn L down the right side of the

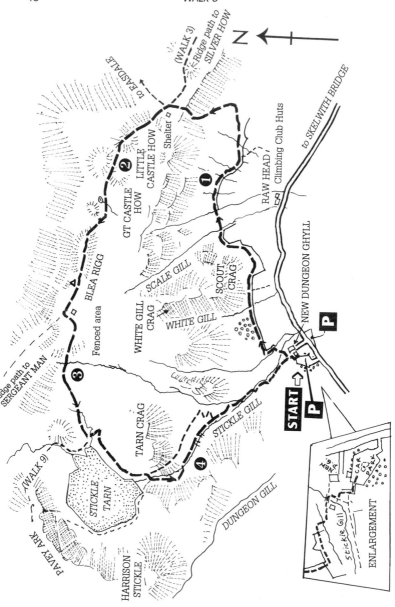

N

(Ridge path to SILVER HOW (WALK 3))

to EASEDALE

to SKELWITH BRIDGE

Shelter

LITTLE CASTLE HOW

②

GT CASTLE HOW

Climbing Club Huts

RAW HEAD

①

BLEA RIGG

Fenced area

SCALE GILL

WHITE GILL CRAG

SCOUT CRAG

WHITE GILL

NEW DUNGEON GHYLL

P

Ridge path to SERGEANT MAN

③

TARN CRAG

START

P

STICKLE GILL

④

STICKLE TARN

(WALK 9)

DUNGEON GILL

PAVEY ARK

HARRISON STICKLE

ENLARGEMENT

NEW DUNGEON GHYLL

CAR PARK

CAR PARK

Stickle Gill

gill on a steep path. (If the water is high take the path down the near side of the gill.) You may think that this is the roughest walking of the day - but persevere. The path has been re-layed, stay on it crossing the stream again and passing waterfalls down to the car park.

Stickle Tarn
Stickle Tarn was dammed to provide a head of water for the Chapel Stile gunpowder factory. The gunpowder was used by the local quarrying industry.

WALK 9: The Langdale Pikes

Loft Crag above Gimmer Crag with Harrison Stickle behind, seen from Pike o' Stickle

SUMMARY: One of the most popular objectives for walkers here are the three bold summits of the Langdale Pikes - Pavey Ark, Harrison Stickle and Pike o' Stickle. Their craggy profiles are a familiar sight to

Distance:	4¹/₂ miles 7¹/₄km
Grade:	Strenuous
Terrain:	High fell walk on rough paths
Summits:	Pavey Ark - 2297ft (700m)
	Harrison Stickle - 2415ft (736m)
	Pike o' Stickle - 2362ft (709m)
Map:	OL6

all visitors to the Lakes, yet their ascent is surprisingly easy, only Pike o' Stickle requiring a little scramble.

The route described takes the old pony track towards Tarn Crag, much pleasanter underfoot than the more obvious route by Stickle Gill, to reach Stickle Tarn. Pavey Ark succumbs to a flanking route on the right of its steep crags, to gain the plateau at its top. Harrison Stickle proves a simple stroll, thence across the head of Dungeon Gill to the final scrambly cone of Pike o' Stickle. Descent is made by a recently laid track above the Dungeon Gill ravine, past the viewpoint of Pike How to finish again on a laid track.

The work of the National Trust in this area deserves praise. Much work has been done in re-laying worn out paths by the old techniques of 'pitching' used centuries ago to make long-lasting pony tracks. Descent of the steep worn paths was a nightmarish experience, now it is a dream.

HOW TO GET THERE AND PARKING: At the New Dungeon Gill car park (refreshments, toilets), Langdale.

THE WALK: From the far end of the car park a path winds through a walled enclosure to reach the side of Stickle Gill, which flows prettily down a series of steps, pools and cascades. The broad paved path rises to cross a bridge where the view is well worth savouring – downstream

across Langdale to Side Pike and Lingmoor, upstream to the cascades of the gill and the rocky knoll of Tarn Crag on the right.

Continue up the pitched stone path, cross a small sidestream and pass a fenced enclosure which protects small saplings. At the next tiny sidestream, don't cross the slab bridge, but take a narrow paved path on the right. (The main path continues to Stickle Tarn and is the choice of most walks, but we recommend the route described. It is quieter, better underfoot and gains height more easily.) No description is needed for a while, just follow the paved way until it ends at a rocky section below Tarn Crag.

Continue at this level traversing a grassy shelf to join the broad, stony path on the right of the main stream. Keep up this path until rewarded by the splendid sight of Stickle Tarn and Pavey Ark.

It is valuable to sit awhile by the dam and study the skyline of Pavey Ark right to left as this is more or less our onward route. Turn R and walk on the tarnside. Note glacial erratic boulders. Cross stepping-stones and ignore a path branching right which leads to Castle How and Easedale.

The tarnside is now rather spongy, but you can use the jumble of stones to keep dry and gain a path on the right of the inlet stream. At the next cairn branch L to cross the stream. Now climb the steepening stony but well cairned path to reach a grassy shoulder. Follow the rake, straight, and sandwiched between the rocks, in a viewless concentrated effort to emerge onto this tame hinterland of the Langdale Pikes. The path bends left. Go through a boggy gap in a wall and wend your way to the conical summit of Pavey Ark (2297ft-700m). *Even though not graced with a cairn the situation is itself stunning for you are perched on top of the crag with Stickle Tarn glinting far below, a situation enjoyed by countless rock climbers and scramblers drawn to the classic climbs and scramble of Jack's Rake.* Before leaving, look at the onward path to Harrison Stickle - our next summit. Continue along the worn rocks of knobbly volcanic ash moving back through the intermittent wall to cross the outlet of a little tarn. The path spreads out with many threads, so keep to the line of the cairns, passing three small tarns, then descend to a gap. Note this spot for our way on. Go straight ahead up the slope to the summit of Harrison Stickle (2415ft-736m) the highest of the Langdale Pikes. The rock summit has several cairns to visit and the crags plunging away on the Langdale side are of rhyolite - a rough knobbly rock so enjoyed by scramblers.

Return to the gap. Turn L on reaching it and look across the shallow valley of Harrison Combe to Pike o' Stickle. Make a quick descent to the flat-bottomed combe, the gathering ground of Dungeon Gill (the path branching left is our descent route to Langdale). Cross the boggy area and stream then keep ahead (W) joining a better path traversing past Loft Crag

Dungeon Gill and Harrison Stickle from Pike How

until the climb to Pike o' Stickle begins. Cross the top of the South Scree stone chute, a wind tunnel on the calmest day and site of the Neolithic stone axe factory. A *notice requesting walkers not to descend the chute is placed at the top.*

The path steepens as we approach the rocky summit cone. There are two ways to conquer the final 100 feet.

a) Turn L opposite a large boulder for the easier scrambling path and return the same way.

b) Keep on the main path until faced with a steep descending cleft. Clamber L up a five-foot rock step followed by a stepped gully to the summit (2362ft-709m). The views are excellent but the star attraction is Gimmer Crag and its rock sport.

Return to the top of South Scree Gully. Keep on the path which passes under Loft Crag to cross the steam at the head of the Dungeon Gill, then turn R. The path is narrow but well trodden and cairned. Now the scene changes to make a sudden and dramatic descent beside the chasm. The path is being pitch-paved at the time of writing and heads straight towards Pike How. The path passes to its right but it is well worth climbing its pimple for a retrospective view of the Pikes. Return to the paved path

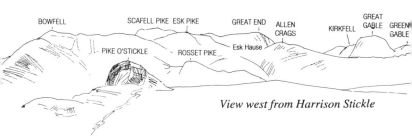

View west from Harrison Stickle

which leads down the steep fellside to a stile in the intake wall, keep ahead and reach a kissing gate on the left. Go through to another kissing gate in the wall on the right. A path leads down the field to the car park.

The Langdale Pikes are composed of the hard volcanic rocks which form the core of central Lakeland. In detail there are distinct differences. There are piles of lava sheets and the bedded ash of old volcanoes, with beds differing greatly in texture and looks, from the rough knobbly rock of Pavey Ark to the smooth pale banded beds on Pike o' Stickle. The very finest grained band of volcanic ash is of a hardness and character similar to flint and it was this bed that was worked for tools and weapons by prehistoric man. The roughly shaped axe heads were transported to coastal settlements for finishing and traded to many parts of Britain and as far afield as Poland.

The Langdale fells are one of the few places in Britain where you may see the mountain ringlet butterfly (dark brown with orange markings). Spot it in June or July.

WALK 10: Little Langdale, Lingmoor Fell & Blea Tarn

Side Pike from Blea Tarn

SUMMARY:
Lingmoor is typical
of Lakeland's lesser
fells - a modest hill
which contains all
the character of the
higher fells with

Distance:	6 miles 9¹/₂km
Grade:	Moderate
Terrain:	Medium fell walk, rough paths in parts
Summits:	Lingmoor Fell (Brown Howe) - 1530ft (467m)
	Side Pike - 1187ft (362m)
Map:	OL6

less effort involved and the advantage of a grandstand viewpoint of its
peers. Quarrying is much in evidence and the old quarrymen's paths make
a pleasing route to the fell top.

There is some rough walking along the crest of the fell and even more
excitement if the craggy knobble of Side Pike is included. The charm of
Blea Tarn and Little Langdale is a pleasing contrast to the fells.

For those who prefer little uphill on their outing, a circuit of Lingmoor
makes a pleasant valley walk.

HOW TO GET THERE AND PARKING: There are three possible starting
places -

1) Above Fell Foot Farm, park on the moor on the Wrynose Pass road.
2) Blea Tarn car park
3) On the roadside below Side Pike in the direction of Wall End.

THE WALK: At Fell Foot Farm the Wrynose Pass road squeezes past the
corner of the seventeenth-century farm building. Go down the road beside
the youthful River Brathay and turn R over its attractive stone bridge,
through a kissing gate, and along the track across the flat valley floor to
another stone bridge over the Greenburn Beck at Bridge End. Although
you may be tempted to stop and admire this lovely old cottage, keep
straight on the track which begins to rise up the valley side and bend
leftwards, from where you can appreciate it in its setting. Both habitations
have been carefully sited in the lee of rocky knolls, Castle How and Hollin
Crag, which protect them from squalls funnelling down the valleys.

Keep on the rising track and soon the miners' track from Greenburn
joins in from the right. At the next fork go L. Little Langdale Tarn, excavated
by glacial action, rests in verdant water meadows and smiles in a circuit of
fells.

The track descends and goes through a gate into a lane, blinkered by
high walls, to High Hall Garth. A spoil heap, escaping from its wall, now
randomly paves the path with tinkling slates as you make your way to Low
Hall Garth. Here is another typical, mainly seventeenth-century cottage.
On reaching the next, still captive spoil heap, turn L through a kissing gate
and cross the field to the renowned Slaters' Bridge. Cross the delicate

Slaters Bridge

stone arch and clapper bridge and continue by the wall and up the ice-smoothed rock by the slaters' footholds (or go round on the grass). From the knoll there is a fine panorama of the head of Little Langdale. Pass by the farm entrance and keep on the lane to the road, public footpath sign.

If you are in need of refreshment the local inn The Three Shires, formerly The Traveller's Rest, is at Little Langdale village just down the road to the right.

Turn L then R on the narrow road to Dale End. In spring the roadside bank is a display of colour with celandine, stitchwort and wood sorrel. Pass Dale End Farm and keep ahead on the bridle track. (*Circuit of Lingmoor continues on the bridle track.) A few yards after the next gate leave civilisation to begin the ascent of Lingmoor Fell. Go through a gap in the wall set back on the left and bear L to a ladder stile by a gate in the next cross wall. Take the path which hugs the left-hand wall at first then rises steadily to another gate and ladder stile over the intake wall.

This wall, from here to be known as *the* wall, is an important landmark. It rises up the ridge and bends west to run the length of Lingmoor and becomes the boundary between Great and Little Langdale. If you have difficulty in mist keep it in sight and it will lead you over the fell top to easy ground.

The path is now the old quarry pony track grassed over. Take the easy zigzags up the hill with the wall on the right. When a cairn is in sight ahead, look for the trace of an old path to the left and leaving the wall traverse L avoiding Bield Crag and zigzag up again on a clearer path. To the right is the summit cairn of Bield Crag and ahead small quarries and their attendant sad, roofless buildings. Looking back, Dale End 600 feet below

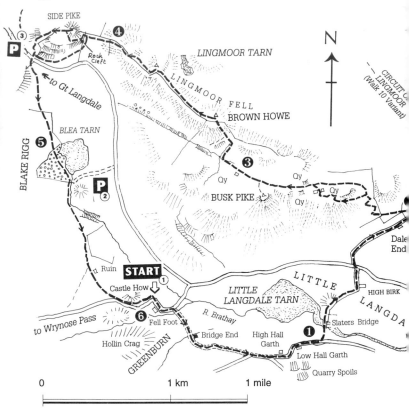

SIDE PIKE
P (3)
Rock Cleft
(4)
LINGMOOR TARN
LINGMOOR FELL
BROWN HOWE
N
CIRCUIT OF LINGMOOR (Walk 10 Variant)
to Gt Langdale
BLEA TARN
BLAKE RIGG
(5)
(3)
Qy
BUSK PIKE
Qy
Qy
Qy
P (2)
Dale End
Ruin
START (1)
Castle How
LITTLE LANGDALE TARN
LITTLE
HIGH BIRK
to Wrynose Pass
(6)
Fell Foot
R. Brathay
LANGDALE
Slaters Bridge
Hollin Crag
Bridge End
High Hall Garth
(1)
GREENBURN
Low Hall Garth
Quarry Spoils
HIGH HALL GARTH

0   1 km   1 mile

appears tiny, whilst Elterwater nestles at the southern end of Langdale and Windermere stretches out its shining length in the far distance .

Go ahead on a grassed shelf then bend rightwards round spiky rocks to the old quarry buildings where you can rest and be thankful that you are here for pleasure and not for a gruelling day's work with your slater's fare, a tin of sandwiches and a bottle of cold tea.

Go up the grass to the right of a quarry working to join a pony track. Turn L and pass more delvings. Soon the path levels and gradually swings right towards the Lingmoor quarry. On the left is the summit of Busk Pike with its cairn and 'neolithic monument' which some strong man has set up recently (long may it stand). Leave the path and make a short diversion to

Busk Pike and 'monument'

the cairn. The view of Wetherlam is worth the little effort. The quarry buildings provide shelter. Pass them and look ahead. The deep cleft is the result of erosion on a joint of weaker rock shattered by faulting and you are on it. Go on the path towards the cleft keeping to the right of a small boggy hollow. Do not enter the fault defile but turn R up a small side stream which leads to a tiny tarn and the wall which ends temporarily in a crag. Turn L on a cairned path. Do not go along the terrace but turn up right holding the direction of the wall (now a fence) and cross it by a stile to the summit cairn of Brown Howe 1530 feet.

From here the northern slopes of the fell are covered with dark ling which spreads an air of desolation around little Lingmoor Tarn. Continue along the fence to the next cairn. Over the fence to the west you can look down on the cheerful face of Blea Tarn with its cap of conifers and to the north the next objective Side Pike with the Langdale Pikes beyond. The friendly fence bends left, follow its path. (The path straight ahead leads to another cairned viewpoint.) The path becomes steep, then very steep down smooth-worn rock which demands care, then easier to cross the wall (née fence) at a stile. Continue down the wallside to the gap between Lingmoor and Side Pike and cross a fence barring the way. (Ordinary mortals turn L down the grassy slopes to the Blea Tarn Road. Turn R on a track above and parallel to the road to gain its highest point.) Those with a sense of adventure and who like a laugh at their companions' expense carry on.

The way on up Side Pike is not as daunting as it appears from here. Climb the stile over the fence and go up to the foot of the crag. Turn L along the base of the crag to a fallen block of rock. Take off your rucksack, breathe in and squeeze behind the block, don't get stuck or you will never hear the last of it. The path continuing beyond the 'fat man's agony' is easy but needs a steady head. After a few yards branch up R on a rising path leaving the crag behind and wind gradually right to join a better path by a low wall (cairn). Step over the gap in the low wall and go up to the summit where shapely rocks substitute for a cairn. After admiring the ever-impressive mountains at the head of Langdale regain the wall end and retrace the path to its crossing point, then follow the better path which is

Side Pike showing the route through the 'squeeze'

cairned to lead you down and round a rocky outcrop to pass a memorial seat. Gain the road at its highest point by a ladder stile. Access to Parking 3. *Circuit of Lingmoor joins here.

Cross the road and take the left-hand path through a gap in the wall. Stride out now you can take your eyes from the path and feast them on beautiful Blea Tarn. To the left on the slopes of Lingmoor the fault line stands prominently as a deep wooded gash. Stop at the junction of a broken wall with a fence corner for from here you can trace the incredulous line of our path across the craggy face of Side Pike. Keep heading for the tarn along a path which serves as a streambed for a while, then pass a progeny of trees, maturing branches of a long-fallen trunk. Keep on to the kissing gate which leads into shady woodland. Go straight on by the rhododendrons then fork L on a narrow path to cross a stream and pass through their evergreen arch. The trees are now groomed to give glimpses of the water and the path restored tastefully.

For Access to Parking 2 turn L over the footbridge and along the path to the car park. NB. *It is worth crossing the bridge for the view described by Wordsworth in his poem 'The Solitary'. In it Wordsworth accompanies the 'Wanderer' over the mountains to visit a friend the 'Solitary' and views from an eminence the little vale chosen by the 'Solitary' as his retreat.*

Keep ahead on the refurbished path to a kissing gate in a wall and gain the open fell. Follow the path by the merry outlet stream which soon plunges in a series of cascades into an open gorge. When a group of boulders is reached the path forks. Keep straight ahead passing to the right of the boulders and make your own way through the mire as the path contours to a wall. The wall bends away left and the path carries on. Fork L on a faint path leading down to a ruined building. *This has an upturned table used for target practice by troops who trained on Wrynose Pass during World War II.* Continue to contour on the line of an old path above the boggy area then rise up the bracken slopes to the Wrynose road. Turn L down the road to the start.

*CIRCUIT OF LINGMOOR

Continue on the rough lane from Dale End Farm towards Elterwater and just over the top of the rise after a gateway take a path L into woods. This descends to join a surfaced lane.Turn L along the road past Baysbrown Farm (Walk 7). Keep straight on above the buildings, over the cattle-grid and along the track. Fork L on a rising quarry track and enter Hag Wood. Branch R from the quarry track, through woodland and along a path to Oak Howe Farm. Turn L past a knoll and follow the path which traverses below the steep slopes of Lingmoor. Pass above Side House and continue to join another path which links the National Trust campsite in Langdale to the Blea Tarn road. Turn L and climb steeply up this to the col.

Fell Foot Farm

Fell Foot Farm is on an old packhorse and smugglers' route over Wrynose Pass. Over the door are the arms of Fletcher Fleming. Behind the farm is a flat platform edged by terraces, almost certainly a Viking 'Thingmount' - a meeting place for ceremony and justice.

Slaters Bridge

Slaters Bridge is a fine example of slate slab and packhorse bridge reputedly built to aid the quarrymen to and from work although its origin could predate the quarries.

WALK 11: Crinkle Crags & Cold Pike from Wrynose Pass

The rocky summit of Cold Pike

Distance:	6 miles 9½km
Grade:	Strenuous
Terrain:	High fell walk, rough and stony paths
Summits:	Crinkle Crags - 2818ft (859m)
	Cold Pike - 2300ft (701m)
Map:	OL6

SUMMARY: Starting from the top of Wrynose Pass enables the walker to reach easily one of Lakeland's highest fells in a short walk. A gentle ascent past many drumlins and ice-strewn boulders to shallow Red Tarn is followed by a short climb

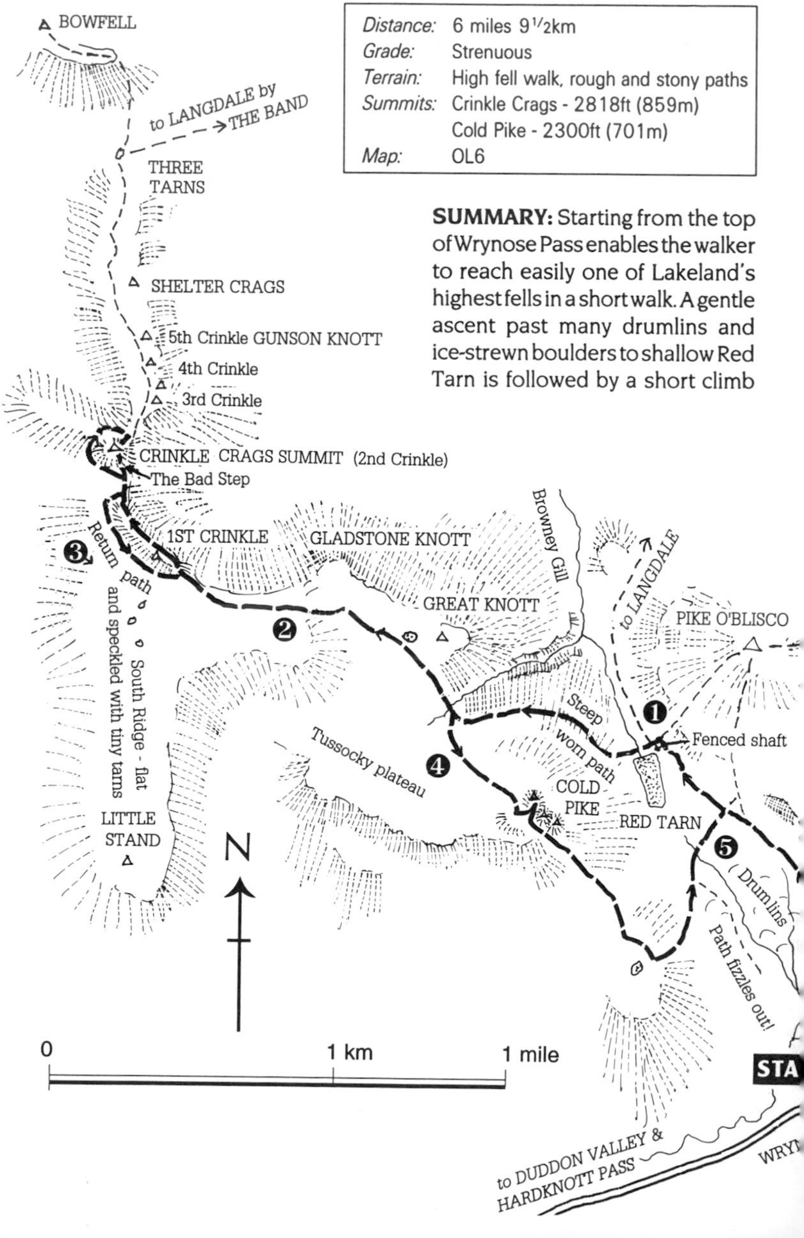

BOWFELL

to LANGDALE by → THE BAND

THREE TARNS

SHELTER CRAGS

5th Crinkle GUNSON KNOTT

4th Crinkle

3rd Crinkle

CRINKLE CRAGS SUMMIT (2nd Crinkle)

The Bad Step

1ST CRINKLE

GLADSTONE KNOTT

GREAT KNOTT

Browney Gill

to LANGDALE

PIKE O'BLISCO

Return path

③

South Ridge - flat and speckled with tiny tarns

②

Steep worn path

④

① Fenced shaft

Tussocky plateau

COLD PIKE

RED TARN

LITTLE STAND

⑤

N

Drumlins

Path fizzles out!

0   1 km   1 mile

to DUDDON VALLEY & HARDKNOTT PASS

STA

WRY

onto a grassy plateau where height is gained easily. An exposed scrambly traverse of the First Crinkle leads to the final rocky hump of the main summit.

Views are widespread, ranging over most of southern Lakeland and in clear weather the Isle of Man floats like a wisp of cloud over a silver sea. Other wisps rise from Sellafield's cooling towers. But where are the lovely little fells of our other short walks? They are there, insignificant foothills overshadowed by the higher mountains.

The character of the ascent is typical of Lakeland's popular high fells, on broad stony paths (although some repair work has eased the worst sections), where it is impossible to lose the way in clear weather. A constant stream of walkers traverses the hills, many of them doing the popular horseshoe walk from Langdale over as many tops as time allows. You are almost certain to meet others on the summit. Our described return offers some quieter alternatives and the diversion over Cold Pike is particulary worthwhile; a fine rocky summit, pleasant grassy tracks and good views over the ascent route. This is a walk to be done in fine, clear weather.

HOW TO GET THERE AND PARKING: Start from the Three Shire Stone at the top of Wrynose Pass. There is limited parking, about 6 cars at the Three Shire Stone and other larger spaces a short distance away on either side. Wrynose Pass is approached by a slow but pretty drive up the narrow lanes of Little Langdale.

BLACK CRAG

Sheepfold

THREE
SHIRE
STONE

THE WALK: From the Three Shire Stone a clear path circumnavigates the roadside bog and stream then heads north on the side of a shallow valley to the right of Roughcrags Gill. There is an immediate view along Wrynose Bottom to Harter Fell, with the grey thread of the road winding up Hard Knott Pass. The path needs no description as you pass through an area of drumlins with its random scattering of ice-borne boulders. When opposite an old circular sheepfold the path forks, but this is only a diversion round a peaty bog which has now had an efficient repair, so keep straight on. The path is now cairned. Pass Long Scar - the line of crag up on the right. When opposite the end of the Scar narrow grass paths join the main path * **.

*   The path to Pike o' Blisco branches right here.
**   The return path from Cold Pike joins here.

1st CRINKLE

Continue past Red Tarn, a lonely, waterfilled scoop, with waterweeds smoothing its surface against the plucking turbulent wind currents in this draughty corridor. *Pollen grains from here prove that it was forested around 5000 BC.*

At the valley head four paths meet by an old iron and copper mine shaft. From this red junction the path R leads up Pike o' Blisco.* Straight on down to Stool End, Langdale, and L to Crinkle Crags.

Turn L, cross the outlet stream and climb up the stony path which steepens as it passes the head of Browney Gill. There are fine views across Langdale to Pike of Stickle with the grey scree chute on its right making a vivid scar which is not all attributable to the prehistoric axe head manufacturers.

Walk at an easier gradient past Great Knott 696m. From here you can easily divert R to its summit.

Pass a small tarn to the R and the summits of Crinkle Crags are now ahead. The path is well cairned.

Make an assault on the first rocky summit, the South Top. It is a bit sporty but there are no difficulties and the reward is an excellent view down Eskdale, and, if the air is clear, the Isle of Man may be seen

The Crinkles and Bowfell from Red Tarn

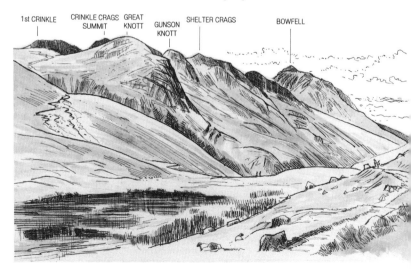

1st CRINKLE   CRINKLE CRAGS   GREAT   GUNSON   SHELTER CRAGS   BOWFELL
               SUMMIT   KNOTT   KNOTT

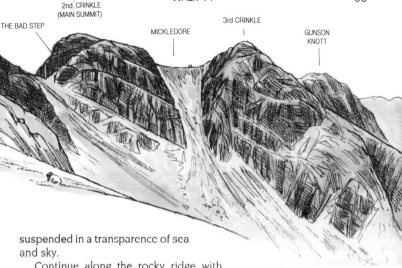

THE BAD STEP

2nd CRINKLE
(MAIN SUMMIT)

MICKLEDORE

3rd CRINKLE

GUNSON
KNOTT

suspended in a transparence of sea
and sky.

Continue along the rocky ridge with
alternate glances into Eskdale or Langdale as the path pendulums in and
out of the rocks. Before descending into the gap look forward at the
onward route then descend to the gap by whichever way suits you. To
reach the next and highest summit there is a choice of path.

a) The Bad Step where a chockstone bars the gully and must be passed by
climbing the steep rock wall 15 feet on its right. Beware of stones being
dislodged from above.

b) A narrow path to the L traverses and then climbs easily and bends back
R to approach the summit.

From the top is a splendid 100-degree panorama but the immense wall
of the Scafell range must monopolise the attention, its proximity allowing
you to study its detail.

RETURN TO WRYNOSE PASS

Although the views have been good they are even better on the return.
Retrace your route to the gap before the Bad Step. From here we
recommend that you bypass the rock summits on their right along a
pleasant grassy shelf with a narrow trod. From here you can peer down
into the Great Moss of Eskdale. Rejoin the main path at the foot of the
rocks and turn R along the outward route. Continue to descend until the
relatively flat area opposite Great Knott.

The path to Cold Pike branches right here.

Continue down the steep section to the red junction. Turn R and follow the path back down the valley to the start.

RETURN OVER COLD PIKE

If you are footweary of the stones, fancy the grass beneath your feet and an hour of solitude away from busy parade, Cold Pike comes highly recommended. You will rarely be out of the sight and security of the path, but far enough to be able to completely ignore it.

Branch R on the gently rising, narrow path to the rocky crown of Cold Pike. The path leads to the right (west) side of the rocks, so make a diversion L to the highest point. This is a "real" summit with a rock castle and a standing block supporting the cairn. It is wonderful to sit on a rough textured perch and take in the new scenery. There is the full face of the Crinkles to the north, the Coniston Fells to the south and the gas rigs of the Irish Sea like flotsam on the western horizon. Return to the path and keep on in the same direction. The path is rather indistinct along the west side of the rocks but quickly improves as you leave the summit behind and begin the descent. The Wrynose road is now in sight far below. Pass a cairn and, off to the right, a small tarn. The descent becomes steeper as you bend L and return to the valley below Red Tarn. On reaching the drumlins look out for a Y-junction. Keep slightly L - aiming for the left end of Long Crag - and join the main path at the point ** on the outward route. Turn R down the valley to the Three Shire Stone.

Three Shire Stone

Until 1974 the Three Shire Stone was the junction of Lancashire, Westmorland and Cumberland.

Mining around Red Tarn

Robinson (1709) stated that a furnace in Langdale was kept in operation by ore found locally in the mountains, mainly around Red Tarn. At about the same time a bloomery in Langstrath worked by the monks of Furness Abbey, used ore from Ore Gap between Hanging Knotts and Bowfell, where there was a large deposit of finest quality haematite, difficult to extract because of its lofty position. At that time timber was more abundant at the valley heads.

Local farmers used the iron red earth as a dye for marking sheep. This was known as 'schmitt' thought to be a reference to the early miners who came from Germany.

The Cathedral, an atmospheric monument to bygone industry (Walk 14)
On the Tilberthwaite Round (Walk 13)

Above:
The old quarry track over
Hole Rake to
Tilberthwaite (Walk 15)

Inset right:
The squeeze on Side Pike
(Walk 10)

WALK 12: Greenburn Copper Mines, Rough Crags & Wrynose Pass

The ruins of Greenburn Copper Mines with Swirl How beyond

SUMMARY: A short easy walk into a quiet secluded valley to the remains of the Greenburn Mines can be varied on the return by an excursion onto the ridge of Rough Crags, which makes a spectacular viewpoint. The top of Wrynose Pass is easily reached to make a gentle descent back to the car.

Those who want to extend the walk could continue along the well marked ridge path to Great Carrs. The continuation of the ridge horseshoe over Swirl How and Wetherlam makes a rough, strenuous day's walk and is beyond the scope of this book.

Distance:	4³/4 miles 7¹/2km
Grade:	Moderate
Terrain:	Valley and medium fell. Mostly on good paths apart from the fell crossing to Wrynose Pass.
Summit:	Rough Crags - 1580ft (482m)
Map:	OL6

Recommended reading - *Coniston Copper Mines - A Field Guide* by Eric Holland (Cicerone Press).

HOW TO GET THERE AND PARKING: Near Fell Foot Farm, Little Langdale. Park on the moor beside the Wrynose Pass road up beyond the steep S-bend above the farm.

THE WALK: At Fell Foot Farm the Wrynose Pass road squeezes past the corner of the seventeenth-century farm building. Go down the road beside the youthful River Brathay and turn R over its attractive stone bridge, through a kissing gate, and along the track across the flat valley floor to another stone bridge over the Greenburn Beck at Bridge End, another lovely old cottage. Keep on the rising track and soon the miners' road from Greenburn joins in from the right.

Turn R and westward into the Greenburn Valley. The gradient is kindly as befits the heavily-laden carts which used it to transport the needs and products of the mines. Go over a stile by the intake wall. From here on the grandeur of the valley can be appreciated. Nature has repaired many of the mining scars and is now mellowing the main industrial complex into an interesting archive. On approaching the mines the road forks. Take the R-hand lower track. The Greenburn Beck splashes noisily down a series of cascades in its sculptured bed.

The first building to the left is the little square powder house, set wisely apart. **WARNING** - keep on the path.

The veins lie on each side and parallel with the path and are stoped. The other buildings, office, smithy, copper store and drying shed lie in ruins but can be identified from Eric Holland's Field Guide. The path rises to the

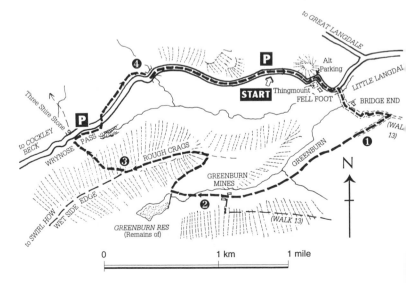

Bridge End

level of the main buildings. *The mine complex was powered by two water-wheels. On the right is the trench of the sump lode - the main source of production. The copper was so pure in colour and texture that, according to W.T.Palmer, a secret smelter and mint was set up in the Rusland valley woods turning out fake 'gold' coins - guineas and half guineas. All the workings go down to 120 fathoms (720ft) and are stoped. The engine shaft top is amongst the ruins and has an iron pump rod protruding at a blockage of stones, so* **BEWARE**. *Eric Holland in his field guide warns against 'probing about - the blockage may clear itself without warning.'* Continuing on, a boggy area contains fenced shafts on the line of the sump lode. Keep well away as *'The water level in here will be the same as the engine shafts, be careful not to fall in as there would be no hope of survival.'*

Our way now leaves the mines and heads for the breached dam of Greenburn Reservoir. *The reservoir supplied water to the beck which was, in turn, conveyed by leat to the two water-wheels. The water was economically used, the tail race from the big wheel (29-foot diameter approx.) fed a smaller wheel, then was finally used for washing the ore, before being returned to the stream.*

From the reservoir you can admire the upper reaches of the Greenburn Valley. A wild, trackless and rough landscape cradled in the magnificent cirque of Rough Crags, Great Carrs, Swirl How and Wetherlam, a dark backdrop to the white cotton grass waving across the now exposed bed of the reservoir.

To begin the ascent of Rough Crags turn sharp three-quarters R, along the top edge of a flat shelf keeping below the level of the bracken. On the skyline a gallant holly which we will pass presently stands amongst spiked rocks. Ignore sheep trods and tractor prints - keep traversing until you meet the ridge path (which comes from lower down Greenburn). Turn L and climb the steep end of the ridge. When below the holly zigzag R to gain

COLD PIKE   CRINKLE CRAGS   BOWFELL   PIKE O'BLISCO

From the top of Rough Crags

the ridge top. This is a wonderful spot for views - especially down Little Langdale. Continue along the ridge passing small rocky outcrops. The path passes the highest one on its left then emerges onto a wide grass col. (Ahead rises the long ridge of Wet Side Edge.) Turn R down the grassy slopes, to the Wrynose Pass. (The pass top can be pinpointed by looking across the road to where a major path descends from Pike o' Blisco.) The descent is easier and shorter than it appears and various elusive paths (which are more evident when you have reached the road) exist.

Turn R down the road to the start.

Wrynose Pass

The road is part of the Roman Xth highway from Ravenglass (Glannaventa) via Hardknott Fort, Hardknott and Wrynose Passes to Ambleside (Galava). It was built by Agricola some time before AD 90 and its 20-foot width indicated its importance as a supply route. Although there was no regular garrison at Hardknott Fort after the end of the second century, the road has been in regular use ever since. The road over Wrynose Pass was used for army training during World War II and re-surfaced with concrete after heavy vehicle damage. Now, coupled with the crossing of Hardknott Pass, it is a popular outing for motorists.

Stope

A vertical fissure which contained the vein, left void by the extraction of ore. To make a useable passage the stope was bridged by timbers then packed with waste rock above known as 'deads'. The floor was of timbers overlaid with rubble and clay to prevent water running into the workings below. With passage of time the state of the timbers is unknown and they could collapse at any moment. The Sump Lode at Greenburn reached a depth of 120 fathoms below the top of the engine shaft.

WALK 13: Tilberthwaite Round

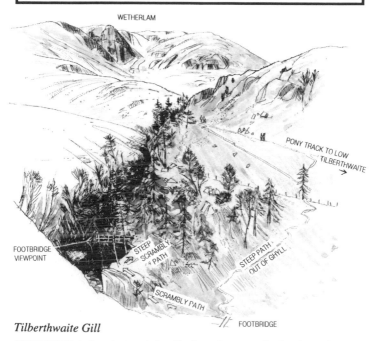

WETHERLAM

PONY TRACK TO LOW TILBERTHWAITE →

FOOTBRIDGE VIEWPOINT

STEEP SCRAMBLY PATH

STEEP PATH OUT OF GHYLL

SCRAMBLY PATH

FOOTBRIDGE

Tilberthwaite Gill

SUMMARY: A short but varied walk where the natural splendour of ravine and rough fell has been modified by Lakeland's traditional industries of quarrying and mining. Old miners' tracks are used in part. A low col gives widespread views.

HOW TO GET THERE AND PARKING: From the A593 Coniston-Ambleside road turn up the road to Tilberthwaite 1½ miles north of Coniston and drive to a large dual parking area a mile up the valley at Low Tilberthwaite.

Distance:	4¾ miles 7½km
Grade:	Moderate
Terrain:	Valley and low fell walk
Summit:	Col above Hellen's Mine - 1200ft (366m)
Map:	OL6

THE WALK: A footpath leaves the lower end of the car park up steps and winds up a heap of quarry rid. On the left is Penny Rigg Slate Quarry. At

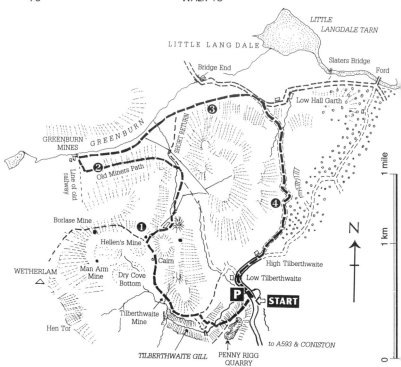

the second entrance it is worth having a peep into the quarry bowl, now used by rock climbers. The best of the quarry's attractive grey stone has long gone leaving a mellowed, sheltered void with delicate vegetation. **Remember, old quarries are dangerous to explore** - return to the main path.

Climb steadily to a path junction at a small ruined hut. Note the path L into a rock cutting leads to the vertical quarry edge! Keep children in check! The rising path forking L is an alternative path which follows the left rim of Tilberthwaite Gill, but we take the R fork which runs level.

This follows the line of an old water race from the gill, which worked the quarry before the higher level Crook Beck race was constructed (seat with view).

Tilberthwaite Gill can be seen - almost - from here, as the ravine begins at a right angled bend in the stream below. In summer a dense covering of trees hides the ravine. Follow the path to a footbridge over the chuckling water. A sign warns that the 'footpath is steep and dangerous beyond this point', so follow the path which almost immediately climbs out of the gill. There is nothing to fear, climb up and go over a high stile onto open ground, up again and fork L where you soon join the broad pony track from Low Tilberthwaite. The sign refers to another way which is indeed steep, eroded, exposed and dangerous to anyone unused to scrambly exposed paths. This adventurous alternative follows the rocky edge of the stream to scramble onto a platform above a right-angled bend at the foot of the ravine. Here you can gain a viewing bridge, with a waterfall trapped between steep rock walls just above. *This is the only remnant of the Victorian walkway which followed the ravine.* A steep path needing care, zigzags from the platform to join the pony track.

Turn L up the pony track which comes close to the steep edge of the ravine. Trees prevent a good view into its depths but the stream can be heard and the treetops, now at eye level, are a bonus for bird watchers.

The head of the gill is a T-junction of streams where our path bends R. Keep R at a fork, although it is worth a short detour L to the stream where Benson's Vein Level is seen across the footbridge. The line of the vein can be traced up the hillside where there is a dead cleft.

Back on the main miners' track cross a side stream above the old Tilberthwaite Mine, an area of extensive ochre waste and dangerous crumbly-edged shafts. One of the fenced depressions is a 540-foot deep

View from the nameless little summit

shaft! Anyone interested in the mines should study Eric Holland's interesting and informative *Coniston Copper Mines - A Field Guide* (Cicerone Press).

The path enters a crag-girt boggy combe near the valley head, below the steep rocky face of Wetherlam. The combe, misleadingly called Dry Cove Bottom, was dammed during the mining heyday, to form a broad lake for a head of water. The path rises to a cairn, a good place to view the ongoing route. The main path passes a black peat bog to some ochre mine spoil at Hellen's mine 300 yards ahead.

Leave the main path at the cairn by Hellen's mine and turn R past a small ruined hut and shaft to a low tree-dotted col. (The main miners' path contours ahead to the Borlase Mine at the valley head.) Retrospective views to the gaunt bulk of Wetherlam are impressive but the onward view from the col is excellent. The eastern fells are displayed from Helvellyn to High Street with the Langdales in the foreground. Descend past the stumps of felled trees into a hollow with a boggy area and fence on its left. Keep to the right of the bog, below trees. (The nameless little hill above is an easy prize for summit baggers with the reward of more extensive views down Yewdale.) Ignore the first stile, defended by the end of the bog and continue to cross the fence at a second stile. Descend by the fenceside and continue to a wall ahead.

TO CONTINUE TO GREENBURN MINES VIA THE MINERS' PATH

On meeting the wall by a wettish patch turn L on an indistinct trod which traverses into the gill. Cross just above a large quartz strung boulder and you are on the right trod. Continue to traverse the slope below small rocky outcrops. The path is fairly level and better than it appears at first sight, also the aspect is wonderful. Pass a cairn and on rounding the shoulder Greenburn is added to the panorama. The path descends a little, (cairns) then levels and rises again. Notice a cairn by a large slab boulder. Beyond the path divides but only to cross the stream and continues to traverse beyond. Keep on to a single metal pole then 100 yards beyond gain the line of the old incline leading directly down to the ruins of the mines. Turn R down the short turf of the incline. As you descend you will notice the odd sleeper still in place. Stay carefully on the incline (to its left is a trial shaft where the the line of the Gossan Lode crosses), and cross the incline causeway over the stream to arrive in the mine complex atop a spoil heap. Straight in front is the old wheel pit, the paved floor of the crusher and the concrete, once lead-lined, settling tanks.

It is wise not to wander and poke about in these workings. Five veins were mined, some to a depth of 120 fathoms, the depth of the engine shaft, and are now stoped with rotting timbers and flooded. If you could study a reconstructed cross section of one of the mines you would certainly do your viewing cautiously from the path.

Turn R along the spoil heap to gain the main track down the valley. It is now a relaxed gentle descent, with the perpetual draught, which creeps down Greenburn in the calmest of weather, at your back, the singing cascades of the beck at your side and the verges lined with small flowers, butterwort, scabious, quatrefoil and ragwort in their season.

Go through the gate in the intake wall. Soon Greenburn merges into the pleasant pastoral scene of Little Langdale.

Short route joins here.*

THE SHORT ROUTE TO LITTLE LANGDALE
Follow the wall and make a steep descent down the smooth grass with care to a high ladder stile. Go over and keep to the right hand side of a small stream, ignoring all other paths left and right. This path drops steeply through a rough fellside directly towards Bridge End, a prominent cottage in Little Langdale below. Views open up Greenburn to its mines and valley head - and across to the Wrynose road, once a Roman road, to shapely Pike o' Blisco. Join the Greenburn track and turn R.*

RETURN TO TILBERTHWAITE
Continue along the track and keep straight on at a junction. At the next fork, just before High Hall Garth, fork R on a stony track which rises gently over a broad grassy shelf. From here the descent is straightforward to the surfaced road at High Tilberthwaite Farm. Go through the yard turning R and along the road to the car park.

Low Tilberthwaite

WALK 14: Holme Fell, Hodge Close & The Cathedral

Hodge Close Quarry

SUMMARY: A short walk which has much of the best character of South Lakeland. There are beautiful natural woodlands; rough fells with a craggy summit and fine views over lakes and hills; a placid tarn; a glimpse of old industry with exciting situations for anyone inspired by rock scenery - and all so easily gained! **Warning: take care in the quarries, rockfalls can occur.**

HOW TO GET THERE AND PARKING: Start at the car park at Tilberthwaite, approached by a side road from the A593 1½ miles north of Coniston.

THE WALK: Standing on Gill Bridge and looking downstream a footpath can be seen on the left stony bank. In the middle distance is the delightful woodland of Low Coppice and beyond, forming the horizon, stretch the many summits of tiny Holme Fell. Go through the gap on

Distance:	5 miles 8km
Grade:	Easy
Terrain:	Low fell and woodland walk
Summit:	Holme Fell - 1010ft (308m)
Maps:	OL6/7

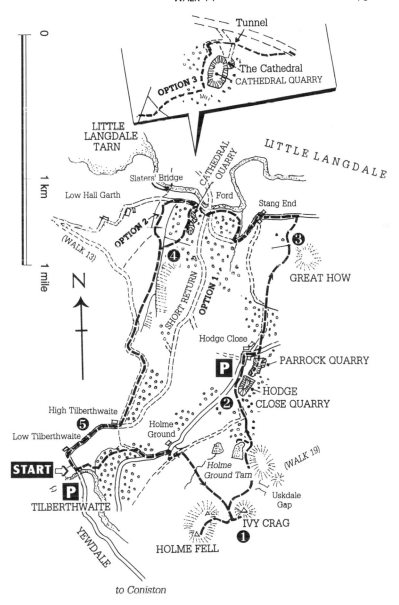

Tunnel

The Cathedral
CATHEDRAL QUARRY

OPTION 3

LITTLE
LANGDALE
TARN

LI7TLE LANGDALE

Slaters' Bridge

CATHEDRAL QUARRY

Ford

Stang End

Low Hall Garth

OPTION 2

(WALK 13)

❹

OPTION 1

SHORT RETURN

❸

GREAT HOW

N

Hodge Close

P

PARROCK QUARRY

❷

HODGE
CLOSE QUARRY

High Tilberthwaite

❺

Holme
Ground

Low Tilberthwaite

*Holme
Ground Tarn*

(WALK 19)

Uskdale
Gap

START

P

TILBERTHWAITE

IVY CRAG

❶

HOLME FELL

YEWDALE

to Coniston

0

1 km

1 mile

to the floodbanks and make your way to a kissing gate into the wood. Low Coppice is a beautiful birch wood. The path rises gently amid silver trunks and down to join a major path coming across the fields from High Tilberthwaite. Turn R passing through a cutting where grooves in the stone indicate its former importance as a wagonway. At the surfaced road turn L. In this little hidden vale you can sense the tranquillity as you approach Holme Ground. On the right, opposite the cottage, a gate swings open across slabs bridging a small stream. There is no footpath sign. Go through the gate on the wide path up the wallside until, after passing a concrete water tank, turn sharp L to pass above the tank. Turning from the intimacy of the pathside the elevation now reveals a pastel view of Tilberthwaite, mine and quarry scars providing shades of blue to complement the greens of Betsy Crag, Blake Rigg and Wetherlam. Go through the next gate, and 20 yards on take a path on the right threading its way uphill between the rowans. As the path levels off Holme Fell and Ivy Crag with its prominent cairn appear suddenly on the horizon.

Spend a minute looking ahead at the route and identifying its features from the map. The path winds up the fellside between the two summits and descends further left in a line below Ivy Crag to the Uskdale Gap. Continue past a cairn, turn L, then pass another cairn. Keep on up this grassy cairned path, crossing a small traversing trod then tackle the final rise to the top. On the summit plateau there is a small juvenile bog to avoid before mounting to the cairn of Ivy Crag on the left. (See the sketch to identify the extensive panorama.)

It would be a shame to leave without exploring the higher summit of Holme Fell for it offers a different dimension to the view over Coniston Water. The short path to gain its summit climbs through a rock band but is easier than it looks. A little cairn notes the return descent from the top.

Back at the bog pass it on its R and go down steadily to the tarn. Keep your inquisitive dependants away from the badly fenced patch of innocent-looking grass on the right (typical of a concealed mine shaft) and continue down the indistinct path on the left of a myrtle-clad spring to

View north east from Ivy Crag

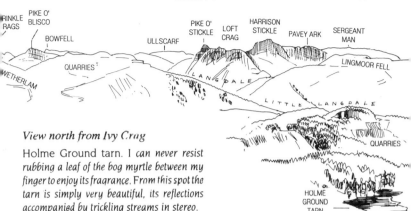

RINKLE RAGS
PIKE O' BLISCO
BOWFELL
WETHERLAM
QUARRIES
ULLSCARF
PIKE O' STICKLE
LOFT CRAG
HARRISON STICKLE
PAVEY ARK
SERGEANT MAN
LINGMOOR FELL
LANGDALE
LITTLE LANGDALE
QUARRIES
HOLME GROUND TARN

View north from Ivy Crag

Holme Ground tarn. *I can never resist rubbing a leaf of the bog myrtle between my finger to enjoy its fragrance. From this spot the tarn is simply very beautiful, its reflections accompanied by trickling streams in stereo.*

Cross over the stream to the R passing a heavy metal box and bend L across a wettish section to join a better path leading from the tarn outlet. Postpone turning right for a moment and go L to the edge of the tarn. The view of Holme Fell across the water is one you will want to fold away in your memory and file as a Lakeland treasure.

Return along the better path and continue downhill past a small quarry building to join a track by a wall. Turn R, go through one gate but stop at the next gate in a fence. Handcuff your children, hobble your dog. When you go through this gate the rather inadequate fence on the right conceals a fearsome drop into Hodge Close Quarry. A cautious approach will reveal the vast extent of the abandoned workings now taken over by rock climbers, abseilers and divers... NEVER THROW STONES INTO HOLES... Turn R along the road to the Old Forge Tea Garden and cottage.

EXCURSION INTO THE QUARRIES

A visit to the lake in the bottom of Hodge Close Quarry is surprisingly easy and certainly an experience but needs a steady foot in sensible footwear.

D SCREES

In 1995 access was stopped for a while after rockfalls. This emphasizes the still eroding nature of the quarries. **Be aware of the danger**. At the cottage leave the road and fork R. Opposite a garage turn R on a path leading down the old incline into Parrock Quarry. Keep on the well trodden stony path along the serene quarry floor, now colonised with delicate young birches, to the huge arch into Hodge Close. This is as far as you can go as the water fills the great void. **Do not** attempt a circus act on the base of the long gone travelling crane, there is insecure rock above, but enjoy the awe from a safe position. *Parrock Quarry and the rocks under the arch are very popular with rock climbers as the climbs have been safeguarded with bolts in continental style. The pool is a favourite venue for sub-aqua divers. It is 30 metres deep and contains several wrecked cars. Divers explore the flooded side tunnels.* Return the way that you came and rejoin the road.

Continue on the road past Wythe How to a gate in the fell wall. As the road bends away left keep straight ahead and hold direction on the shadow of a path which tracks above the flat rushy expanse of The Dubs on the right. Over your shoulder Holme Fell recedes into the distance. Pass by a wall end to a stile in a wall/fence. Bend L by a fine oak and down the field into Little Langdale. Across the flat valley of the River Brathay rise the slopes of Lingmoor Fell and at our feet the narrow road leads up the dale. Turn L along the road to pass Stang End and on to cross the bridge over Pierce How beck. Now turn R on a path, shaded by oaks, which follows the stream down until it joins the Brathay then bends upriver to join the road at the ford and footbridge. (*Refreshments at Three Shires pub*)

*OPTION 1
SHORT RETURN: Turn L along the rough road which follows the valley of the Pierce How Beck to High Tilberthwaite, Low Tilberthwaite and the car park.

Do not cross the river but continue on the road up the wooded valley, with a right fork after half a mile.

*OPTION 2
TO CONTINUE THE ROUTE: Keep along the road towards Low Hall Garth until just before the footpath which leads right to the Slaters' Bridge. Take the narrow quarry track on the left. Follow the footpath signs into and up a steep meadow with a stile at the top. Keep L to the wallside to join the excursion route to the quarry.

*OPTION 3
EXCURSION TO THE CATHEDRAL QUARRY:
WARNING: Rockfalls can and do occur in old slate quarries, enter at your oun risk and take care. This quarry may not be as vast as Hodge Close but as its name suggests it is something worth seeing. From the ford go along the road towards Low Hall Garth for 100 yards. Just before a gate mount the wall on a set of protruding stones and take a steep path up the side of the spoil to the quarry dressing floor where you turn R. As you walk along the flat expanse look for a tunnel on the left.

The tunnel is cut through solid rock and is short enough to negotiate without the use of a torch. However, it holds a few inches of water. There are good stepping-stones and it is easy to get to the end of the tunnel without wet feet. *The vast cavern is well named. The roof arch is supported by a column of living rock and high in the wall ethereal green and yellow light filters through a veil of leaves giving the green stone an air of unreality.*

WARNING: Stay in the end of the tunnel and do not wander about in the half-light. The water beyond the column is very deep. Rockfalls can occur.

From the flat floor take the quarry track L. It winds up past various buildings with viewpoints into the quarries until it bends right to a flat clearing high above the quarry face. Turn R up a green pathway to the right of the spoil heap. The path bends to the right and levels, traversing to a wall. Go through a broken gap and angle R towards another wall with two awkward old stiles (take your choice) to gain the open fell. (Junction with route from Slaters' Bridge.)

Proceed up the fell keeping the wall on your left past the remains of a cross wall to a brow by a building and wind-bent yew. Even though the position is elevated the distant views are curtailed and the skyscape and silence dominates except when the working quarry, hidden on the left, is in full blast. Pass half a ruin with a hawthorn tenant and keep ahead to join a grey stone track. As you turn L along it the horizon in front becomes immediately familiar - Holme Fell. Go pleasantly down to the Tilberthwaite valley road at High Tilberthwaite. Turn R passing Low Tilberthwaite famous for its spinning gallery and on to the car park at Gill Bridge.

Slate Quarrying in the Lake District

The best slates in the area are found in the hard volcanic rocks. Excellent quality slates are found in a band which runs diagonally SW to NE through Brown Pike, Coniston Old Man, Tilberthwaite, Elterwater, Troutbeck and the head of Longsleddale. The colour of the best slate is varied with pleasing textures and hues of green, far superior in looks to the drab grey Welsh slates - or the neighbouring dark blue of the Silurian rocks which were formed by deposits of fine volcanic ash and dust fallen in successive showers into a lake.

Quarries, always a source of local building stone, flourished in the eighteenth and nineteenth centuries when vast quantities were used for roofing in the emerging industrial towns.

WALK 15: Old Tracks on the Yewdale Fells

Penny Rigg Copper Mill and quarries

SUMMARY: The double crossing of the Yewdale Fells, which this walk achieves, on old green tracks once used by quarrymen and miners, is traversed now only by the discerning walker.

The first part of the route, over attractive lonely fells feels more remote than it really is, and few people are encountered in this beautiful quiet corner of Lakeland. Care is needed in following the directions - it is easy to miss the way. Return is by an easy-to-follow path with splendid views. A walk for clear weather, especially attractive in spring or autumn when the rich colours are at their best. Wet underfoot in parts.

Distance:	5 miles 8km
Grade:	Moderate
Terrain:	Low fell. Rough paths
Summit:	1000ft (305m)
Map:	OL6

HOW TO GET THERE AND PARKING:
From the A593 Coniston-Ambleside road turn up the road to Tilberthwaite 1½ miles north of Coniston and drive to a large dual parking area a mile up the valley at Low Tilberthwaite.

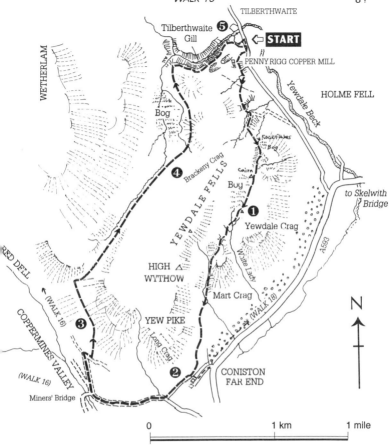

THE WALK: *The car park is set amid quarry spoil heaps and is a history lesson in itself. See Eric Holland and Postlethwaite for a deeper background than this publication can provide.*

Ignore the signed steps leading from the parking area, they are our return route.

From the car park go back down the valley road for 100 yards. Immediately, the top of the rise gives a splendid view of Yewdale Beck in its tree-clad valley with the slopes of Holme Fell to the left (east) and the Yewdale Fells, the way of our route to the R (west). Opposite the end of the

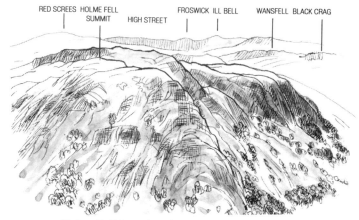

RED SCREES   HOLME FELL   FROSWICK ILL BELL   WANSFELL BLACK CRAG
             SUMMIT   HIGH STREET

Holme Fell from the miners' path above Yewdale

iron fence turn R up a prominent vehicle track beside a tiny stream to the
derelict buildings and two-tone spoil heaps of the Penny Rigg Copper Mill
and quarry. *The grey spoil is quarry rid, the ochre spoil heaps denote mineral workings,
sometimes almost buried by quarry rid. Ore was brought here from the Tilberthwaite
Mine along the 3240-foot Horse Crag level.*

Pass the mine entrance with rails in place and a business-like appearance.
The danger sign is serious so keep out. *This is a private enterprise being worked
by a local quarryman for grey roofing slate. (A different vein from the greenstone quarry
across and higher up the valley, also worked by another small local firm.) The entrance
tunnel was the lowest adit level of the Tilberthwaite Mine and is now used as the haulage
road from the underground quarry.*

Continue past a sound building to a tiny establishment on the left - the
dynamite store which was usually set apart at a safe distance. Turn R up
the fellside on a small path through the bracken heading towards a gap
with a lone tree on the skyline. Go almost straight across a green track and
up the continuation of the small path to reach the gap which proves to
have a remnant of wall. Cross the stream and gain an old green track where
you turn R. *The track has edging stones still in place and has been hewn from the solid
rock. The fellside is clothed in juniper, yew and holly, their colours and scents must surely
have lifted the hearts of the miners and quarrymen as they made their way home after
dusty hours underground.*

In 250 yards the track squeezes between a stream and a rock slab. Bend
L here. (Ignore the broad green way which carries straight on. If you cross
the stream you have gone too far.) Keep on the level path to a cluster of

rock flakes. The path now forks but both branches lead into a little boggy hollow which is circled on its right. Keep on the path as it leaves the hollow. A break in the rocks to the left gives a fine view over the Tarn Hows woodlands and the lower Yewdale valley. Jump across a tiny stream and mount to the next gap passing rocks with a small pinnacle to emerge at an upland shelf. Pass a small bog on the left as you move along to the first cairn. Brackeny Crag up to the right (north) is well named with the russet expanse of Yewdale Crag Moss at its feet.

The path is now indistinct but has occasional marker cairns in places to keep you on the line. (The one we are making for is the marker cairn visible at the far end of the flat shelf ahead.) To get there descend slightly to a small dry trod which skirts the edge of the Moss - a multi-coloured bog busy with summer dragonflies - or use the vestiges of the old track which can be traced at a higher level.

At the marker cairn survey the terrain ahead. Coniston Water can be seen shining through the gap on the skyline. Our route uses the gap higher and to the right. Descend onto the flat area and step over its meandering stream. Leap over another stream and go ahead on a rising path, very narrow, sometimes obscured by bracken, but sound underfoot. Bend gradually R into a little side valley leaving the streams to meander on before suddenly plunging into Yewdale down the White Gill Falls.

Continue up the side valley (cairn) towards the gap we pinpointed earlier. Pass ice-scratched rocks and up to the right a crag, its fallen rocks favoured by a lone holly. On approaching the gap do not dash on, by moving a few yards off the path to the left you can blend into the lonesome fellside and absorb the birds-eye vista of Yewdale.

Through the gap arrive at a level area occupied by a red bog. Go along its left-hand side then begin the descent beside its outlet stream, muttering in its deep yet narrow channel beside the path.

After 100 yards cross over and leave the stream. Coniston village can be seen below. The valley is now rocky, narrows to a gully and steepens. Keep to the path just off the edge of the screes, or pick your way down the left-hand spur.

Care is needed as the path disappears in the erosion and the descent is steep. At the rocky end of the spur the scree in the gully becomes finer and easier underfoot. Go down this for 50 yards to a large hawthorn to meet a traversing path by squeezing past a gorse bush and breathing a sigh of relief now the difficulties are passed. Continue along the gently descending traverse path passing the fine rock scenery of Long Crag to a wall. Turn R along the wall to a stile and the Coppermines road. (Coniston Village is quarter of a mile down the road to the left.)

To continue turn R up the Coppermines road.

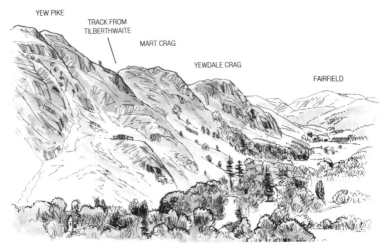

YEW PIKE

TRACK FROM TILBERTHWAITE

MART CRAG

YEWDALE CRAG

FAIRFIELD

The steep wall of the Yewdale Fells lies along a geological fault as seen from the Walna Scar road above Coniston

Church Beck cascades down the narrow valley its waters gathered from a grand circle of mountains above. L to R The Old Man of Coniston, Brim Fell, Great How, Swirl How and Wetherlam which surround the bowl of Levers Water and Red Dell. Rich in ore - copper with a high silver content - the open valley ahead was occupied by a vast mining enterprise from 1599 to 1942 which delved to depths of 1200ft and extended along the veins into the neighbouring valley of Tilberthwaite. The workings were powered by water until steam arrived to lend a helping hand.

Immediately below Miners' Bridge, Church Beck thunders over a fall, its power freed from the wheels of industry, and across the beck in the spray of the fall is the entrance to an ancient mine trial. It was unproductive, but of interest to mine buffs as it still possesses its wooden rails, preserved by a few inches of water.

Keep on the road which levels then fork R on a major track. This upper track gives a superior view of the site remains. *Excellent drawings of the buildings, water-wheels, leats and tracks in Eric Holland's Coniston Copper - A Field Guide (Cicerone Press) bring the dramatic area to life again. It also gives a realistic appraisal of the hardships endured by the miners. I was impressed by a picture of young maidens, their fingers covered with copper rings, not from a false sense of vanity but to protect their fingers from the heavy hammers as they bucked the ore. The row of cottages immediately below is Irish Row, once the home of Irish miners.*

The track forks by some large spoil heaps. Branch R and begin to gain height passing the spoil heaps on the right to the next path junction. Do not cross the stream but fork R then go left onto a green path by a cairn. The gently graded path across the aptly named Above Beck Fells proves a good vantage point and after gaining considerable height a zigzag makes the final assault on the pass. (The path leaving to the L is the Wetherlam ridge path.)

The unnamed pass with its captive tarn is a banqueting place for swallows. Past the watershed the facing view shows the Tilberthwaite valley again. Pass a mine entrance (**dangerous**) and ruined hut and continue down the wide bowl with the great bare slopes of Wetherlam to the NW.

Balance over a stream which plunges prettily in a rowan-hung waterfall. Keep on the neat path (cairn) over a little rise and continue with ease to circle the bowl. Across the bog the spoil of the Tilberthwaite workings pinpoints the entrances to the mines; Man Arm, Borlase, Hellen's, Haystack and Birk Fell Hause. At a cairn keep ahead but do not cross the stream. Bend R along the side of Tilberthwaite Gill on a path which now demands your attention as it traverses above the gorge, following the line of an old water leat which once brought water to the quarry and mine workings below. Continue down past a cairn on a spoil heap to a rocky step with a tree which provides a handhold for crossing the sidestream. Keep on down the path past quarries to the car park.

WALK 16: Coniston Coppermines Valley, Levers Water & The Goose Bield

Levers Water and the Goose Bield

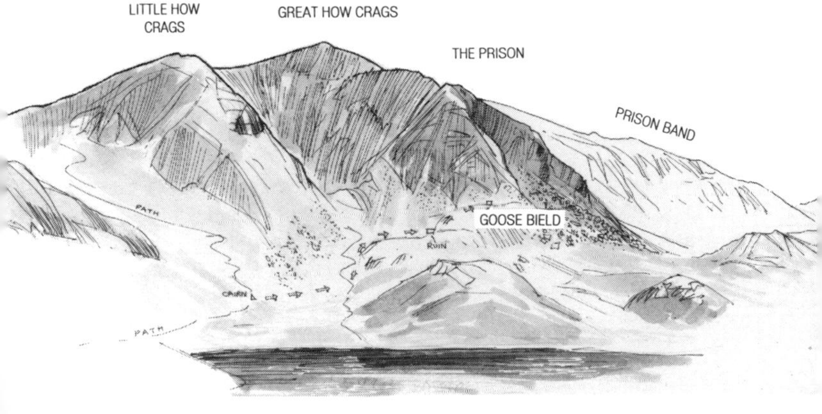

SWIRL HOW

GREAT HOW

LITTLE HOW

Goose
Bield

N

LEVERS
WATER

RED DELL

Thriddle Incline

Bonsor Mines

(WALK 15)

Simon's
Nick

Gill Cove

Raven Tor

BRIM FELL

LOW WATER

PADDY
END

YH

COPPERMINES VALLEY

Pudding
Stone

CONISTON OLD MAN

(WALK 17)

Miners' Bridg

to V

0   1 km   1 mile

SUMMARY: A walk steeped in the history of Lakeland mining, the relics of which are constantly visible, yet are now part of the landscape. There are good paths as far as Levers Water but the extension to see the Goose Bield is over rough fellside, wet in parts - boots recommended.

Distance:	5³/₄ miles 9¹/₄km
Grade:	Moderate
Terrain:	Medium fell walk. Rough in parts
Summit:	1600ft (488m)
Map:	OL6

HOW TO GET THERE AND PARKING:
Take the Walna Scar and Seathwaite road out of Coniston village. As the road steepens turn L. Parking opposite the Mountain Rescue Depot, at the old railway station.

THE WALK: Go back to the Walna Scar Road and turn R towards the village. In 50 yards turn L, then L again just before the Sun Inn, signed Public Footpath to Old Man & Levers Water. Every building is full of character but in 100 yards look for the gate at Dixon Ground Farm, signed with an arrow to the YHA. It leads into a field and the village is left behind. Follow the track across the field. To the right Church Beck tumbles down its rocky bed and up to the left is the bridge which carried the old carriage way from the railway terminus to the Coppermines Valley. Cross the slab bridge over Mealy Gill and noting the yellow arrow waymarks climb the rising track to a kissing gate. The track is steep and stony, and deep in its gorge the Church Beck rumbles and tumbles. *As your body warms to the exercise let your heart warm to the memory of the hundreds of workers, men, women and children who have toiled up this path to work at the mines.*

On approaching Miners' Bridge the glint of a waterfall attracts the eye. To get a better view you need more stable footing than the overhanging vegetation by the trackside. Cross the bridge then walk downstream for a few yards to see the fall. On the left of the plunge pool in a gloomy cleft is the entrance to a trial mine level. Inside the shallow water has preserved the wooden rails. The floor and roof are safe but it is only possible to see inside in dry weather. (For futher details see *Coniston Copper Mines* - A Field Guide.)

to Skelwith Bridge
(WALK 15)
The Sun
CONISTON
P
P
START
to Torver

Turn back up the valley where the stream, now on the left, flows in a captivating harmony of blue water-sculptured rock.

The gradient flattens and the open valley reveals an unnatural, yet strangely fascinating, sight; tidy spoil heaps and smart buildings amongst ruins, all backed by an impressive circle of mountains heedless of the extraction of their roots. Veins of silver rich copper were worked by miners from 1599. The mining heyday was in the mid-1800's and work ceased in 1942. The area around Coppermines Valley is now designated as an area of historical and scientific interest.

After 150 yards fork R on a gently ascending path passing the bottom tunnel (collapsed) of the Blue Quarries and its spoil heaps. Keep R where the track forks and continue uphill bending L at the next junction. The path can be seen stretching on for half a mile and the route well ahead can be identified. The line of the water-cut from Red Dell to Paddy End Copper Mill runs across the face of Kernal Crag well above the white Youth Hostel (formerly the mine office and manager's house surrounded by the Bonsor

*The site of the Old Engine Shaft, Red Dell and the
Thriddle Incline behind*

Dressing Floors) and away to the west the return path can be identified above the lower working quarry.

The track turns into a smooth green path with ice-planed rocks alongside. *The striations showing the direction of the ice flow are highlighted by lines of moss.* The two ruined pits to the left of the path were the wheel pit and engine house of the Bonsor East Wheel. The path crosses over the mine entrance which is blocked. Continue to the site of the Old Engine Shaft, its ruined towers still standing with strength and dignity. The mine entrance leading 20 yards to the engine shaft is on the right. *A line of metal spikes in the wall supported rollers and wooden push rods which transmitted the water-driven wheel power to the engine shaft for raising ore and pumping water.* **This shaft is dangerous***, it is 1395ft deep. Two white chains across the tunnel guard its approach. Only if you have a responsible attitude and a strong torch can you make the 20-yard approach to the chains. Beyond is a 15-foot drop to the balance-bob platform. Square holes in the sides held a wooden walkway, and the remains of the massive timbers used to support the works below can be seen.*

The path continues between two stone leat supports and goes down to the footbridge over Red Dell Beck. Cross and turn L between the stream and the fenced area.

Danger: *the fenced area with its innocent looking hole in the grass contains the Bonsor Shaft, the site of some tragic accidents.*

Gain the little path which runs along the bank of the water-cut to traverse the hillside. Clamber over a rocky bar near an old sluice gate. About 10 yards beyond is the pipeline where the water supply ran off to run a water-wheel which powered a compressor. Continue along this interesting balcony until the way is barred by a rocky knob. Here the water flowed through a tunnel but go round R or L, to rejoin the cut on the other side. At the base of a crag keep ahead where a path joins from the Paddy End workings below. (*From here make a mental note of the scene.) Then shortly after leave the cut and take the next fork R rising up the fellside to begin the ascent of the Levers Valley. The next feature is a little arched tunnel. Join the major track from the valley and keep ahead uphill. The next mine to the right is the entrance to the Kernal Level. **Not to be entered** but the stonework is to be admired. The track now presents a steep stony climb up to Levers Water, a natural lake enlarged by damming to serve the mines. The skyline is dominated by the ragged ochre gashes of Simon's Nick. *The mine was named after the miner who found the lode. It is said that the lode's secret was shown to him by the fairies, but years later, on revealing the source of his information, the lode ran out. Another version is that he sold his soul to the Devil in exchange for riches in copper. Today the cascading beck from Levers Water makes a gallant attempt to restore some beauty to the stricken vale.*

Turn L and cross the granite causeway of the outlet and make your way along the dam. On even the hottest summer day the water always looks dark, deep, cold and uninvitingly reflects the grey stony mountainsides; which is as well because it is Coniston's water supply.

The route now passes the Simon's Nick workings which descend 480

*Old sluice
gate on the
water cut
between
Red Dell
and
Paddy End*

feet to the level of the Paddy End (*where you made the mental note) and
further in flooded levels below.

EXCURSION TO THE GOOSE BIELD (see page 7)

Continue along the path around the left, western side of Levers Water to
the stream of Cove Beck. The path swings up and left in Gill Cove, so we
must leave it at a cairn. Cross the next slight stream and ascend the left side
of a spur which flattens below the steep crags of Great How crags. The
Goose Bield is on this platform below large scree boulders. No one knows
how old this structure is, but the builders had a marvellous view. Return
the same way.

TO CONTINUE keep on the waterside path for 20 yards then take a rising
leftward path to the mine. The danger areas are fenced. **Do not venture
into these areas**, the Danger notices mean what they say. Turn L before
the next fenced shaft and up a grassy bank where a path develops and
goes through the gap. Pass between ochre spoil heaps and begin the drop
into Boulder Valley. This is a pleasing grassy descent facing a fine view of
Coniston village and Water. Even the blue stone of the spoil heaps on
Coniston Old Man is not unsightly to the sympathetic eye. Cross the bridge
and old pipeline by the Pudding Stone, the largest of many in Boulder
Valley. The stream is Low Water Beck which leaves Low Water to fall in a
beautiful cascade from its hanging valley. The path continues through an
area of boulders, helped by a little bank of steps, and on to join a mine track
at a dressing floor. Keep on this track, its high terrace position allowing a
study of the working quarry over the fronds of juniper. At the T-junction
turn L and in 20 yards turn L again. Here we begin a gentle descent into the
Copper Mines valley and the full extent of the Paddy End workings can be
seen. Go over a stile in a cross wall from which the path leads on to a gap
in the next wall. Here the worn traditional way has been re-routed, a fence
barring its use, but the new way has quickly become well trodden. Follow
this to a ladder stile over the next wall from where the path continues
uninterrupted to the Miners' Bridge. Stay on the right side of Church Beck
and retrace the outward route to the start.

Goose Bield

The Goose Bield is a fine example of a fox trap, a bell-shaped thick walled
structure which was baited with a dead goose. The fox attracted by the
prey walked along a plank which then tipped the fox into the trap from
which it could not escape. There is another example in Ennerdale and a
name on the map suggests another site above Eskdale.

WALK 17:
Coniston Old Man & Goat's Water from the Walna Scar Road

Dow Crag dominates Goat's Water

GOAT'S HAUSE ❸

BRIM FELL

(WALK 16)

0

LOW WATER

❹

Remains of haulage way

(WALK 16)

THE BELL △

Old Quarries

DOW CRAG △

GOAT'S WATER

CONISTON OLD MAN △

SADDLESTONE QUARRIES

❺

BUSK PIKE △

❷ Rocky scramble

Quarry Ridg

Old Quarries

BURSTING STONE QUARRIES

Quarry Road

P

START

BLIND TARN

BROWN PIKE △

WALNA   SCAR   TRACK

Cairn   Rock cuttings

WALNA SCAR TRACK

to DUDDON VALLEY   (WALK 20)

(WALK 20)

❶

SUMMARY:
Once the highest point of Lancashire before county boundary

reorganisation, Coniston Old Man still retains its magnetic attraction. It is a mountain everyone climbs: the uninformed straight up and down by the old quarry tracks, unpleasantly bouldery; the discerning by the more varied route past dark Goat's Water in its stony hollow below the great crags of Dow.

Much of the walking is typical of the high fells, on eroded but clearly defined paths. It can be confusing in mist, so choose a nice day when the extensive summit views over much of South Lakeland and the Irish Sea can be savoured to the full. Boots recommended. Take care if the descent path is icy - it stays a long time in the shade in winter.

Distance:	5½ miles 9 km
Grade:	Strenuous
Terrain:	High fell walk, rough and stony paths
Summit:	Coniston Old Man - 2634ft (803m)
Map:	OL6

km   1 mile

N

CONISTON

Very steep

P

A593

to SKELWITH BRIDGE & AMBLESIDE

to TORVER

HOW TO GET THERE AND PARKING: From Coniston village A593 by the river bridge turn up the Walna Scar road (signed Walna Scar track and Seathwaite). Go straight on up the narrow and very steep road to the fell gate. Large parking areas through the gate, beside the track.

THE WALK: Set off along the broad stony Walna Scar road which runs westward along the lower slopes of the Old Man. *The first part of the way is well beaten by the lorries of Bursting Stone Quarry seen above. The route is very popular and weekends bring the tramp of many feet. The slopes of the mountain appear stark yet visitors' muted voices are gaily drowned by the resident skylarks' song. The flat boggy area you pass on the left was once a thriving community in prehistoric times, when trees covered much of the moor.*

The many stones and boulders along the wayside give no indication to the untrained eye and hammerless hand that to the left lies Silurian Windermere rock, to the right the Borrowdale Volcanics and in between the thin layer of Coniston Limestone *(now unhappily renamed The Dent Subgroup by the academics).* Keep straight on where the quarry road bends away to the right and enjoy the now widening views. *Across Coniston Water you can see Top o' Selside (walk 28) and to the west of the Water lies The Beacon and the Pool Scar round (walk 25).*

Continue until Brown Pike rises against the sky ahead and the road passes through two rock cuttings. Cross a stream to the meeting of four ways at a great cairn. Turn R up a broad green swathe, leaving the Walna Scar road to climb over the pass into the Duddon valley. (The path left goes down the fell to the A593 at Torver.)

Make your way up the path now rising towards Goat's Water along the western foot of The Old Man. *On this walk you never really see the*

The second rock cutting

The Summit of Coniston Old Man

mountain in its entirety and, though its presence is felt, the eye is drawn to the opposite side of the valley. From the Walna Scar pass rises Brown Pike with its quarried slopes and a grey line of glacial moraine hiding Blind Tarn. Red screes run down from Buck Pike and the dramatic jagged skyline of Dow Crag gradually smoothes into the col of Goat's Hause at the head of the valley. As progress is made up the valley the black cleft of Great Gully in Dow Crag East Buttress cannot be mistaken. It was the first recorded climb on the crag in 1866. The blue box below on its right is the Mountain Rescue first aid box.

Continue as the path steepens and scramble up a rocky bar below Goat Crag to be rewarded by the sight of Goat's Water reflecting its dark combe.

The crags are an extensive and popular traditional rock climbing area and climbers can usually be seen across the water and novices practising the sport dangle about on Goat Crag. The first impression of a gloomy atmosphere will grow into an absorbing appreciation of the subtle shapes and colours if you take a short break here.

Keep parallel to the shore where the path disappears amongst stones then continue up the steep, wide zig-zagging path to Goat's Hause, where a view appears over the Duddon and Eskdale valleys to the Scafell range. You have now joined the ridge path from Dow Crag. Turn R on the rising path. You are now on the broad, open upper slopes of the mountain so keep an eye on the weather. Stay carefully on the braided path which gradually makes a rising bend right to join a path from Brim Fell. Turn R along the summit ridge (**Take great care in mist** - to the left E of the path is a plunging crag). Low Water and, beyond Brim Fell, Levers Water can be seen below as you go along to the great summit cairn of The Old Man of Coniston. The panorama is excellent. The various facets of the structure give some shelter from the wind but this is not the spot to linger in bad weather.

Leave on the opposite side of the structure from your arrival, to the south-east for a few yards before the path veers left down steep slopes. The path winds down through upended strata, its rocks like piles of slates bordering the path. The way is very eroded and steep but reasonable if you skilfully pick out the old zigzags. At a large cairn on a shoulder go L. (Ignore the cairned path leading right and down above the quarry.) Continue down zigzags through old quarry workings. Tread warily if there is a nip in the air. Lingering frost, snow or ice in this sunless combe can render the path dangerous in winter.

Stay on the quarry track unless you want to turn aside to Low Water. Pass between the cuttings and quarry rid.

Away on the left the waterfalls of Low Water Beck plunge to the valley below. In the nineteenth century its waters were captured in a dam just below the Pudding Stone and taken by a race to work the Paddy End ore dressing floors, raced away again to work the mine sawmill, next to help power the Bonsor dressing floor then on to drive various crushing rolls, wheels, stamps, and jigs until eventually being returned to the beck.

Keep progressing down the track. Pass on the right a quarry heap in unstable, untidy chaos contrasting with the neat little stone arch of a tunnel. Neither to be entered. The remaining old set stones give a good grip underfoot for a while. Step over rusting cables and make your way down the track, now a stream, or keep to the little side-trod. Pass cairns and go through an ochre cutting with large cairns every few yards beyond. At a Y junction turn R (a good spot from which to survey the remains of the mine complex). Go through the gap and on the user-friendly path for ¼ mile back to the start.

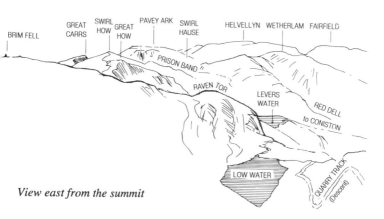

View east from the summit

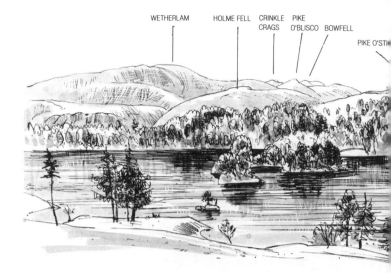

WETHERLAM   HOLME FELL CRINKLE PIKE
                          CRAGS   O'BLISCO BOWFELL
                                                PIKE O'STI

WALK 18:   Tarn Hows from Coniston

SUMMARY: Tarn Hows is a renowned beauty spot and therefore a busy place, yet this walk has its quieter stretches - and its noisy ones too, with the traffic drone of a nearby road. However, the woodland walking is delightful, the Yewdale fells impressively rugged, and the viewpoint of Tom Heights, the little fell above Tarn Hows, is well worth the effort. A good mixture.

HOW TO GET THERE AND PARKING: Park at the Coniston Old Railway Station car park, Coniston which lies a short distance up the Walna Scar road, on the left.

Distance:	7³/₄ miles 11³/₄km
Grade:	Moderate
Terrain:	Valley, low fell and woodland
Summit:	Tom Heights - 895ft (269m)
Map:	OL7

THE WALK: Turn R down the Walna Scar road for 50 yards then L. Pass the sixteenth-century Sun Hotel and continue down the road to the river bridge. *Coniston now is a well known tourist spot but in past*

centuries it was a busy mining and quarrying community leaving a legacy of architecture and industrial archaeology to mingle, little changed, with the self-serve units of today. Turn L over the bridge, then L again across the front of the Black Bull then L immediately on a lane down the side of the pub and out of the threat of the traffic. There is a brief chance to enjoy the character of the village, until after passing the Ruskin Museum the village is left behind.

The road begins to climb on its way to the Coppermines Valley. After quarter of a mile the surface ends. As the right-hand wall angles away right by a warning notice, read and turn R, go over a stile in a fence to gain a path running by the wall. Towering above are the slopes of Yew Pike and by choosing a shelf of soil-creep to walk on you can capture a choice view of the Yewdale Valley and Coniston Water with the dark crimped horizon of the Grizedale Forest.

Keep following the wall, pass a water hole covered by stone slabs and at a gate in the wall turn R into a stony walled path leading to the road. Go L in front of a row of picturesque cottages at the far end to the busy Coniston to Ambleside main road. Make a 20-yard dash L to a gap in the wall and National Trust sign (public footpath to Skelwith Bridge avoiding road). As you wander along the path the noise of the traffic, at first obtrusive, gradually fades from notice amid the unspoilt woodland of birch coppiced with standard oaks and a springtime carpet of bluebells,

celandine and sorrel. Cross two wooden bridges
and continue on the path which traces a spring line,
the rocky hillside of Yewdale Crag collecting the
waters above. A wall approaches the path from the
right and on the left White Gill pours its water down
the hillside. When the weather is poor the 'White
Lady' displays an exquisite cascade.

Cross the gill bridge and although there is recent
forestry work the path is clear to follow. *You may be
able to see a limekiln in the field below. The farmers knew that
there was a thin band of poor quality limestone (The Coniston
Limestone) which was a useful resource.* At a cross wall
take the ladder stile on the right, where the path
continues to a another ladder stile. The road
is now close by and the buildings of Low
Yewdale Farm appear huddled around
their tree-crowned wind shelter.
Primroses and early stitchwort
decorate the path, but as all good
things come to an end, the path
meets the main road. Take
care along this 500-yard
stretch for the road is
narrow and busy. Pass the
Tilberthwaite road end. Do
not let the view of Raven
Crag Buttress, seen to
advantage as the valley
bends towards Tilber-
thwaite, take your attention
from the traffic. Turn L
signed Hodge Close, and
cross the Shepherd's Bridge
(or ford the Yewdale Beck)
to gain a gate on the right -
sign to Skelwith Bridge. The
path by the wall is green
and inviting with the gentle
swathe of woodlands hiding
Tarn Hows ahead con-
trasting with the gaunt
bouldery flanks of Ivy Crag

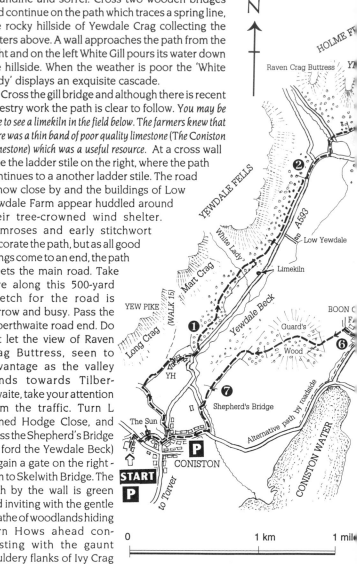

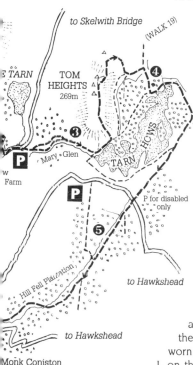

to Skelwith Bridge

(WALK 19)

E *TARN*

TOM
HEIGHTS
269m

P

Mary Glen

w
Farm

P

TARN HOWS

P for disabled
only

Hill Fell Plantation

to Hawkshead

to Hawkshead

Monk Coniston

to the left. Go through a gate, cross the field keeping by the wall to go through the next facing gate. The ensuing broad path winds over a rise to another gate (waymark). Continue past a group of old pines standing above Yew Tree Farm. Cross a high ladder stile R and down the track to the road. Pause to look at Yew Tree Farm, with its (much photographed) spinning gallery. Cross the bridge, turn L along the road for 25 yards and cross to the Glen Mary car park. Do not go on the bridleway but cross over the wooden footbridge and turn R on the public footpath to Tarn Hows. Stay on the left-hand side of the stream where the path climbs, passing cascading Tom Gill to the outlet at the Tarn. (For fuller description see walk 19.)

After the effort of the climb you are sure to want to relax enthralled by the scene, and here are suitable rocks worn smooth by a thousand bottoms. Turn L on the well made path which circles the Tarn. Pass a fenced area beyond which the path rises over a promontory, here turn L up a small path which climbs steeply up bracken slopes. There is a brief respite by way of a shelf with beautiful clusters of larch and silver birch. Keep ahead and up again onto the Heights and the sudden view from here is just a starter. Follow the path which trends north-east winding around rocky humps and a boggy hollow, then mount the first summit of Tom Heights. The views west are bountiful. Continue north-east passing a small cairn left to the larger one ahead. Here at the second summit the northern aspect unfolds. On again to the third cairn and the east scene completes the banquet. Continue along the path (E) which runs softly down grassy slopes which allow you to extract the last crumbs of pleasure the Heights offer. Drop into a gap (not the smaller gap just before!) where paths cross (small cairn on knoll ahead is not visited). Turn R and descend 25 yards then R again. Take the first small path left and down, passing a huge broken tree

on the right to join a major path -
the Cumbria Way. Turn R and soon
the water of Tarn Hows is glimpsed
again through the trees. At a
triangular path trend L onto the
Tarnside circular path where artistic
blends of leaf and water excel. Go
through the kissing gate and over
the little bridge of the tarn inlet
stream. Bog myrtle scents the path
and as the way rises away from the
water's edge, tree roots pave

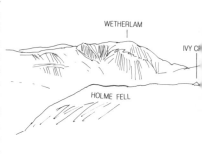

underfoot. Continue for half a mile until the tarn is once more in view and
paths meet in a K junction. Keep L on the high way, then in 50 yards go R
along a 'belvedere', the magic of its view undiminished by countless
reproductions.

Continue past a plantation to a kissing gate and through the 'Parking
for the Disabled' to the road. Cross to a public footpath and proceed down
a broad descending path by a wall. In 100 yards branch R on a narrower
path keeping beside the wall. As it descends the path becomes wider and
more important with the imprint of forestry work.

March on for quarter of a mile keeping ahead where a track from the
right curves in. Rhododendrons now occupy the sunlit spaces. At the next
junction go R and cross the stream. Straight on and, ignoring forking paths,
continue to follow the stream downhill. The track now crosses to the right-
hand bank and becomes steeper with the stream beginning a merry
chatter as it cascades below. Pass a series of pools, hewn from the rock
and filled with yellow iris and carry on to meet a surfaced lane and the edge
of the woodland. Cross the lane to continue along a NT signed path which
runs parallel to the main road. (Monk Coniston lies across the road.)

After 250 yards turn R at a farm drive. (The path to Coniston continues
by the roadside but is inferior to the route we describe.) Pass a woodyard
with the aromatic pine smell which the French manage to capture so
tastefully in their *sucre-de-pin* sweets, and on up an old lane. Pass Boon Crag
Farm with its neat grey stone barn, and just beyond where the lane bends
right take a stile on the L into a field. A green path leads on and up to where
a gate allows entrance to High Guards Wood. Continue on the path and
look for arrow waymarks to Coniston. At a National Trust sign keep on the
R fork uphill. The way is poorly marked with supposedly white-topped, but
rather mouldy-looking, poles through the rhododendron-skirted trees
and over the top of the hill. Pass over a stile and as you descend to the
woodland's edge Coniston can be seen below. Go through a stile into a

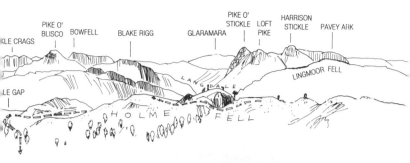

View from Tom Heights, showing the later part of the walk 19 over Holme Fell

field, waymarkers indicating the direction of the path, across the field and through a gathering of gorse to a gate. Follow the line of the left-hand fence to a ruin. Cross through the fence at a gate and still keeping by the fence carry straight on to a stile by the bank of Yewdale Beck. Climb the stone stile in the bridge parapet and cross the bridge to the road. Turn L for 150 yards to a junction. Turn R along Tilberthwaite Avenue passing car park and toilets on the left. Pass the church, cross the bridge where you turn R to retrace the outward route past the Sun Hotel to the start.

Monk Coniston

Monk Coniston was named by the monks of Furness Abbey, whose grange extended as far as this point, to distinguish it from Church Coniston, the present village. It was once the home of J.G.Marshall an eminent geologist. Now it is a Holiday Fellowship Centre. The Marshalls built the dam at Tarn Hows to make a single tarn from three smaller ones. In the grounds of the hall are several outstanding tall trees which you may be able to distinguish from the road - a 90-foot high Himalayan silver fir, a 127-foot high western hemlock (both the tallest in England) and a rare 50-foot high mountain hemlock.

Western Hemlock

WALK 19: Tarn Hows, Black Crag & Holme Fell

Black Crag

SUMMARY: A cocktail of pleasure! Wooded glen, delectable tarn, an isolated craggy summit, and an intricate return over a little-visited rugged fell with fine views. Some rough walking is encountered on the return along Holme Fell, but this could be avoided by a noisy path near the road.

HOW TO GET THERE AND PARKING: On the Coniston-Ambleside road A593, 400 yards south of Yew Tree Tarn, there are three ample parking areas by the Tom Gill bridge, at the foot of Glen Mary.

THE WALK: Gain the left-hand side of the stream and take the path up its left bank through the oakwood. Pretty cascades, enhanced by dappled sunlight on the shining mica-rich rocks, accompany the pathway. Pass a clearing newly planted in harmony with the surrounding woodland. When level with the waterfalls take the lower path which allows more intimate views of the tumbling spray. Go through a kissing gate in a fence. Where the water

Distance:	6¼ miles 10km
Grade:	Moderate
Terrain:	Valley, low fell and woodland
Summit:	Black Crag - 1056ft (322m)
	Holme Fell - 930ft (284m)
Map:	OL7

disappears under a bed of stones, the climb is almost over and the tarn outlet is at hand. The first sight of the tarn will make a lasting impression and you should look with tolerance on the crowds who are continually drawn to this beautiful spot. Turn L along the well maintained footpath, part of The Cumbria Way. Keep on the main path at a fork. The path rises over a rocky ridge and down the other side meets a crosspath. Our way lies L, but before you go, take the R fork and make your way to the waters' edge. The tarn lies in a perfect setting. A well known calendar scene but real, vibrant with light and shade, and emitting a spirit to stir the poet in you.

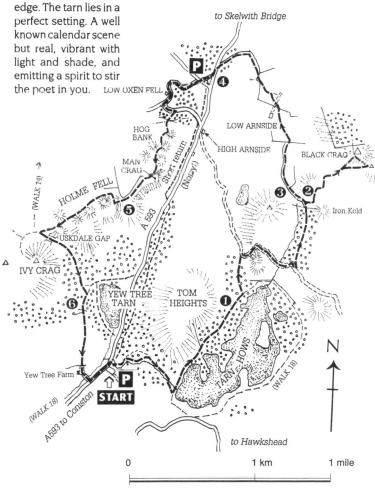

The path follows a little valley, clad with silver birches and bracken, to a stile at the Old Mountain Road. Here the Cumbria Way turns left but our route goes R. The road climbs the slopes of Arnside Intake and views to the west open out. At Iron Keld plantation look for a Public Bridleway sign to Black Crag on the left. Go over a stile into a larch plantation and continue to go through a gate at the edge of the forest. Turn L and go through an open gateway then bend back sharp R (cairn) onto a narrow cairned path. The path progresses through short turf studded with tormentil up the slopes of Iron Keld and at the top the view is promising. To the north-west Bowfell seems to wear a dark shadowy frown whilst across the Langdale valley the Pikes stand perky in the sun. There are two cairns ahead on Black Crag, the left-hand triangulation point at 322m is our objective. The path passes a flat hollow to the right with a quartet of larches, then makes for the top. The promised view has now blossomed and if you stay to examine its inexhaustible detail the grass may grow over your boots. Surfice it to say that the second part of this walk can be traced to the west backed by the great flanks of Wetherlam.

Do not go over the ladder stile but return down the path to the cairn by the forest. Turn R and continue on the path passing a gateway and a cross wall to Low Arnside Farm, a picturesque Lakeland farmstead. Keep straight ahead through a gap in a wall into a pasture. Look now for arrow waymarks. Bear L (blue arrow) and at the signpost L again (yellow arrow). The path is faint, but keep down the field to a gate (yellow arrow reverse

Low Arnside Farm

direction). Go down more steeply, ignore a gate on the right at the bottom of the field, and stay on the main rising path. A gate leads into woodland, and along the track to meet the main road. Cross onto a minor lane, alternative parking.

SHORT RETURN: Turn L and follow the line of the main road back to the start. The road is narrow and busy but to avoid its horrors a parallel footpath is available in the adjacent field or wood, at first on the right, then on the left.

TO CONTINUE: Take the L-hand minor road and go past a seat, a stream, up the hill past Low Oxen Fell cottage and take the next fork L. Do not scorn the road walk as much height has been easily gained. Immediately past a wallend turn right through a gate leading onto the fell.

(The route now gains the wide ridge-top of Holme Fell and progresses along its knolls and undulations over Man Crag, to the Uskdale Gap, all the while holding a general south-west direction. If the following descriptions do not fit exactly do not worry. We have tried to pinpoint reassuring features as the path is sometimes obscured by bracken and animal tracks come and go; however when you get to the Uskdale Gap you will recognise it.)

Go up the path by the fence following the line of the electricity wires to their first pole. Turn right for about 25yds then angle L up the slope and under the wires on a little trod shrouded in bracken. The path improves and continues gently uphill bearing away from the wires and running below the crest of the rising ridge. Looking back there is an unusual view of the Langdales. Pass a group of birch and rowan and go up and through a green trough, then to the right of a small screeslope to a wide lawn on the ridge overlooked by a graceful larch which mimics a tuning fork in winter. The elevated ridge provides extensive views south to Black Crag and north over the Tilberthwaite quarries to the central fells.

Continue to a little col with a rock pyramid. A perch offering a perspective of Coniston Water. The path continues through a rock gap then bends right with the lie of the ridge. (Look ahead and note an antique iron fence on the skyline.) Carry on into a gap then up the slope to the iron fence. Go over the stile and turn R along the fenceside. (Look ahead past the intervening knolls to the Uskdale Gap and Ivy Crag beyond.) Descend to the fence corner and follow its line R by the easiest trod to its L bend and about 100yds along to a fine holly where the fence dives away right. Bend diagonally L and progress up onto more open ground. Skirt to the R of the knobs and up L to a grassy corridor. Ivy Crag with its triangular cairn can be seen on the R. Turn R along the corridor towards it passing two large untarnished silver birches. Go R of a larch tree on a more obvious rising path where the road and Yew Tree Tarn can be seen below. The path now traverses a slope and sidles round an airy corner before crossing a green lawn of cropped grass where many sheep have staked their claim. Continue to traverse round another knoll where you are suddenly confronted by the final slope into the Uskdale Gap supervised by the masterful pyramid of Ivy Crag.

THE ASCENT OF IVY CRAG is described in Walk 14 page 74. Turn R to meet the crag path at the gap then return to this point to continue.

TO CONTINUE: Turn L (SE) and descend the stony path into the valley. At a huge boulder Yew Tree Tarn can be seen. Bend R to join a waymarked path at a large cairn and keep R passing large boulders (waymark white arrow). Go through a gate in the left-hand fence and keep on the path which bends R along a damp reedy trough to a winter feeding station for sheep. Go over a stile by the gate above Yew Tree Farm and make your way L along the wallside. The farm is famous for its spinning gallery. At the main road turn L for 100 yards to the start.

WALK 20: Walna Scar & Brown Pike from Torver

SUMMARY: Another walk steeped in history. An upland shelf, once home to prehistoric man, when trees flourished almost to the fell tops, is traversed past now silent quarry holes. Blind Tarn, with no

Distance:	6³/₄ miles 10³/₄km
Grade:	Strenuous
Terrain:	Medium fell, high fell
Summit:	Brown Pike - 2237ft (682m)
Map:	OL6

outlet, is well worth the diversion from the popular path nearby, whilst Brown Pike is easily accessible for those who like to tick a summit. There are wet patches on this walk, but fine views and interesting details make it very worthwhile.

The Walna Scar road was an old packhorse route between Coniston and the Duddon.

HOW TO GET THERE AND PARKING: Park at Torver on the A5084 using a spur of old road in front of the campsite.

THE WALK: At the junction of the A5084 and the A593 at Torver turn R towards Coniston. Walk a most interesting furlong passing the old Station House (the railway was built in 1859 and was closed in 1958). The Church House Inn, the church and the school (its old bell silent in its niche). Turn L on the narrow lane signed Coniston Old Man & Walna Scar. Begin a steady ascent zigzagging past campsites and cottages. The lane becomes high-walled and unsurfaced. Go through a gate where the aspect is now pleasant. A steep section has its set stones still intact. This was a quarry

CONISTON OLD MAN

Brown Pike and Coniston Old Man fom Ashgill Quarries

road, laid to carry heavy loads. Go through a gate by a barn, ignoring a track left, and bend R along the bridleway. The small roadside quarry soon passed on the left shows clearly the cleavage of the rock, and on its flat

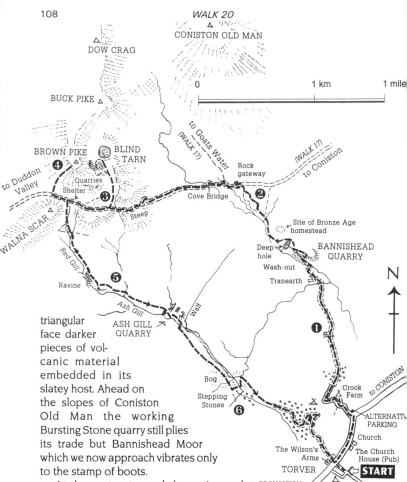

WALK 20
△
CONISTON OLD MAN

DOW CRAG △

BUCK PIKE △

0   1 km   1 mile

BROWN PIKE △   BLIND TARN
❹
Quarries Shelter   ❸
to Duddon Valley

WALNA SCAR

Red Gill

Ravine   ❺

Ash Gill

ASH GILL QUARRY

to Goats Water (WALK 17)

Rock gateway

(WALK 17) to Coniston

Cove Bridge   ❷

Steep

Site of Bronze Age homestead

BANNISHEAD QUARRY

Deep hole

Wash-out

Tranearth

Wall

N

❶

to CONISTON

triangular face darker pieces of volcanic material embedded in its slatey host. Ahead on the slopes of Coniston Old Man the working Bursting Stone quarry still plies its trade but Bannishead Moor which we now approach vibrates only to the stamp of boots.

Bog

Stepping Stones   ❻

Crook Farm

ALTERNATIVE PARKING

Church

The Wilson's Arms

The Church House (Pub)

TORVER   START

to BROUGHTON   to GREENODD

At the next gate read the notice and remember its advice. Continue over the Ash Gill bridge, passing an access track to Tranearth, now a Climbing Club cottage, and on towards Bannishead Quarry. Go through the first gate then take the kissing gate, the right-hand of two gates ahead. Turn immediately R to the next gate and bridge. Bend L at the waymark post (not applicable to our route) and advance along the path between the spoil heaps until halted by a recent sign. There has been a washout and the stream has taken the path with it.

Bannishead Quarry

Turn R on the steep path arranged up the spoil heap and turn L at the top along the grassy shelf. It is interesting to imagine the moor covered with trees, as pollen tests assure us that it once was. Also interesting to have a potter about to investigate how the washout occurred and view its results. Continue up the path, the trees on the left camouflaging the quarry access and circle the huge fenced quarry hole, completely flooded and fed by a waterfall. The path forks - both lead up to the Walna Scar road but take the left-hand one. Walk on up to the next shelf where thereabouts was a Neolithic settlement. There are several green paths ahead through the bracken. Choose the one ahead and go on to meet the Walna Scar road.

The Walna Scar road is an ancient pony track from the Duddon Valley to Coniston rising to almost 2000 feet in its crossing of Walna Scar.

Turn L through a rock cutting and a few yards brings you to a large cairn, landmark at the major junction where the path to Goat's Water, Coniston Old Man and Dow Crag leaves the pony track. (Walk 17)

Continue along the Walna Scar road enjoying views stretching to the sea, to cross the packhorse bridge over the Torver Beck. *The beautiful arch was widened to take the laden carts from the quarries and now carries the ugly burden of a grey and rusting side-rail.* After the bridge the road becomes more eroded but there is foot-soft turf alongside. Mount the steeper zigzags - cairns - passing a small quarry on the right. Continue through a cut section then

Blind Tarn and Buck Pike

look out for a cairn about 20 yards after a small stream, Lee How Gutter. Turn R on a path which has a rushy start. Keep on this path up the shallow Gutter valley until it begins to climb through a spoil heap, where you move R along the shelf at the base of the stones to the undrained corrie of Blind Tarn. *It is a place of soaring rocky slopes and desolation. A place where the chirp of a bird echoes and the water waits captive for the touch of a breeze, a place to linger and experience the peace.* Return to the Walna Scar road and turn R up the stony road once more.

A few yards on the left the old green track lies untrod beside its stony usurper. Pass a little shelter on the right. Just fine for one, cosy for two, possible for more in proportion to the ferocity of the weather.

NB In the next few yards look down left for a slight trod leading down into the hollow below. Note it for this is our return route.

Continue to the pass - cairn - between Brown Pike and Walna Scar (the raised ridge leading SW culminates in the White Maiden). It is worth going on a few yards to see the view into the Duddon valley and over the western fells.

Turn R and mount the broad cairned path to the summit of Brown Pike 2237ft. From here the view is certainly splendid, showing the trickling streams feeding the mountain tarn of Goat's Water, the birth of the Torver Beck, its adolescent leap to Coniston Lake where it joins the River Crake in its march to the sea.

Return to the cairn on the pass. Turn L and return down the road for

50yds past an area of rushes then turn R off the road down the grassy trod previously noted. We are heading for the deeply gashed ravine of Red Gill Beck far below. Keep down a grassy spur between developing streamlets. Cross the trace of an old grassed over quarry path. Keep on down the grass slopes parallel to a stream to reach the side of the ravine where there is a slight path. Continue down the left-hand side of Ash Gill to old quarry workings. *Ash Gill is popular with geologists; odd scrapings and decapitated rocks indicate their search of the Coniston Limestone for the elusive fossils trilobites and brachiopods.* By keeping well to the left you can avoid the bracken. Pass huge boulders and find a good sheep trod which leads to the fence of the Ash Gill Quarry. Keep to the path. Pass between the fence and the deep hole then straight on for 25yds where you bend L to gain the level of the roofless buildings. Cross the haulage way to a flat area. Turn R and go below the spoil heap to cross the stream by the haulage bridge. Bend slightly L and follow the line of the stream. Cross a tributary stream and keep on to an area of reeds and rushes where there are stepping stones across the pool. Look for a stile by a gate in the left-hand wall. Go over and turn R (making a necessary circuit of a foul boghole first) on a good path by a fence then a wall. Go through a gate in a wall corner into a path-cum-streambed. Continue down the path which develops into a walled lane. Pass the plantation to a ladder stile on the L. Continue on the green lane round the front of a cottage and straight on to Torver at the Wilson's Arms.

Old quarryman's shelter on the Walna Scar Road

WALK 21:

The Lickle Valley & The White Maiden

The upper Lickle Valley and White Pike

SUMMARY: A pleasant walk partly along an ancient green track well away from the crowds of central Lakeland. There is a short return through the conifers along a forest road, but the full walk described gains the top of White Maiden quite easily, whence a steep rough descent joins the shorter walk at the edge of the forest. Boots for the full round, as there are wet patches.

HOW TO GET THERE AND PARKING: Take the Broughton Mills road which leaves the A593 1 mile north of Broughton, and in 200 yards turn R on a lane which runs along the crest of a low hill. After 1¾ miles keep L at a fork, down to the Appletree Worth Beck. Car park on the R over the bridge.

Distance:	7½ miles 11½ km
Grade:	Moderate
Terrain:	Valley, medium fell
Summits:	Walna Scar - 2035ft (621m)
	White Maiden - 2001ft (610m)
Map:	OL6

THE WALK: Leave the car park and turn right up the road. Caw with Stickle Pike to its left, is well seen. The road runs through forest but soon the trees on the left end and the lovely valley of the River Lickle is revealed. The

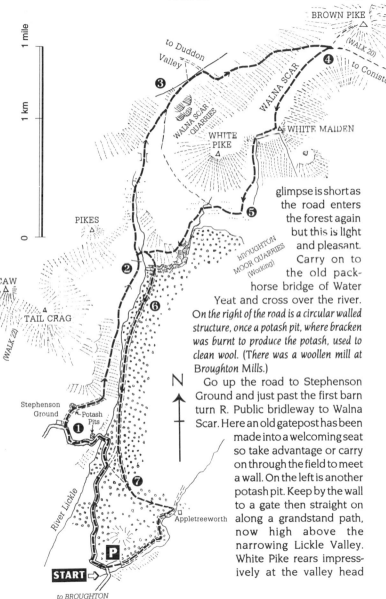

glimpse is short as the road enters the forest again but this is light and pleasant. Carry on to the old packhorse bridge of Water Yeat and cross over the river. *On the right of the road is a circular walled structure, once a potash pit, where bracken was burnt to produce the potash, used to clean wool. (There was a woollen mill at Broughton Mills.)*

Go up the road to Stephenson Ground and just past the first barn turn R. Public bridleway to Walna Scar. Here an old gatepost has been made into a welcoming seat so take advantage or carry on through the field to meet a wall. On the left is another potash pit. Keep by the wall to a gate then straight on along a grandstand path, now high above the narrowing Lickle Valley. White Pike rears impressively at the valley head

START ⇨

to BROUGHTON

looking greater than its almost 2000 feet. Go through a gateway in the intake wall and after crossing a stream zigzag up the rising ground to a gap in another wall. Down to the right the infant Lickle is joined by its tributary, the Yewry Sike, a merry stream in a rocky bed and spanned by a wooden footbridge which is crossed on the return. Keep ahead to a path junction.

SHORT RETURN: Turn R and make your way past a spongy area to the bridge.

N.B. It is well worth continuing to the gap near Dawson Pike, a mere half mile further and 200 feet higher, where you will be rewarded with a wonderful view of Dunnerdale and its surrounding fells. Retrace your route to the short return. (Short Return continued ***)

TO CONTINUE: Bear L still on the bridle track following its imprint in the green swathe and rising up the valley with the craggy top of Pikes on the left. The track now tries to dodge Yaud Mire. Avoid the wet bits with common sense and when you reach the gap at the rim of its hollow by Dawson Pike, the view into the Duddon Valley is superb.

The track now becomes a balcony and leads along the foot of White Pike to the Walna Scar Quarries. Pass along the silent dressing floor. *Roofless stone buildings offer seats, shelter and reminiscences of a time when the place bustled with industry.*

At the far side of the floor the route ahead can be examined. Take heart, the Walna Scar pass merges into the hillside below the skyline and does not climb the summit of Brown Pike although the prominently visible path would have us think otherwise. Where the track approaches a wall bear away R to another spoil heap and up to the next dressing floor. In 100 yards our bridle track now joins the Walna Scar road. Turn R uphill and if you want to take the grind out of the climb stop and stare north-west at Harter Fell, bursting out of its girdle of conifers, the Wallowbarrow gorge swallowing the Duddon at its feet. On reaching the pass Coniston Old Man and Coniston Water appear to the east.

At the cairn turn R up the smooth, grassy, pathless wide ridge and wander along to another cairn. Maintain direction along the ridge top. This is the Walna Scar. Not the usual idea of a scar but more like

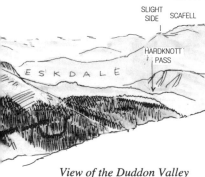

View of the Duddon Valley

a tonic putting a spring in the step and dispensing a feeling of elevation. The vestige of a path appears, then evaporates. Descend slightly to a saddle then rise passing a tiny tarn to the stony outcrop on the top of White Maiden. The summit stands proud allowing a bird's eye view in all directions but at its foot the drab working quarries of Broughton Moor bring back to industrial reality the nostalgic thoughts developed in the blue ruins of the Walna Scar.

From the cairn follow the wall R continuing along the ridge towards White Pike until reaching the saddle between White Maiden and White Pike. (Diversion to the summit of White Pike from this point.) The wall bends away left. Keep by the wallside and descend very steeply down the grassy slope. When the quarry buildings away to the right disappear from sight begin to make your way gradually R to the foot of the lowest rocky spur of White Pike. Pick up a slight crosspath and go to the R along it as it avoids Caw Moss. The forest will now be drawing nearer and the Lickle Valley recognisable. Keep on the improving path over a little clapper bridge and along through a cut gap to a boggy impasse which is crossed by the leap and hope method. At a cross path turn L and down to the wooden footbridge.

The central fells from Walna Scar

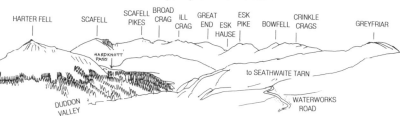

Short return joins in here.*

Cross the footbridge taking special care if you are left-handed - there is only one handrail - then go over the stile into the forest. The intimate leafy shade makes a welcome contrast after the open fell. Go straight on the path which gains importance and after passing a turning circle becomes a mature forest track. At the Y-junction keep L on the main track and L again at the T-junction. About a mile and a half has been covered in the forest. You have rounded the Knott which is entombed in the trees and have entered the valley of the Appletree Worth Beck. Its water is just below on the right and also the ruins of Appletree Worth farm. Turn sharp R and follow the track by the beck passing an area of exposed metamorphosed rock - hardened by volcanic heat, to the forest fence and the car park at the start.

Potash pits

There are several of these located in South Lakeland. Bracken and birch twigs were burnt to produce the potash. Lime was added to produce caustic potash which when boiled with tallow, produced soft soap used in the cleaning of wool. Potash was produced in this fashion between 1545 and the late 1700s.

Grounds

In 1509 and 1532 Furness Abbey made agreement to allow illegal settlers to enclose small areas and build a farmstead. Each of these settlements was called a 'Ground' coupled with the name of the family. There are over 36 grounds in High Furness, several in the Lickle Valley.

Potash pit above Stephenson Ground

WALK 22: Stickle Pike & Caw

Hovel Knott and Little Stickle

SUMMARY: A route which encompasses in miniature the best qualities of Lakeland fellwalking - pleasant grassy paths (not like the worn out tracks of the higher fells!), shapely craggy summits set in an intricate necklace of sparkling tarns, and widespread views of the higher peaks. The complete round is quite strenuous, but easier options can be taken. The area is quiet and peaceful but rough in parts - boots advised.

HOW TO GET THERE AND PARKING: At Broughton Mills, a tiny hamlet astride the River Lickle in the Dunnerdale Fells, 2½ miles north of Broughton village. Once the site of a woollen mill, which later became a bobbin mill. A corn mill also operated. The Blacksmith's Arms dates from the eighteenth century.

Distance:	7½miles 11½km
Grade:	Strenuous
Terrain:	Medium Fell
Summits:	Great Stickle - 1001ft (305m)
	Stickle Pike - 1231ft (375m)
	Caw - 1735ft (529m)
Map:	OL6

Parking is limited but a few spaces are to be found where the single track road widens before and after the bridge. Please take especial care to park considerately. The roads are liberally provided with passing places. Do not use them for parking. More liberal parking can be found where the route crosses the Seathwaite road at its highest point.

THE WALK (from Broughton Mills): Cross the river bridge and take the narrow lane to Green Bank Farm. Continue past the farm to a cottage then take the track opposite into a wood with a wall on the left. At a gate leave the wood and keep ahead up the slope to a green, walled lane. Bend L at a fork (where the path fom Scrithwaite Farm joins in).

Go on the grassy track through a gateway, then bear R. As height is gained views over the Lickle Valley and the estuary of the Duddon will draw your eye. The low walls of the lane appear again and over on the right gorse is aglow in March, enhanced by colourful bullfinches.

Staying on the lane decend and cross Stickletongue Beck, go through a gate and after passing a barn on the left, the next gate leads through the intake wall onto the open fell. Keep L by the wallside a few yards then branch R on an obvious path which leads directly up the col between Hovel Knott and Little Stickle.

Turn R, and make your way by little paths up the hummocky ridge, past the shoulder of Little Stickle to the rocky summit of Great Stickle, 1001 feet.

(An alternative longer but less steep route takes the main path round the base of Hovel Knott. The path rises to a low col (where the main track bears left towards Ulpha). Keep straight on below the steep flanks of Great Stickle to another ascent and path junction. The summit of Great Stickle lies a few minutes away on the right.)

Pass between the cairn and the triangulation point and survey the route ahead. To the north is a tarn, this is our next objective. Take an imaginary path down the initial steep slope then make your own way towards the tarn. *The crystal clear water will tempt you to linger and peer at the wealth*

Great Stickle

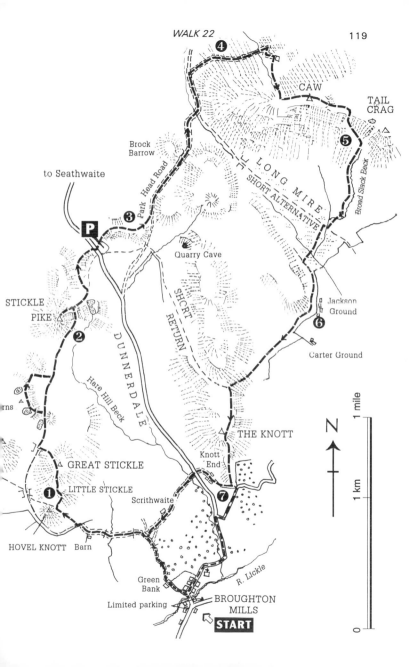

to Seathwaite

P

3 Park Head Road

Brock
Barrow

4

CAW

TAIL
CRAG

5

L O N G   M I R E

SHORT ALTERNATIVE

Broad Slack Beck

STICKLE
PIKE

2

Quarry Cave

S
H
O
R
T

R
E
T
U
R
N

D
U
N
N
E
R
D
A
L
E

Hare Hill Beck

rns

Jackson
Ground

6

Carter Ground

GREAT STICKLE

1   LITTLE STICKLE

THE KNOTT

Knott
End

7

Scrithwaite

HOVEL KNOTT   Barn

N

1 mile

1 km

Green
Bank

R. Lickle

Limited parking

BROUGHTON
MILLS

START

0

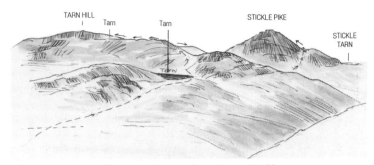

TARN HILL   Tarn   Tarn   STICKLE PIKE

                                                    STICKLE
                                                    TARN

The onward route from Great Stickle

of busy water creatures, whilst above, skylarks sing and if you search the ground many owl pellets hint at the popularity to wildlife of this delightful spot. Walk round the right-hand side of the tarn and go over the gap which frames Stickle Pike ahead.

Direct route towards Stickle Pike

Descend towards a shallow U-shaped valley then take the path which contours left round its head at a lower level.

Diversion to the Tarns

From the gap turn L onto Tarn Hill, where over the immediate rise is hidden yet another mirror-like tarn, go round its right-hand edge and bear L to a cairn on the summit. It leaves no doubt why Tarn Hill is named, from this cairn is a five-tarn panorama.

From the cairn a slight path circles the hillocks at the valley head. As you pass another tarn turn your back on it to see the perfect U-shaped valley, complete with erratic boulder. A text book example of glaciation.

Descend the grassy slopes to the right, thus avoiding the steep rocky slopes on the hidden far side of the next knoll, to join the direct route contouring path from the gap.

A broad path leads easily up the right shoulder of Stickle Pike. At the first cairn on the shoulder a glance back will reveal the mirror tarn reflecting in the distance. Go to a second cairn then turn L where the steep, pink stony path to the summit promotes a real mountain atmosphere. Do not descend the stony path but turn north at the cairn and make your way down the more amenable grassy slopes on the right returning to the second cairn. Turn L and down to pass Stickle Tarn bulging out of its hollow on the right. Keep ahead through the gap which frames Caw, our next mountain. The path now ambles down wide and clear gradually pulling round rightwards to join the road.

Parking. Short return to Broughton Mills - turn R along the road down Dunnerdale.

CAW

Cross the road and take the track on the left. Follow this until you meet another major track. This is the Park Head Road. Turn L on the 'road' for three-quarters of a mile. Progress is rapid round the flanks of knobbly hills and over Brockbarrow Pass. As you walk along, the northern aspect is pleasing with the forested slopes of Harter Fell and the Wallowbarrow Gorge seen over Dunnerdale.

The 'road' descends to cross Long Mire Beck. (A return can be made from here by following the Beck up its valley, see map.) From this point the ascent of crag girt Caw looks somewhat formidable, but be encouraged, it is far easier than it looks. Just after crossing the bridging stones of the next small side stream look for a green track which branches to the right and rises up the hillside. The track leads to a disused quarry and provides an easy way to gain height up the steep and inhospitable slopes of Caw. At the huge spoil heaps the track winds up to the retired buildings where plenty of flat slabs and walls offer a sheltered seat.

A makeshift cairn on the slope to the right of the entrance level indicates a very faint path straight up the fell to a depression in the skyline. As you toil upwards there appears more of a path by a tiny stream with small encouraging cairns every now and then. On gaining the top of the depression bend L and ahead the triangulation point comes into view. Fork L by some angular rocks to the fine summit. A special atmosphere of isolation rests on Caw. Once a hive of quarrying, the swarm has gone and few visit this worthy summit. Leave to the east, heading for the col between Caw and Tail Crag but there are no paths to help you. Keep to the ridge top on the grass. Do not go up a slight rise, but bear R down a gap on grass to avoid steep rocky ground. An indistinct shelf slopes diagonally left on grass to the gap. Do not go on as far as the tarn but turn R and move down to a depression. Swing L to a bright green spongy area from which a spring emerges to form a

The summit of Caw

useful guideline trickle, whilst up on the left the bizarre rocks of Tail Crag point their strata at the sky. Follow the growing Broad Slack Beck to the flat expanse of Jackson Ground. At a stream junction ignore a path to the right. Keep straight on across the valley floor to the intake wall corner. A sheep trod in line with the wallside leads to Jackson Ground Farm. Keep on the path above the farm and continue by the intake wall passing a barn. The wall bends away but the path contours and now heads for the spur between Raven's Crag and The Knott. Cross a stream and pass by an old mine level on a well established path, the scene dominated by erratic glacial boulders. On reaching the spur at a broken wall where the path bends right cross the wall left and go along the ridge. At the cairn on The Knott you can make a panoramic summary of the route before continuing straight into the summit hollow. At its lip look R for a ridge to use as a way down. It is a steep grassy slope demanding care, go straight on to a stile and gate in a wall.

Either -

a) Over the stile turn R on a lane down the hill, L at the next junction and half a mile down the road is Broughton Mills.

Or -

b) Turn R along the track to Knott End Farm. Go through the farmyard and along the track to join the road by the Scrithwaite Farm gate. The farm lane crosses a stream and winds up pastures between a wooded knoll and a rocky knoll. By the time the farm comes into view you will have sensed that the whole area is bathed in a haze of tranquillity (if the bull is not at home). Go straight through the farmyard and through a gate into a green lane. Fork left to descend to Broughton Mills.

Stickle Pike from Tarn Hill

CHAPTER 2

Around Coniston Water & Windermere

The lower hills around Coniston Water and Windermere are composed of Coniston Grits and Silurian Slates, softer rocks than the hard rugged volcanics of the central fells. Thus the landscape is gentler, more rounded and often clothed in woodland. Much of the Furness fells have long lost their covering of trees due in parts to extensive use for charcoal burning, however, a lot remains elsewhere, supplemented by more recent planting of conifers.

Walking in this area is often quiet, unspoilt and utterly charming. The viewpoints provide grand panoramas of the high fells, often as a backdrop to a boat-dappled lake.

Not all the forest is conifer, indeed most of the walks are through more interesting varied woodland, with fine little summits here and there. When the higher fells are shrouded in mist this area can give delightful walking. Every season has its attractions here and all-year-round sheltered walking is available. Forest walking is not to everyone's taste, but those who do enjoy it appreciate the interplay of light on foliage and branches; the tranquillity of jewel-like tarns enclosed by the sheltering trees; the rich carpet of mosses; the glimpse of deer and birds. Occasional distant views are all the better for the scarcity. And of course, the wonderfully sited sculptures in the Grizedale Forest are worth seeking by anyone imaginative or artistic.

WALK 23: The Woodland Valley from Broughton-in-Furness

The market square and stone fish slabs at Broughton-in-Furness

SUMMARY: This is Lakeland at its quietest, a circuit of the entire Woodland Valley, which includes a flat flood plain - remnant of glacial times, a low hill with a fine panorama from the Coniston Fells to the sea, intricate paths through meadows, woods and bracken covered hillsides, a jewel-like tarn and a jungle-like streamside track. It is quite a lengthy walk compared with

Distance:	10 miles 16km
Grade:	Moderate
Terrain:	Valley and woodland, low fell
	By the Short Return
Distance:	5¼ miles 8½km
Grade:	Easy
Map:	OL6 and PF626

others in this book, with some rough going at its apex. It could be split into two shorter walks, both worthwhile, but the best lies in the second half.

HOW TO GET THERE AND PARKING: At the market square, Broughton-in-Furness.

THE WALK: Start from the market square. Pass by the stone tables (*the stone tables were once used for sale of the fish caught in the River Duddon and the estuary*), and exit towards the toilets, keep to the 'Gents' side and turn R along a lane. Cross the line of the old railway, (*Broughton-in-Furness to Torver and Coniston branch 1859 - 1958*), and over the stone stairway-stile beyond. Look for a yellow arrow waymarked route and turn L parallel to the line. Go through a field and a gateway. At the next wall turn R to a slit stile then keep by the wallside and straight over the rise. There are odd snippets of views towards Woodland as you carry on to a thin-leg stile. Turn L towards Wall End Farm. The way is now more colourful with tansy, yarrow and dog rose in the hedgerow. On approaching the farm look for a waymark to the R. Go steeply down to a stile in a lane, cross the surfaced road and enter the woodland track at the public footpath sign. Keep L and down past the

CAW PIKES WHITE PIKE WHITE MAIDEN BROWN PIKE CONISTON OLD MAN THE KNOTT
TAIL CRAG DOW CRAG

The bridge below Latter Rigg

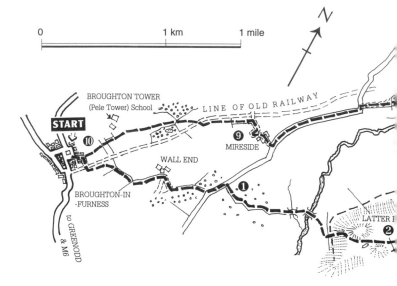

plantation to the road. Turn L along the road for 100 yds then R on the public footpath to Woodland Hall by a gate supported on a huge stone slab.

Across the valley stands Latter Rigg, its modest 80m enhanced by the contrast with the flat valley floor. *The Woodland mosses (Black Moss, Middlescough White Moss and Heathwaite Moss) are separated from those of the Duddon Estuary by Wreaks Causeway which carries the main road.* Keep ahead by the wall on a vehicle track over the rough heathland pasture. *The air is full of chirps, trills and twitters; a buzzard is often seen wheeling overhead while smaller birds flit in and out of the clumps of Turks Head grass, the walkers' nightmare.* Cross the bridge over the drainage cut then head for a stile and bridge (which looks like a fence as the water is hidden deep in its retaining channel) straight across the field. Cross the bridge and strike out straight across the field for the slopes of Latter Rigg where a green path can be seen rising towards the summit. An isolated remnant of stone wall containing a gateway and stile allows access to the foot of the Rigg. Brace muscles and go straight up the hill. Bend L to a large hawthorn, here bear R and zigzag up to a shelf. Turn L up grass and rock to the summit cairn. From here a splendid landscape of wood, hill and vale is on view. Yet this Rigg is little visited and the unworn grass transmits hints of exploration to your feet.

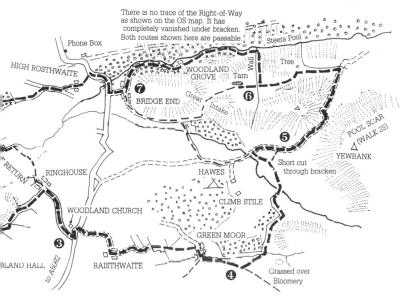

From the summit observe a belt of trees to the NE and a stony track, your onwards route. Keep along the ridge to a slight hollow. Descend R past a reedy pool to a gate in a wall. Go straight on a green path to rise and join a stony track to Woodland Hall.

Proceed through the farmyard gate, pass the stables and turn L into a field. Go straight across keeping right of a concrete storage tank to a stile by a clump of trees. Stay by the left-hand fence which is soon crossed by a stile. Follow the fence line and then left of a copse to the wall end which is supported by a four-holed slab - half an old pole gate. Straight on then follow remains of an old wall high up on the left. At the field corner is a stile which leads into a lane at Ringhouse Farm.

SHORT RETURN

Turn L to Ringhouse Farm and straight through the yard. The gate leads out onto a green way. Keep on to another gate with a yellow waymark arrow. The path hugs the left-hand wall round a corner (for a few yards) and we are in open country again. Bend R on a narrow grassy path to face into the valley. A pleasant atmosphere pervades the scene and scattered birches and rocky knolls invite a halt to enjoy it. Descend into the valley. At a crosspath keep L then bend R to resume the general direction of descent into the valley walking beside a wall overhung with hazel catkins. Cross the wall by a ladder stile, then the beck by a footbridge made from a sturdy second-hand beam. Go ahead to the next ladder stile. Keep along the left edge of the field by the embankment. Pass by a gateway and along the wall to a little footbridge over a stream. Keep on towards the wood, not to the broken gap in the wall ahead, but accept the challenge of finding the bench mark on an excellent little stile in the wall corner. Go over and turn R to a stile in the woodland fence. Carry on past the remains of a mossy wall. Turn L and in 20yds meet the major path and turn L joining the longer route on its return through the wood. *** [Ignore the yellow w/m arrow which leads up to the road.]

TO CONTINUE

Turn R down the hill then L at Woodland and the church of St John on its little knoll. *The present church, its stone walls dulled by pebbledash, is unspectacular and dates from 1865 but an earlier one was marked on a map of Lancashire by Saxton in 1577. (A bridleway - The Monks' Walk - was used to bring coffins from Torver, to Woodland, by the monks of Furness Abbey.) In spring however, the graveyard becomes alive with golden daffodils under a graceful canopy of yew.*

Opposite the church gate turn R on the public footpath along the farm access road to Green Moor. Go through the pasture to the farm and out of the gate at the end of the tarmac into an old green walled lane. The walls are low enough to display the serene valley. Go through the gate at the end of the lane and up the bank ahead. Turn R to a gateway in the field corner. Pass the curve of the wall on the left and head across the field to a big tree to the L of two barns at Green Moor. On the west lie the trees of Green Moor Wood and to the east the bracken-clad slopes of Woodland Fell. Go through a stile under an ash tree and turn R to the fell gate. Go over a

clapper bridge over Green Moor Beck and turn L. The path runs by a gurgling water then rises gently through the bracken slopes until looking down on the now muted stream and the edge of the wood. Cross a little side stream, pass a hawthorn bush and continue rising to fork L at the next hawthorn tree. We are now aiming for the corner of the wood on a tiny trod. Descend to a ford by the wood corner. Cross the ford and follow the edge of the woodland. Keep by the wall bending L onto the shoulder of the hill - a good

Carving on porch
at Woodland Church

viewpoint. The wall swings away to the left for awhile. Keep on to meet the wandering wall again and stay by it. At a gate and tin sheep pen don't go through, but bend R and go through a fold in the land to a wall end and a ford on Hodge Wife Gill, with holly and alder. From here turn your back to the stream and look to the onward horizon - left of centre is a lone tree and col north of The Knott, which is our objective. Keep in line with the stream and wall and where they bend away straight on through a fence by an abandoned Bamfords mower. As the path drops into the valley head look for a short cut R. Use it to cross the stream and turn R on the broad green path which runs up the valley. Climb up to the col 207m between The Knott and Yewbank where another fine prospect awaits. From the col the wooded vale of Steers Pool lies tranquil and apparently remote yet hidden on its slopes are the A593 and the disused railway (from Broughton-in-Furness to Torver). Descend a zigzag and continue down the path to a wall and gate with notices. Do not go through. Turn L along the wallside into a no-man's land - a secluded trough running along the western face of The Knott where only a few discerning walkers seek out its pleasures. At a stand of larches the wall bends away to the right. The route is now pathless for a while as the old path is lost in the bracken. Stay along the trough at the L edge of the bog along the foot of the rocky hillside. When 30 yards from a lone pine standing in the centre of a colourful bog, look for a path forking and rising L through the bracken to a higher level below a rock slab. Continue almost level to a ladder stile over a high wall (the right of way footpath is wrongly marked on the O.S. map and not reliable). Note that the ladder stile has replaced an old step stile, so you need to go 5 yards L to find the continuation of the path. It is necessary to divert round watery depressions but continue in the same direction to the beautiful little unnamed tarn, edged with a rock band overhung by an old oak admiring itself in the water. Now a choice of return:

1) Via Steers Pool and Woodland Grove. This is certainly the most attractive and adventurous way.

2) Via Great Intake. This is slightly shorter.

1) RETURN VIA STEERS POOL AND WOODLAND GROVE

Return to the wall and over the ladder stile. Turn L down the wallside, finding the least difficult route through the bracken, to the stream. Turn L over an awkward step stile in the wall - a friendly shoulder would help - to gain the small path beside the stream. The walk beside the stream, often on its very brink, is a real pleasure and too soon you reach the secluded Woodland Grove, the site of an old mill. Pass straight by onto the access track. The way is still beside the stream which has increased in volume and is tumbling merrily down a series of cascades and under an old clapper bridge. Mixed woodland lines the track and even in winter the pink flowers of herb robert peep from the grassy verge. At Bridge End Farm join the Return 2.

2) RETURN VIA GREAT INTAKE

Pass the tarn and keep on the path which stays level through the bracken past an old stone - beware of paths branching right and veering off down the hillside. The wide green path bends over the ridge of Great Intake and reveals a view of the Woodland Valley again. Bend L by three silver birch trees and descend steeply towards a belt of woods. Bend R and follow the wall to a gate giving access to a farm lane. Turn R and continue to join Return 1 at Bridge End Farm.

From Bridge End Farm go down the access lane to the road. Turn R on the road, cross the bridge and climb up through the wood. Where the woods end turn L on a track (public footpath sign). Go through the field and down to High Rosthwaite Farm. Go through the farmyard onto the access lane, and down the hill with an outlook over the flat valley. At a T-junction turn R past a cottage and barn to a public footpath on the L. We are now on an old pathway with open views to Latter Rigg. After a gate the path narrows and becomes invaded by a small stream. Rise up into a wood with a straight, leaf-strewn path to a gate at the wood's edge.*** (The Short Return joins halfway through the wood.) Keep straight on and through the next gate into an enclosed path leading to a surfaced lane. Turn L and after a speedy half mile along the road turn R and to Mireside Farm. Go through the farmyard to a gate ahead and keep R up a green lane which bends L through a rock cutting. Go over a stile on the L just below the old railway. The path runs parallel to the trackway. Go through a gate in a wall. Keep ahead with a hedge/wall on the right. After passing a large oak look for a three-stone stile on the R. Make a rising diagonal line towards a gate in the crosswall. Keep along the upper edge of the next pasture for 100 yards and find a stone-step stile to cross the old railway to the field opposite. Follow the wall to a gate and then bear R to a kissing gate beneath pines into the park of Broughton Hall. Keep by the fence through the gentle parkland. Pass a trio of evergreens on the left and head over a little hillock to the enclosed garden wall and kissing gate with a turnstile. Keep along the wall through a small wood to the next gate and into Broughton's recreation field with seats. A few yards away is a gate near the public toilets.

A variety of refreshments are available in the town.

Broughton-in-Furness

Broughton-in-Furness was once the centre of the wool trade and the manufacture of oak swills (baskets). It was mentioned in the Domesday Book. On August 1st, the Reading of the Charter (Elizabethan charter to hold a fair), is carried out at noon when pennies are thrown for the children.

WALK 24: Blawith Knott, Tottlebank Height and Great Burney

Blawith Knott

SUMMARY: A peaceful walk which links three small but interesting hills, with widespread views. It is difficult to imagine these bracken-clad hills clothed in woodland, which they were until all the timber was used to fire 'bloomeries' in medieval times for the production of iron. Bracken is prolific at the height of its growth, but the walk uses small paths which should

Distance:	6³/₄ miles 11km
Grade:	Moderate
Terrain:	Low fell
Summits:	Blawith Knott - 806ft (246m)
	Tottlebank Height - 775ft (236m)
	Great Burney - 979ft (298m)
Map:	PF626

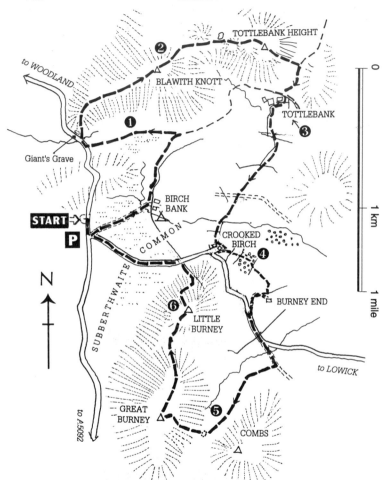

improve with use. Look out for yellow hammers, they live in areas of bracken.

HOW TO GET THERE AND PARKING: On the A592 at the top of the hill between the Crake Valley and the Duddon Valley a narrow unfenced lane signed 'Woodland' branches north. This runs along the base of Great

Burney to the flat moss of Subberthwaite Common. Just past a lane on the R to Crooked Birch, park in an old quarry on the left.

THE WALK: From the parking turn R a few yards, turn L then fork L immediately along the farm road towards Birch Bank (camping). (You could walk along the road north to Giant's Grave, but the way described is more pleasant.)

At the farm swing L on the bridleway and keep along the wallside. (Ignore the blue arrow when you come to the gate on the right.) On approaching the foot of Blawith Knott the track bends right to join a substantial cross path along the base of the fell. Turn L. Just in view to the south are the controversial wind powered generators on Kirkby Fell. Presently the path rises, keep on the main path R and on a small shoulder there are remnants of old bloomeries. At the road turn R, cross a small stream and turn R on a path between the stream and boulders.

Giant's Grave is a Bronze Age barrow, by the roadside - not the first cluster of boulders but the less prominent shallow hollow with a single sentinel rock.

The path makes a steep ascent of the west ridge of Blawith Knott and arrives at a rocky outcrop topped by a cairn. Here are all the ingredients of a fine summit, including the fact that, on arrival, it is not the top. However, the rich view rises to the occasion with the gentle Woodland Valley backed by the sturdy little hills of Stickle Pike and Caw and on their right the mass of the Coniston Fells. The angle relents, pass a lesser cairn on the left and the next small cairn along is the true summit. To the south Hoad Hill Monument (see page 205) above Ulverston points a strict finger to the sky but the wind generators completely overshadow our final objective, Great Burney.

View NE from Blawith Knott

Progress 50 yards along the summit ridge to the next cairn, then spy out the summit of Tottlebank Height with a little tarn amongst the knolls to its left. The path now descends and slants to the left crossing a shallow col. Skirt the first knoll on the right, then straight over the next knoll to pass the tarn on its right. Keep straight on around another knoll towards the cairn on Tottlebank Height. The path is intermittent but the cairn is soon reached.

Go on a few yards to a better viewpoint on top of a 12-foot slab which is not visible from your angle of approach. The wooded Crake Valley is diplayed from the sea to Coniston Water. Turn L following a shallow trough in the direction of Beacon Fell to descend a narrow trod through bracken, at first towards Cockenskell Farm. Past a boulder turn R on a cross path which traverses the fellside and improves as it runs down a tiny valley with a miniature triangle of scree. Continue to meet the road at Tottlebank Farm.

Turn L a few yards to the start of the tarmac. Go R through the gate by an attractive duckpond, public footpath signpost, then turn L through a gate into a field, waymark arrow. Look past the telegraph post to a gate and kissing gate and cross the field to it. Keep R by a wall to another kissing gate, hidden by hawthorns in the corner. Keep a straight course for Crooked Birch Farm on the hillside ahead. Go through a pair of gates and down the field to a stile in a fence. Cross the brisk stream by a footbridge then go up the field to the right of electricity poles and an old broken wall to a stile in the next fence. Keep to the L of the farm, going through a gate to its left which leads into the field above the farm.

SHORT RETURN. Turn R along the fence side above the farm, go through a fancy gateway to meet the farm lane, which joins the road. Turn R and a short walk along this regains the car.

TO CONTINUE. From the field above Crooked Birch turn L (waymark) through a gate. Ignore another waymark on the left, but keep straight across the field into a small plantation. The path is difficult to see, but cross it to a fence where another stile is found a few yards higher. Pass between rock outcrops ahead to a stile in the fence just before Burney End. Bear R and gain the farm lane through a gate. Turn R and in a few yards join the road then turn L along it. Just through the fell gate at the base of a broad shallow valley, branch R on a green track which can be seen winding up the hillside ahead. Cross a small stream and after a slight rise turn R on a path leading up the wide valley of Combs. This uses a bracken-covered spur to reach a lone stone. A view of the Crake valley has already materialised.

Now look at the way ahead. In front stretches a large area of bog and, although it seems nearer and is possible to cut across to go up the slopes of Great Burney using sheep trods, it is more satisfying to pass the bog on its left and visit the ancient cairn at the path-meet on the col, from where the sight of the shining Duddon Estuary demands another pause. Turn R, fix your eye on the summit triangulation point and wend your way up the steep slopes of the hill to reach it.

The summit of Great Burney 298m is known for its stone circles. On arrival the ancient remains are rather meagre but the view is 100%. Turn R (N) to Hanging Stone and along the Grey Stone Moss ridge to Little Burney, taking care not to drop back into the Combs Valley now down on the right. The path is but a sheep trod, bear L and head in the direction of Birch Bank Farm which is clearly visible to the north. Cross the shallow hollow of Grey Stone Moss before rising onto Little Burney. To gain the road descend the steep end of Little Burney making for the gate in a crosswall to meet a path. Do not go through but turn L and follow the path to the road.

Turn L along the road crossing Subberthwaite Common and R at the junction to the start.

The ancient cairn on the col below Great Burney is overlooked by the modern wind power generators on Kirkby Moor

WALK 25: The Furness Fells Horseshoe -
Pool Scar, Yew Bank and The Beacon

Ancient cairn between Yew Bank and Rattan How

SUMMARY: The Furness fells feel pleasantly remote, giving rough walking reminiscent of the Scottish Highlands with heather underfoot. Good tracks are rare along the horseshoe ridge walk. Ignore the mish mash of electricity poles and savour the area's roughness, with its host of shapely little hills, miniatures against their loftier neighbours, the Coniston Fells. It is difficult to imagine that these bare hills were richly wooded in medieval times when the wood fuelled the 'bloomeries' to smelt iron ore.

This is a walk for a clear day, for it would be very confusing in mist, and the splendid views of the Coniston Fells should not be missed.

The Beacon is the only popular peak on the walk, whose 'tourist' ascent is described in Walk 26.

HOW TO GET THERE AND PARKING: Park on the NE side of the A5084 Greenodd to Coniston road, on R 200 yards from Sunny Bank if approaching from the south, opposite the little side valley of Mere Beck. *Toilets 1 mile south at Brown Howe lake side car park.*

Distance:	5¾ miles 9¼km
Grade:	Strenuous
Terrain:	Low fell
Summits:	Green How - 550ft (168m)
	Yew Bank - 673ft (205m)
	Fisher High - 700ft (213m)
	The Beacon - 835m (254m)
Map:	OL6

THE WALK: Cross the road and go over the stile at the Torver

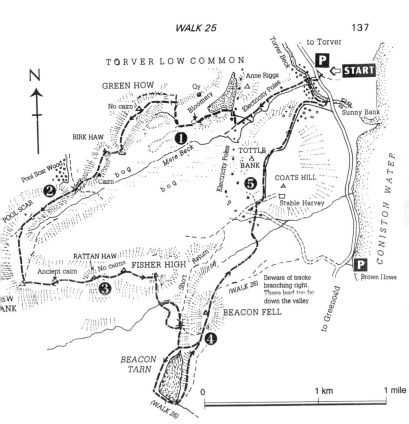

Commons sign. A path leads down to a ford over the chuckling Torver Beck but use the footbridge poised over a merry cascade. Keep ahead up the tributary valley of Mere Beck. The valley has an attractive unkempt look, invaded by short bracken, juniper and holly, and overlooked from above by a few mature silver birches. The path rises gently to cross a small stream. This is the outflow from an old tarn its level raised as a reservoir. Continue up the path for 60 yards to where the valley opens suddenly into a wide bowl. Turn R, then jump across the stream again in its meander and go onto the little dam. From here Coniston Old Man is reflected in the water and to the NE the end of the tarn frames the Fairfield fells. Turn L and cross the dam and the outlet and make your way along the tarnside to its end, where it is replaced by an area of tussocky bog. (The skyline ahead is the onward circuit.) Keep ahead on the rising, drier path to the site of a bloomery, a circular area of grassed over uneven mounds *(see page 147 for fuller description).

About 50 yards past the bloomery turn R and cross the bog at its highest point on a sheep trod. Wind up a bracken slope by a lone larch tree and a tiny stream to where its miniature valley bends away to the left. Keep straight up the slope, with the larch at your back and the nose of Coniston Old Man ahead, to the protruding rocks on the brow. Turn L to gain the ridgetop. The view of nearby tarns, hollows and valleys, with the spread of Coniston's Fells on the horizon is an almost embarrassing reward for the meagre effort made to attain it.

Turn W (left) along the ridge to the summit of Green How with its seven tarn view. The Mere Beck valley lies to the south and on the far western horizon stands Black Combe.

From Green How look at the route ahead. The next modest summit, Birk Haw, has a prominent rock cairn. Drop into the hollow ahead and slightly left. Pass a rock tooth and continue past a small tarn on the left to Birk Haw. On arrival the cairn is more modest than it appeared but is given prominence by riding on the back of a rocky horse.

Keep parallel to the upper Mere Beck Valley keeping to the highest ground. Pass a cairn situated 30 yards from the path on the left, then go through a rock gap, down and over a little heathery rise to a col containing a distinct path. Identify the col by looking down to the right where the intake wall encloses Pool Scar wood. Cross the col and make the steep climb up a peaty path on the hillside of Pool Scar. The path soon improves as we walk along the ridge parallel to the rising Mere Beck Valley. Pass through a slight rock defile and the crest of the ridge allows an uninterrupted scan of the Woodland valley. (Cairn 30 yards on right.) The path now curves gradually south to meet the path junction at the head of the Mere Beck Valley.

Turn L on the path leading to the tall cairn on Yew Bank. This summit has a little sister cairn a few yards away. It is worth moving to it for an improved view of the Duddon Estuary and to look down and spot the tiny tarn visited on Walk 23.

We now turn our backs on the Woodland Valley and take the narrow path east towards Rattan Haw. The broad heathery ridge leads to an ancient cairn, a prominent doughnut of stones. The path onward is more imaginary than real but the direction of progress is the important thing. Cross a shallowing and take the line of the grass between heathery humps. A better path is met at the next gap, bear L along it for a short distance. A small scree across a boggy flat now to your left pinpointing your progress. The path traverses the north slope of Rattan Haw. Take care not to lose any height but mount the slope right through the heather to the flat topped summit of the broad ridge. Ahead Beacon Fell begins to dominate the view.

Make your way over the pathless short heather to Fisher High, directed by a few cairns for easiest walking. Keep on the highest ground towards Beacon Fell. After a few ups and downs arrive at the stones and cairn on Fisher High summit, a distinctive end to the horseshoe ridge, with The Beacon now dominant in front.

From your prominent position survey the next section of the route. On leaving Fisher High you will be confronted by a deep hollow holding a bog. A major path skirts the bog along the base of The Beacon and climbs to the col between the Fell and Tarn Riggs. The next aim is to join this path without getting your boots full of bog.

At Fisher High summit turn R (SW) and wind steeply down aiming to cross the stream where it shakes free from the mire. After crossing turn L along the edge of the dry ground. Do not be tempted to cut across to the major path too soon. It is wetter than it looks. Join the major path.

SHORT RETURN TO THE START: Turn L and follow the path past the bog and along a gentle descending traverse round the foot of the fell. At a junction of paths bend L to cross a small stream and continue to another stream. Keep straight up a grassy knoll and under the power line to join the tarmac road (see below*).

TO CONTINUE THE ROUTE TO BEACON TARN AND THE BEACON: Turn R and go up the major path to the col. After the bog, bracken and

The summit of The Beacon

heather the contrasting beauty of Beacon Tarn will take you by surprise. The way up the fell branches left but the circuit of the tarn is short and most rewarding.

The path up the fell has more ends than a frayed rope but keep curving up and left and you will arrive on the path which beaks easily through a rock bar to the summit. It is a fitting climax, with a view of the whole route and a circular horizon.

Leave the summit to the north along the ridge. A narrow slit in the rock (or go round to avoid it) will put you on the right path which descends, guarded on its right by a spiky rock rib, to a green platform. (An alternative smooth green path runs parallel on the right, but take care to fork L. All the tracks leading right take you too low into the little valley.) Branch left to cross a small stream. The path is now wider and a bit soggy but soon improves becoming a nice green way passing through bracken slopes. Cross another stream and on under the power line. Go straight across a track and along the shelf of a rock outcrop. Beware of stepping into a bath-shaped hole carved into the rock of the shelf. Cross the next stream and join the surfaced road. Go L up the road.

(If you find that you have strayed onto the wrong track down the fell, you will eventually meet the road, turn L and rejoin the correct route.)

*SHORT RETURN JOINS HERE:
Go past the Public Bridleway and turn L on the public footpath at the farm gate and the intake wall. Follow the wall side over the gap between Tottle Bank and Coats Hill. The path has been repaired at a boggy section. Keep down by the wall through scattered junipers to the slopes above Torver Beck. Before a small sidestream turn L down the grass to a path above the beck. Turn L along the path with the cascading beck playing a fine finale below. Cross Mere Beck and the wooden footbridge over Torver Beck. Return up the wallside path and over the road to the start.

Sunny Bank Mill produced wooden bobbins used in the Lancashire cotton industry. Its heyday was 1847-1870. The last working bobbin mill in South Lakeland, at Stott Park near Lakeside, has been preserved and is open to the public. See page 192.

The Beacon
Sometimes known as Beacon Fell, this was an important link in the chain used to warn the local inhabitants of impending invasion - notably the Spanish Armada. Neighbouring beacons were at Black Combe and across Morecambe Bay at Warton Crag.

WALK 26: Beacon Tarn and The Beacon from Blawith Common

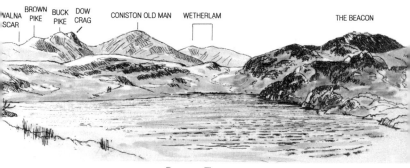

| VALNA SCAR | BROWN PIKE | BUCK PIKE | DOW CRAG | CONISTON OLD MAN | WETHERLAM | THE BEACON |

Beacon Tarn

SUMMARY: The Beacon, on Blawith Fells, is a lowly hill, but its isolated position gives a commanding view of the Cumbrian coast and Coniston fells, hence its use as a beacon hill. At its foot Beacon Tarn nestles in a lonely hollow amongst rough knolls, a tranquil spot. We visit the fell on Walk 25, but this is a delightful little walk in its own right, ideal for children.

HOW TO GET THERE AND PARKING: Start on the A5084 2½ miles south of Torver near the foot of Coniston Water, where Brown Howe car park (*toilets*) is by the lakeside and is popular for picnics. There is alternative roadside parking on Blawith Common three-quarters of a mile south.

THE WALK: From the car park entrance turn L along the road. There is no roadside path, but cross the bridge, pass a lane end. Keep along the road or better, branch R towards a quarry. Here you will discover a green path which runs parallel to the road. Keep high over a small knoll on a crunchy bracken path which descends to a glade. Pass Copper Beech Lodge (seen on the road below). Now forced onto the road again continue to Blawith Common signs (¼ mile). Go through a rock cutting then 100 yards beyond

Distance:	3¾ miles 5¾ km
Grade:	Moderate
Terrain:	Low fell
Summit:	The Beacon - 835ft (254m)
Map:	OL6, PF626

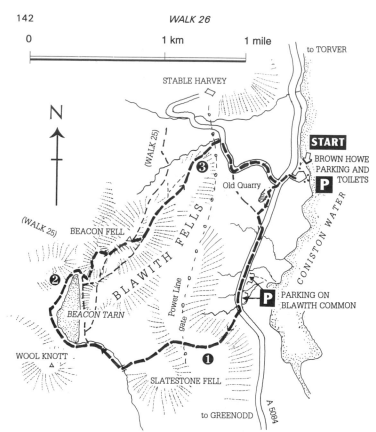

branch R on a broad green path snaking up the hillside. Ignore the various side paths but be sure to stop on a grassy platform for the first of the many wonderful panoramas that is in store. Cross and re-cross the stream and pass an upright rock bearing the tiny holes for some long-gone sign. A steady climb soon reaches level ground at power lines. Cross a boggy patch in the depression using good stepping-stones and under the second line, to a steep climb up the shoulder of Slatestone Fell to a cairn. A forward view to Wool Knott over Tarn Beck in its myrtle-clad valley accompanies the descent to the valley path. Turn R over the bridge and up a recently improved path to meet Tarn Beck. Do not cross but keep on the L side of the beck to outlet of the tarn.

Encircled by rocky knolls and bracken-clad slopes sprinkled with heather, Beacon Tarn lies tranquil in its ice-scooped hollow with the Old Man of Coniston and his companions on the northern horizon. From the Tarn shore paths radiate in all directions.

1). The L side of the Tarn - we recommend and describe this path for the splendid views of the Beacon.
2). The R side of the Tarn - the path is exposed in places.
3). Rising traverse of Bleak Knott which misses out the joy of the lapping water.

Keep L round the Tarn. Note the green path rising up the Beacon from the inlet (north). This is the path we take. Cross the inlet stream and meet the path leading from the low col. (Walk 25 from Fisher High joins in here.) Cross this path and go up the path slanting diagonally R which develops into the path previously noted up the fellside. The green path runs through cushions of heather, which give a wonderful wine-coloured spread in summer, with the delicate pink of its dried flowers lasting to cheer the bare winter.

Gain a shelf holding a boggy patch and as you approach a steep rocky barrier turn R for 10 yards to join a more prominent path, then L on it, up the edge of the rocks. Go along the wide ridge to the summit cairn which is a few yards off the path to the left.

The name of The Beacon is truly deserved, what a splendid outlook! The knotts and commons form a colourful yet complex landscape horizon, a fringe of overlapping mountains strung from coast to coast.

From the summit our approach path looks almost man-made - a neat green swathe between the rocks. Return to it and carry on. Now facing Coniston Water, Peel Island can be seen below. Here is the setting for Arthur Ransome's children's adventure story *Swallows and Amazons*. Keep on down the smooth wide path but do not become too involved in a detailed perusal of the lake shore for the site of the old jetty and furnace at Low Nibthwaite, or speculating on the exact spot near the end of the lake where the Gondola was found and raised - a steeper stony part demands attention before the path becomes smooth and green again. At a fork take the R turn. Pass by a minute pool and rock slab to meet a crosspath. Turn R and in a short distance a fine holly tree to the right will pinpoint your progress. Turn L and before you descend, it is best to preview the onward route from here. Ahead are power lines, the valley of Black Beck and Stable Harvey Farm on the slopes of Coats Hill beyond. Many paths lead down. We are aiming well to the right of the farm where its access lane runs down the valley. Continue down (do not go over a little rock bar with an inviting path), to go under the power lines past a hardy oak tree. Edge steeply down a bank and make an exploratory foray to cross the narrow stream and gain the surfaced lane. Turn R down the lane. (At a bend the public footpath to the R cuts off a corner for those who have parked at the Blawith Common car park.) The lane runs through a dainty birch wood to the A5084 road. Turn L and the Brown Howe parking is a few yards away on the R. (Turn R and Blawith Common is half a mile along the road.)

WALK 27: Torver Back Common, Coniston Water West Shore & Coniston Hall

Coniston Old Hall

SUMMARY: The walk along the west shore of Coniston Water is one of Lakeland's gems, a beautiful blend of lake, woods and hills, with some relics of long gone industry. Combining the shore path with the airy walk over Torver Back Common makes a delightful but short outing.

Distance:	5³/₄ miles 9¹/₄km
Grade:	Easy
Terrain:	Valley, low fell, woodland
Summit:	Torver Back Common - 500ft (152m)
Map:	OL6

You may not choose to extend the walk through a busy campsite to visit Coniston Hall (it is best out of season), but the hall is one of the architectural treasures of the area. It is hoped the National Trust will restore it sufficiently to open it to the public.

In summer you will meet a lot of people on this path for the nearby campsites are very popular. The lake is a hive of activity with windsurfers flitting silently across the water. Anyone who dislikes the noise of Windermere will find Coniston Water more tranquil, for the only powered boat allowed is the steamship 'Gondola'.

HOW TO GET THERE AND PARKING: A5084 1 mile S of Torver, 500 yards N of Sunnybank Mill. Parking place for 6 cars.

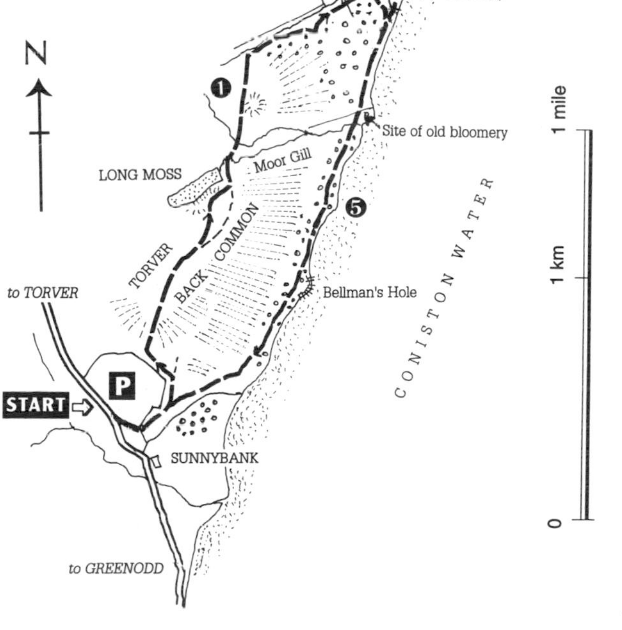

to CONISTON

Sailing 145
Club

CONISTON HALL

❸

CONISTON HALL, CAMPSITE (WATER PARK)

Windsurfers

Bloomery

HOATHWAITE LANDING

End of Torver Common Area ❷ ❹

Circular stone ruin

Site of old bloomery

N

Site of old bloomery

LONG MOSS   Moor Gill

❶

❺

TORVER BACK COMMON

Bellman's Hole

CONISTON WATER

1 mile

1 km

to TORVER

START ➡   **P**

SUNNYBANK

to GREENODD

0

THE WALK: The track winds round the hill to the first stile/gate. Go along the level green path for 100 yards. Coniston Water is in sight but better views lie in wait. Do not descend but branch L onto a narrow path, which may be obscured by bracken in summer, heading for a wall. Follow the line of the wall up the hillside onto Torver Back Common. On reaching the broad crest turn R aiming for the highest point until you strike a path along the crest. *From here is a grandstand view of the mountains to the north, but do not let the Old Man of Coniston monopolise your attention, for the view south down the lake and Crake Valley is equally attractive.*

Proceed northwards along the ridgetop path. Walking is easy and a view of the northern end of Coniston Valley is revealed. When you are halted by a steep bank at Long Moss Tarn turn R and descend to cross the outlet stream (look for carnivorous plants - sundew, butterwort, also other bog loving plants).

Make your way over a boggy area to the gap left of a pointed knoll on the skyline. The path now begins the descent to the lakeside keeping right of the stream. Pass through a scattering of gnarled junipers into a shallow valley. Go through a gate into a once-coppiced birch wood and continue down to join the path along the lake shore.* Turn L and through a gate. This peaceful woodland was once a site of activity with bloomeries and charcoal burning. The path passes through mature woodland and because of its proximity to Coniston Hall campsite is well used. Go through a gap in a wall and on through the plantation. After crossing a stream the path stays close to the shore. The next stile/wall is the boundary of the Torver Back Common area. The water hereabouts is often occupied by colourful windsurfers and the shoreside rocks and jetty at Hoathwaite Landing by their admirers. Continue the route crossing a footbridge and wall/stile. *Progress can be gauged by the proximity of the white house on the opposite side of the lake. This is Brantwood - home of John Ruskin and now a museum to his memory (see walk 29).*

Cross a field to a kissing gate and through the camping ground. The huge cylindrical chimneys of Coniston Hall soon come into sight. Go along the surfaced road to the entrance gate at the Hall. *Coniston Hall is a working farm with a campsite shop (open end March - end October) where canned drinks, ice-cream etc. can be obtained - NO snack bar or restaurant. It is a rather dowdy-looking building on approach, yet it retains some elegance in its chimneys, windows and great hall.*

Return by the same route to the entrance to Torver Back Common. Continue on the shore path past the plantation. Ignore the footpath right which leads to Torver village. Walking along under a mixture of evergreens, birch and oak makes this section a real pleasure. Tough hollies cling to the land, their roots exposed above the shingle. Go through a gate and meet the outward path from the shallow valley.* Keep south along the shore

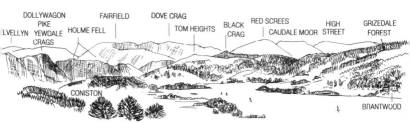

View from Torver Back Common

path which is now narrower, but has been repaired in places. Cross Moor Gill - then look for the flat site of a bloomery, indicated by tell-tale slag on the beach. As progress is made the woodland gradually gives way to a more open fellside of bracken and gorse interspersed with slender silver birch saplings. The narrow path undulates. *This is a lovely section of the shore in spring where primroses sprout from the waterline rock crevices and waytails search the emerging springs.* At the little bay of Bellman's Hole a jutting rock promontory provides a viewpoint looking across the water to Top o' Selside and the dark green blanket of the Grizedale Forest. The path now rises over a lakeside crag then returns to lake level. Pass a seat where we say goodbye to the shore as the path turns away from the lake climbing beside a wall. At a fan of paths keep straight ahead uphill towards an upper wall. On meeting a cross path turn L to the first stile/gate. Follow the track round the end of the hill to the start.

Bloomeries and Charcoal Burning

Iron smelting was a thriving industry in South Lakeland from ancient times until the 1960s. The ore was smelted in 'bloomeries,' small iron furnaces dating from Norman times. Coniston shore was a very convenient site and bloomeries flourished along its length. Along the beach and by every stream was a bloomery. The ore was brought by packhorse and boat from Low Furness, to be smelted with charcoal. Yew was particularly good for charcoal. Although much woodland remains along Coniston shore, elsewhere in Furness many of the woods were destroyed. In 1565 the residents of High Furness requested a Royal Edict to prevent the bloomeries destroying more woodland.

Close to the bloomeries were the charcoal burners' pitsteads - hollowed circular areas still visible for the potash rich soil now grows a richer flora. You can spot remains of the charcoal burners' huts, small stone-walled enclosures which were roofed by turves (see the replica in Grizedale Forest).

The small bloomeries were superseded by larger furnaces in the Crake Valley at Nibthwaite, Penny Bridge and Spark Bridge, in the Rusland Valley at Force Forge and in the Leven Valley at Backbarrow Ironworks which closed in 1965.

Coniston Hall

Coniston Hall was the seat of the Flemings from 1270 to the 1700s. Originally it was a pele tower which was converted to a Great Hall. Its cruck frame is rare in the Lake District, but the tall cylindrical chimneys are typical. It is gradually being restored. The nearby settlement of Bowmanstead was the home of the bowmen who defended the hall.

Before the building of the railway, ore from the Coniston mines was carted to the lake at Coniston Hall, shipped to Nibthwaite quay at the south end of the lake, then carted to Greenodd on the Leven estuary.

Coniston Water

Coniston Water is an ice-gouged lake, with two deep basins, the deepest being 184 feet. The length and straightness of the lake made it a venue for attempts at the world water speed records, culminating in the death of Donald Campbell in 1967. His body was never recovered.

In winter the lake attracts whooper swans; in summer mergansers and sandpipers. Dippers and grey wagtails frequent the shores.

WALK 28: Coniston East - Top o' Selside and Bethecar Moor

SUMMARY: A gradual easy ascent with fine views over Coniston Water and the high fells is followed by a rough moorland walk where route-finding ability is required to link sheep tracks through a maze of interesting little rocky summits. The character is more akin to Scotland than South Lakeland. Avoid it in misty conditions and wear boots!

Distance:	5¼miles 8½km
Grade:	Moderate
Terrain:	Low fell
Summits:	Top o' Selside - 1091ft (333m)
	Arnsbarrow Hill - 1025ft (313m)
Map:	OL6

HOW TO GET THERE AND PARKING: There is no parking in High Nibthwaite itself but to the north of the village there is room for a few cars beside the high wall bordering Water Park. A further quarter of a mile along the Coniston lake shore road is a car park in the woods which also serves visitors to the southern end of the lake.

THE WALK: Start by walking back to the village. *The quay at the end of the lake, was a busy spot before the railway was built to Coniston. Copper ore and gunpowder was shipped here to be carted on to the coast. The large high barn on the left as you enter the*

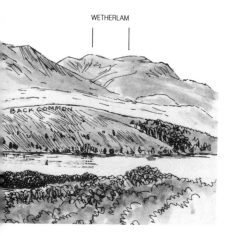
WETHERLAM

BACK COMMON

village was possibly a storehouse.

 Start at the public footpath signpost pointing up a short lane, between the telephone box and the post box. Go through the gate and onto a rough track which is followed for 1½ miles and at first rises pleasantly below a low tree-decked cragline. Keep on the track as it sweeps away from the wall in an S-bend

View from track above Nibthwaite

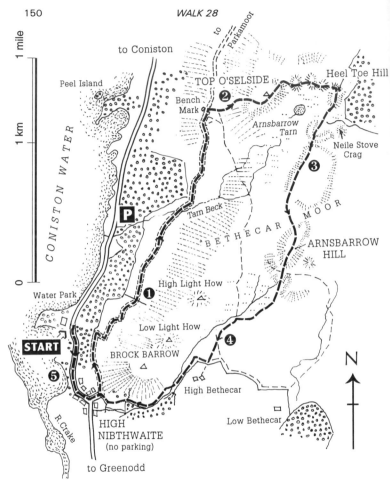

where the change of direction brings a view of the lower Crake Valley, a scene of Lakeland husbandry, and the rocky fringe of Brock Barrow nodding above. Continue steadily, yet scenelessly, easily gaining height until suddenly a magnificent panorama unfolds. Top o' Selside lies ahead whilst across shining Coniston Water the Old Man and its companion mountains beckon.

Progress along the track through an open area of bracken and juniper. Ignore a path right across the moor to a stone barn. The views are still

Nibthwaite, with Brock Barrow behind

excellent, the Coniston mountains being close enough to allow detailed identification and little Beacon Fell to the west, so often merged into a moorland background, stands bold, proud and inviting. Pass a Private way on the R. Soon walls enclose the track which now levels and passes an area of woodland. Cross Tarn Beck then begin to climb once more to the sound of the trickling water. Keep on the main track where the stream and a narrow path move away to the R. The track now becomes rougher and as the view returns Top o' Selside appears much nearer. Cross a small stream and pass a small cairn on the R. Continue to the highest point on the track identified by an OS Bench Mark carved in a rock to the left and a small cairn on the right (on a level with Peel Island).

Here you leave the track for the open moor - a complete contrast of situation with little or no paths and a feeling of real isolation, a rare commodity today to be relished and enjoyed. The description which follows is an attempt to identify features of the moorland which will help you to pinpoint your position as you take the route to - Top o' Selside - Heel Toe Hill - Arnsbarrow Hill arriving at Caws Beck where the waymarked footpath is met.

Turn R up the grassy path and fork L in 20 yards. Follow this path which gently strays up the fellside to a large cairn on the summit Top o' Selside (1091ft). The distant views to the NE are splendid and nearer at hand the green forest above Monk Coniston and around Carron Crag cloaks the land. From here survey the onward route.

In the hollow to the SE lies a perfect circle of water - Arnsborrow Tarn. We take a high level route round this to the east. Beyond the tarn to the S can be seen a triple triangle rock on a flat topped hill and further south the pimple cairn on Arnsbarrow Hill. Note their positions. Leave the summit on a path E (the opposite direction to your approach) and keeping on the higher ground use sheep trods as they appear. Cross a distinct trough and continue up the other side. The next dip has a boghole in the bottom and a single wooden stake on the top of the rise beyond. Climb the bilberry slope to the stake and you will be by the cairn on Heel Toe Hill. The map shows a "marked stone" which I failed to find! Set off again to the S (parallel to the forest edge) passing a lone rowan. The pyramid rock ahead across the heathery waste is Neile Stove Crag. Keep round to the right of a depression and pick up a grassy path on the far side of its boggy hollow, a nursery of many butterwort.

The path disappears leaving you to feel the solitude, and stick to a southerly course by gaining the high points. Hold direction helped by looking back over your left shoulder to Heel Toe, over your right shoulder to Top o' Selside, then ahead to the triple triangle rocks on the north end of Arnsbarrow Hill. Use your map, compass and common sense if in doubt. A trod takes a terrace on the right (W) of the triangular rocks where there is a definite narrow path and the pimple of the main summit of Arnsbarrow Hill is ahead. The path evaporates but at the next narrow trough becomes distinguishable. After passing a boulder in a narrowing gap, go L up the peaty brown bank to the pimple cairn. This gives a good viewpoint over the lower Crake valley and out to sea. A clear path leads on south down a steep ridge to meet a cross path. Carry straight on down the now dispersing ridge where the path fades. Ahead is a large myrtle-filled hollow and beyond the pointed, cairned peaklet of Brock Barrow with the Caw Beck valley on its left. We are making for this valley. Pass the flat area of bog myrtle on its left by using various sheep trods until a small meandering stream is noticed and the valley sides close and begin to pleat into interlocking folds. A better path comes from the right and crosses the stream to enhance our unsteady trod. Keep on the left bank and make easier progress as the path leaves the valley bottom to become smooth and green. Do not let your attention wander in the euphoria of a real path as you stride out over a brow. Look out for a weary cairn and fork R on a smaller path to a wall with gate, stile and waymarks. Turn R for Nibthwaite.

Keep by the wall and now that the route-finding has eased the last three-quarters of a mile to the village can be fully enjoyed. The western horizon hosts a prolifera of miniature summits, each with its own individually shaped cairn, and the valley ahead is beautiful. Negotiate a short steeper section of path, then go straight past a high ladder stile on the L and descend into the narrow valley. Cross the stream and after rising up the bank the path runs on down the widening valley. The oaks of High Wood shade the southern side while the rocky face of Brock Barrow shelters the north. Ignore a small trod making off right and keep down the gently winding path to the village.

At the track turn left through the gate to the start.

Low Nibthwaite

Low Nibthwaite, was the site of one of the most important eighteenth-century iron ore furnaces in the area. It is said that cannon balls were made here for the Duke of Cumberland's use in the 1745 rebellion. Two bobbin mills were later built on the site of the furnace, one later becoming a sawmill.

The Silurian plateau

This plateau around Top o' Selside is one of several in South Lakeland. Hard gritty bands give rise to many ice smoothed rocky knolls. The rough heather cover is reminiscent of the Scottish Highlands.

Peel Island

Anyone who has read the book or seen the TV film of Arthur Ransome's famous children's novel *Swallows and Amazons* will recognise his use of Peel Island as a setting. Ransome loved the Coniston area and incorporated much of its atmosphere into his books. He vividly describes charcoal burning in the woods.

WALK 29: Coniston East - Parkamoor to Brantwood (Gondola Walk)

The SS Gondola on Coniston Water

Distance:	4³/₄ miles 7¹/₂km
Grade:	Moderate
Terrain:	Woodland, forest, low fell
Summit:	High Park - 975ft (297m)
Map:	OL6

To Coniston - additional 2 miles
Brantwood to Dodgson Wood Car
Park by the lakeshore road - additional
2 miles

SUMMARY: This is a linear walk well above the eastern shore of Coniston Water from Parkamoor jetty to Brantwood. The walk climbs through National Trust woodland from Parkamoor along permissive paths to reach right-of-way tracks along the crest of the hills above Coniston Water, giving fine views along the length of the lake with the fells behind. A gradual descent through forest culminates in another delightful stretch of woodland walking along the Brantwood Nature Trail.

Parkamoor jetty lies 1³/₄ miles north of Nibthwaite, about a third of the way along Coniston Water. It is the furthest call on the Gondola service which plies from Coniston - Parkamoor - Brantwood - Coniston. Sailings (in 1993) leave Coniston at 11.00am, 12.05pm, 1.40pm, 2.50pm from 27th March to 3rd November. There is an additional 4.00 sailing in summer. The service is exceedingly popular in the summer high season and is often full. Note that a pick up cannot be guaranteed at either end and dogs are not allowed in the saloons on the Gondola. 'The Ruskin' sails between Coniston and Brantwood.

HOW TO GET THERE AND PARKING: Park near Brantwood, (public car parks a few hundred yards south along the road.). There are many permutations, for example you could start and finish at Coniston, by extending the walk along the lanes around the head of Coniston. However, our recommendation is to get the first boat from Brantwood (11.45am) to Coniston, then the second sailing (12.05pm) to Parkamoor. This gives a magnificent day out enjoying a trip on the Gondola, a fine walk, and a visit to Brantwood (*refreshments*).

The Coniston fells from Parkamoor jetty.

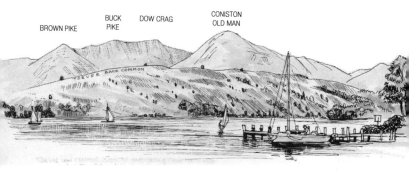

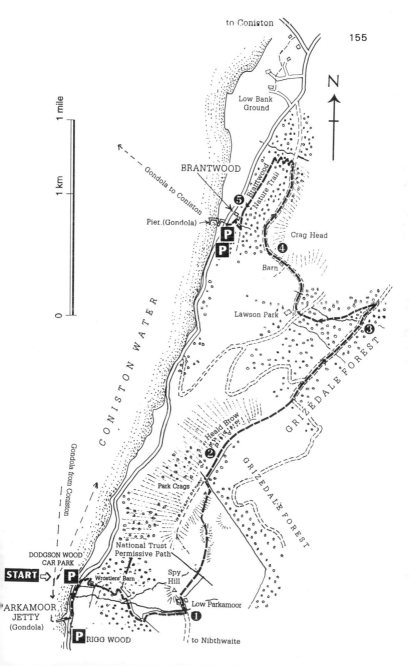

to Coniston

N

Low Bank Ground

BRANTWOOD

Gondola to Coniston

❺

Pier. (Gondola)

P

P

Crag Head

❹

Barn

Lawson Park

❸

GRIZEDALE FOREST

C O N I S T O N   W A T E R

Head Brow

❷

Park Crags

GRIZEDALE FOREST

Gondola from Coniston

DODGSON WOOD
CAR PARK

START ⇨ P

Wrestlers' Barn

National Trust
Permissive Path

Spy
Hill

Low Parkamoor

❶

ARKAMOOR
JETTY
(Gondola)

P

RIGG WOOD

to Nibthwaite

1 mile

1 km

0

View from Hield Brow

If you prefer to do the walk without recourse to the Gondola it is best to park at Parkamoor (Dodgson Wood National Trust car park), and return by the pleasant but sometimes busy lane along the edge of the lake.

THE WALK: Start from Parkamoor jetty. The road along the eastern length of the side of Coniston Water runs by the shore. From the jetty turn L along the road for 400 yards to Dodgson Wood car park on the right. Take the permissive path, waymarked with white posts through the woodland to Wrostler's Barn. *The unusual name, a derivation of wrestler, describes the roofing slabs each side protruding over the other on the apex. Go up the bank behind the barn to see.*

Continue to a gate with a stile and ignoring other tracks follow the white posts to a wider path. At a cross track turn L. Across the stream are two lovely glades, often used by, and ideal for, the Boy Scouts to learn camping. Cross a little stream then as the track bends left through a wall slant R to cross the main stream. Keep parallel to the woodland edge then turn sharp L to a stile in the fence. The simple old path in a crease beside the wall now gives splendid vistas over the lake to Coniston's stately mountains, not forgetting pretty little Spy Hill close by Low Parkamoor. Go over the stile onto the bridle path (right of way Nibthwaite to Parkamoor). Turn L and go through gate/stile to the old farmhouse.

Cross the front of Low Parkamoor farmhouse then immediately L through the gap in the wall then R onto the green path rising between two grassy humps. Once again a widespread view to the north shows a fine display of the Coniston fells. Advance to a boggy gateway in a cross wall. An offset stile allows you to pass dryshod. Ignore the path left and keep ahead, the small right-of-way trod heading towards the forest. A little ridge, which keeps the path clear of the bog, ends. Do a spongy sprint then follow the rising path through the myrtle to High Park 302m. (Summit to the left of the path.) Continue to the wall, turn L over the ridge and descend to turn R at a 'welcome' gate with stile into the newly felled forest.

Note The wide path worn by mountain bikers etc. leading from the gate is not a right-of-way. Good viewpoint 20yards west (left) of the gate.

The path now follows the crest of Heald Brow. The way is soggy at first, but it becomes more solid and the surrounding forest, felled to the west, allows views to measure progress along the lake.

Turn L on the gravel road, bright-edged with ragwort, tansy, foxglove and brambles, giving a chance for boots to dry. Ignore the road left and carry on for half a mile. Descend to cross a stream (right of way path left on O.S. map obsolete). After a 250-yard gentle rise take a wide path L which bends sharply back and downhill. The trees are close and their shade exudes a resinous perfume. In a clearing below stands Lawson Park. Keep straight ahead (sign Coniston) onto a path running above a wall. Go through a gate and continue. The path now traverses Crag Head through lush vegetation and high bracken in summer. Cross a stream where the yellow waymarks of The Brantwood Nature Trail are met. Ignore the yellow arrow on the right just before a small barn, and carry on ahead. Continue along beside Crag Coppice to a new stile L just before a curving bridge over a major stream. Go over this stile and down the recently-constructed zigzag path. Cross a stream by a stone chair, turn R and R again. Turn R down a rustic path to Brantwood (*refreshments, toilets*). Cross the road and descend the signed path to the jetty for the Gondola to Coniston.

If you miss the boat:

Return by road to Coniston 2 miles

Return by road to Parkamoor (Dodgson Wood car park) 2 miles

At the time of writing the last boat to Coniston was 4.45pm.

Brantwood

Brantwood House was the home of John Ruskin, artist, writer and philosopher, from 1872 to 1900. It is open to the public and contains a collection of Ruskin's drawings and watercolours and a more recent collection of Wainwright's work. Wainwright was the author of fell walking guides to the Lake District, inspiring thousands of people.

The 'Parks'

Lawson Park and Parkamoor (alternatively spelt Park-a-Moor) were outlying sheep farms created by the monks of Furness Abbey during the middle of the fourteenth century. 'Park' is from a French word meaning 'enclosed ground for pasture or arable farming'.

Wrostler's Barn

WALK 30:   The Grizedale Forest

'The Ancient Forester'
Sculpture by David Kemp

SUMMARY: Low forested hills around a flat-bottomed green valley provide one of the most attractive woodland areas of northern England. The Forestry Commission must be commended for its efforts to provide a tourist attraction in a working environment. There is a visitor centre with bookshop, café, gardens, mountain bike hire, art gallery and a unique children's playground. And of course, the sculpture - a collection of over 80 works sited throughout the forest. Anyone with imagination or artistic appreciation is sure to be impressed. Some of the pieces are easy to understand, others are amusing, or puzzling, but all add interest to a walk. The artists use materials from the forest which harmonize so well with their surroundings. New works are constantly being added whilst some fall into decay; indeed one piece was eaten by deer! Some are very delicate - please keep your children under control to avoid accidental damage, they can climb on the ones in the childrens' playground. A leaflet on sale at the Visitor Centre shows the locations of all but the most recent sculptures. It is a unique open-air gallery started in 1977 which won, in 1990, the prestigious Prudential Award for the Arts.

The Forestry Commission encourages walkers and mountain bikers, and has devised a number of waymarked trails. Colour-coded posts ensure that the visitor does not get lost Posts with an 'S' denote sculpture nearby. Remember it is a working forest and occasionally sections of paths are closed during felling operations. Please heed any diversion signs.

HOW TO GET THERE AND PARKING: If coming from Central Lakeland, take the Newby Bridge road from Hawkshead and after a quarter of a mile turn R up the hill and over the forested brow into the hidden valley of Grizedale.

From the south take the A590 past Newby Bridge and just past the Haverthwaite Railway terminus turn R signed Bouth and Rusland. The sign has a special Grizedale Forest sign. Follow the forest signs along a maze of lanes up the Rusland Valley. Note a long line of tall trees which line the right side of the road, these are the renowned Rusland beeches, specially attractive in autumn.

THE SILURIAN WAY

Distance: 9½ miles   15km   Green banded pole waymarks

A route map which marks the Silurian Way is available from the Visitor Centre. However, the centre is closed in winter which is a time when many walkers appreciate the sheltered nature of forest walking. The following notes should be sufficient to see you round.

Much of the Silurian Way is along forest roads which are not to everyone's taste and the walker intent on hurrying round will miss much of its attractions. Many of the sculptures are located close to the way and each deserves inspection.

From the Visitor Centre start eastwards up an old bridle path which joins forest roads past the reedy pools of Ormandy Intake. Near a bend is an impressive carving, in red sandstone, of a fox. Grizedale Tarn, a popular but peaceful lake enclosed by trees is one of the highlights of the walk, but make sure you visit the more easterly tarn which has been enlarged by damming and is now a haven for birds. The sculpture here takes the form of an elaborate bird watchers' hide.

Thence the route, still on forest roads, crosses a felled area to reveal the forests on the far side of the Dale Park Valley. The southern part of the way leaves forest roads behind on a delightful woodland stretch, followed by a beautiful riverside path

Replica of a charcoal burner's hut

close to the road and cascades above Force Forge. Another interesting woodland stretch leads past several outstanding sculptures and a replica of a charcoal burner's hut. After crossing the stream of Farra Grain there is a fine ascent through old woodlands to reach a devastated felled area. The traverse of Carron Crag provides a fine panorama before descending, almost entirely on forest roads, back to the Grizedale Centre.

A good walk for a windy day! The Silurian Way route map, or even the Sculpture map, on sale at the centre shows some, but not all, of the route permutations.

Other waymarked trails are as follows:

FROM THE GRIZEDALE CENTRE

Yellow Route:	*The Millwood Habitat Trail*	1½ miles

Part suitable for wheelchairs

Blue Route:	*Ridding Wood Walk*	1 mile

Part suitable for wheelchairs. There are several interesting sculptures on this walk, including musical ones!

Red Route:	*Carron Crag Walk*	3 miles

This is the short version of our Walk 30A

White Route:	*Grizedale Tarn Walk*	3¼ miles

This uses the Silurian Way to reach the tarn, then makes a steep descent through the forest to return along the Ridding Wood Walk.

FROM THE BOGLE CRAG CAR PARK

Bogle Crag car park lies to the east of the road midway between Satterthwaite and the Grizedale Centre. It makes a quieter entry to the forest. A path parallel to, but at a higher level than, the road connects with the Grizedale Centre.

Yellow Route: ¾ mile   *Red Route:* 3 miles   *Blue Route:* 3¾ miles

WALK 30A: Carron Crag

SUMMARY: The summit of Carron Crag is a worthy objective, traversed by the Silurian Way which has several interesting sculptures for those who care to seek them. Some are easily missed! Return is easy along the base of the forest - watch out for mountain bikers. This is a good way to walk a

Distance:	4¼ miles 6¾km
Grade:	Easy
Terrain:	Woodland, forest, low fell
Summit	Carron Crag - 1030ft (314m)
Map:	OL7

short section of the Silurian Way, but much of the walk is along forest road.

THE WALK: Start from the main car park at the Grizedale Visitor

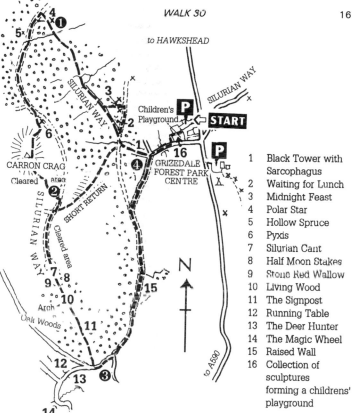

to HAWKSHEAD

SILURIAN WAY

SILURIAN WAY

Children's
Playground

P

START

SILURIAN WAY

CARRON CRAG

Cleared area

P

16

GRIZEDALE
FOREST PARK
CENTRE

SHORT RETURN

SILURIAN WAY

Cleared area

Arch

Oak Woods

N

to A590

1   Black Tower with
      Sarcophagus
2   Waiting for Lunch
3   Midnight Feast
4   Polar Star
5   Hollow Spruce
6   Pyxis
7   Silurian Cant
8   Half Moon Stakes
9   Stone Red Wallow
10   Living Wood
11   The Signpost
12   Running Table
13   The Deer Hunter
14   The Magic Wheel
15   Raised Wall
16   Collection of
       sculptures
       forming a childrens'
       playground

Centre, on the west side of the road.

Cross the little bridge over the stream (toilets on left) and turn R on the track between the walled Nursery Garden and the stream. At the road turn R over the Grizedale Hall bridge. The remains of an old clapper bridge are on the downstream side, its deficiency made up by a slab of concrete. The first track to the left is the return track. Take the next path L, waymark pole green/red/yellow signed 'Coniston 3 miles'. The footpath climbs steeply and your efforts are not exactly cheered by the morbid looking sculpture of 'Black Tower with Sarcophagus'. Keep plodding up the path (used for the short return) and meet a forest road by a hurrying stream. At the forest road turn R and just past a pole branch left. This path is the Silurian Way, waymark pole green/red but we recommend a short excursion to two

The summit of Carron Crag as it was in 1994

nearby sculptures.

Short excursion (10*mins*) The first 'Waiting for lunch' is 20yards straight along the forest road, (waymark pole yellow), and on the left. Continue along the road for 250yards to a S marker pole by a stream. Turn left up the hillside to the 'Midnight feast'. To rejoin the route, keep uphill on the path behind the sculpture and on meeting the main path turn R.

We now walk through agreeable woodland. Old sycamore trees edge the forest, and a couple of sweet chestnuts splay their branches. The steady climb continues until the wall ends at an overgrown old lane with residual gateposts. Look over the right-hand wall as there is a fine view of the High Street range. Keep on through the plantations. There are no signs for a while but keep on to a brow then you cross two-and-a-half streams. To the right is a yellow sculpture named Polar Star. Shortcut L to join the next forest road. Turn L and in ¼ mile look for a 'S' post on the right. Take care not to miss it for this is a sculpture you will never forget. About 60 yards on a narrow path into the dense forest is 'Hollow Spruce' which you must enter to appreciate the artistry. Back on the road the edge of the forest is soon reached at another junction. The main height has now been gained and the summit is in view so keep straight on and pass through a new gate in the deer fence on the right. Note the little sculpture 'Pyxis' to the left. Go steeply up the path through the open but newly planted terrain to the summit. The rocky apex and its immediate surroundings have been left unplanted, ensuring an unrestricted view when the trees are fully grown, and what a fine viewpoint it is. Despite its modest height 1,025ft (314m) the circular panorama is given an extra dimension by the dark shades of the rolling forests and the valleys to the north appear like gateways into the wilderness. The strange shapes seen from the valley turn out to be nothing more than a triangulation point and a firewatcher's hut. The sturdy hut, which is perched uncomfortably astride a pointed rock, is firmly anchored against the wind and secured against vandals so do not rely on it for shelter. (Not so firmly anchored as we thought, it blew away in 1995.)

Continue over the summit and follow poles which mark the descent through short bracken, roots and stumps. Turn L on meeting a wider track and make your way down to a gate at the forest road (Brilliant new forester sculpture). Go R a little way to the crossroads.

Short Return

Turn L (waymark red) on the track which follows a little valley and soon enters the forest. At the junction with the forest road go straight across and down the steep outward route to Grizedale Hall bridge. Enter the centre by a gate in the wall of the enclosed garden.

To continue

Go straight on at the crossroads (waymark green) with open views until the young larches spread their boughs. Just before the end of the road is a sculpture pole, but there is no access and the sculpture of the bird man seems to have flown. Follow the green waymark past the Silurian Cant. The path continues through attractive woods passing sculptures including the arch of 'Living Wood' and arrives at a forest road. Here turn L. (If you want to see some more interesting sculptures turn R to a Y junction then fork back L to see the 'Running Table' then cross the stream and the 'Deer Hunter' is in the wood on the left. If you continue on the forest road to the next bend you will see another sculpture, The Magic Wheel.)

Back at the Y junction continue down the road. There are pleasant scenes over the gentle valley floor, a study in shades of green, as we walk along the edge of the old oak woodland. Pass a group of Monkey Puzzle trees, the pattern of their distinctive trunks like armour, to a sculpture, Raised Wall, beautiful stonework by two Dutch artists. As you keep on over the rise beware speeding cyclists on this multipurpose road. At the next junction keep R over the cattle grid and through the pasture to Home Farm. Turn R over the bridge and enter the Centre by the gate into the walled garden.

WALK 30B: Sculpture Walk from Bogle Crag

Distance:	2 miles 3¹/₄km
Grade:	Easy
Terrain:	Woodland, forest
Map:	OL7

SUMMARY: A good walk for youngsters who will find some of the sculptures most interesting. Most of the walk is along a forest road, with a return on a woodland path.

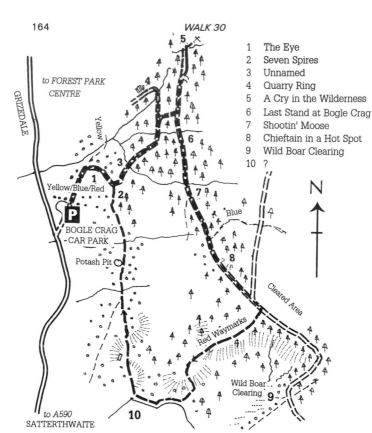

1 The Eye
2 Seven Spires
3 Unnamed
4 Quarry Ring
5 A Cry in the Wilderness
6 Last Stand at Bogle Crag
7 Shootin' Moose
8 Chieftain in a Hot Spot
9 Wild Boar Clearing
10 ?

THE WALK: Start from the Bogle Crag car park to the east of the road midway between Satterthwaite and the Grizedale Visitor Centre.

Walk up the forest road. The first sculpture - The Eye - is by the right hand bend and looks down from its elevated position. Continue along the road to the next bend where the Seven Spires sculpture blend almost invisibly with the trees. Carry on along the road passing a rather strange abstract on the left to a road junction.

Our route goes to the right but first continue along the road to visit another sculpture. A small quarry just beyond a stream has the next small sculpture carved on its face. The artist has utilised the beautiful blend of shades and textures, which reveal their most delicate hues when wet.

Return to the junction and proceed up the road 25 yards to a bend. The next sculpture is well worth seeing and is reached by taking the rough track

L. The track ends but keep by the wall until you see a remarkably life-like hound in the act of jumping the wall. Over the wall in the woods is another hound and their prey, a deer. Return to the main forest road.

Continue up the gently rising road, entertained by the imaginative 'Last Stand at Bogle Crag', 'Shootin' Moose' and 'Chieftain in a Hot Spot'. Ignore a road branching L and keep straight on for 25 yards. Look for a red topped waymark pole on the right just before the road begins to descend. Our route goes R here into the woods, but if you have time to visit another outstanding sculpture keep straight on down the road round a bend to the next junction. Immediately before the junction is a red S-marker pole on the right. A narrow path leads over a stream and descends into Wild Boar Clearing, which must surely be one of the finest works of art in the forest. Return to the red topped pole way back along the road.

Turn down the path to a wall. Our path now bends right keeping above the wall. At the wall end another sculpture is seen down the hillside on the left. Cross a little stream and on across an open glade. Just past a broken wall on the left is a viewpoint seat. Its position on the top of Bogle Crag gives a fine view of the outspread Grizedale valley and Carron Crag.

Continue along the path. Another path (blue waymark) joins from the left. Keep R on the blue/red waymark trail.

On top of the next rise is an old circular stone pit, once used to burn bracken to produce potash, which when boiled with animal fat gave a reasonable soap. Carry on, soon arriving at the Seven Spires sculpture. Turn L down the forest road to the car park.

Grizedale Hall

Once the home of the Brocklebanks in the early 1900s. Henry Brocklebank, who owned the Cunard Shipping Line, planted much of the moorland with trees, some of the plantations named after places his ships had visited. On the Silurian Way near Grizedale Tarn you may notice a funnel by a cluster of rocks in a cleared area. This bore a warning flag when shooting was in progress. During World War II, Grizedale Hall was used as a prisoner of war camp and was demolished in 1956. The site is now a car park and its grounds host an attractive campsite well placed for exploring South Lakeland.

Foxglove

WALK 31: **Around the Dale Park Valley**

The Dale Park Valley from High Dale Park

SUMMARY: This walk is a succession of low forested hill crossings, first from the Dale Park Valley to the Grizedale Valley, then back using old rights of way paths. Another crossing links to the Windermere side of the forest, again using old paths which were once important ways to the ferry.

Dale Park retains its park-like character. In 1516 Abbot Bankes of Furness turned out his tenants, descendants of Norse settlers, to make a deer hunting park. Deer are still common in the woods - look for their tracks and trees stripped of bark.

A good sheltered walk for a windy day, but surprisingly varied.

HOW TO GET THERE AND PARKING: Approach 1) from Newby Bridge - take the A590 towards Barrow. Just past the Lakeside & Haverthwaite Railway terminus turn R signed Bouth, Grizedale Forest and Satterthwaite. Follow the forest signs but after 3½

Distance:	5³/₄ miles 9¹/₄km
Grade:	Moderate
Terrain:	Woodland, forest, valley
Map:	OL7

miles at a fork keep straight on towards Hawkshead (sign Hawkshead 4m). In 500yds parking and picnic area on L at Low Dale Park.

Approach 2) from Hawkshead - take the Newby Bridge road for 1½ miles where a lane on the R leads over the forested hill onto the Dale Park Valley with the picnic area at its foot on the R at Low Dale Park.

THE WALK: The Dale Park Beck runs crystal clear beside the picnic area crossed by a ford and a footbridge. Cross it and set off up the woodland path. The ascent is through mature woodland, a blend of beech, birch and oak with the occasional evergreen making a colour-code to please whatever the season.

At a forest road (The Silurian Way) go almost straight across very slightly L, to a path beside a broken down wall. *Watch carefully in the trees to the right for a large intricate cairn, one of the many sculptures which add interest to the Grizedale Forest ways. This one is a heap of scrap built subtly by the artist into a designer cairn worthy of a noble summit.* Carry on along the track to the forest road where the plantation timber has been newly felled. Turn R and go round the bend then on to a Y-junction (sign 6). Leave the road on a path between the forks. The way is now downhill to a gate at the edge of the wood and the Grizedale valley is spread ahead. Pass by the first houses of Satterthwaite village then a tarmac road begins. Turn R and proceed to the church.

A few yards along the road on the left is the 'Eagle's Head' open for lunchtime refreshments.

Turn R by a barn in front of the church then fork R between a fine-looking bank barn, a relic of the days when the valley had more agriculture, and a studio. Take the next turn R to leave the village .

Pepper House, an Elizabethan farmhouse, serves tea and cakes but no children under 8 or dogs are allowed.

Climb steeply past the graveyard, which must occupy one of the prime sites in the valley, towards Breasty Haw. On the R opposite a house two paths leave the road. Take the R hand one, the public bridleway to Dale Park.(Ignore the blue waymarked path which leads to Bogle Crag.) We are now on the old path from Satterthwaite to the Windermere ferry. Go on the bridleway through an area of once-coppiced trees passing a tiny dam and a piece of nature's geometrical sculpture to the edge of a young beechwood. Continue over the clappered ditch, into an area of felled trees where surviving birches sway in the breeze having escaped the fate of their 34 year growth-ring companions. Pass a small overgrown pond on the left then join a road.

Look out for the S-topped post on the left which denotes a short path over a small stream and ahead into the Wild Boar Clearing, one of the outstanding but rapidly weathering sculptures in the forest.

WALK 31

Go straight across the road keeping to the the old pathway. At the top of the rise - Breasty Haw - pass worm-eaten gateposts and continue downhill now. (Ignore a gateway in a wall corner on the right.) Keep straight on up a rise to the next sculpture. *It is in a clearing on the right and titled 'Axis of the earth' by the Japanese artist Masao Ueno.* In a few yards arrive at the next forest road.

Ignore the various signs around, turn R along the road for 100 yards, then L (yellow waymark) into a narrow path running downhill.

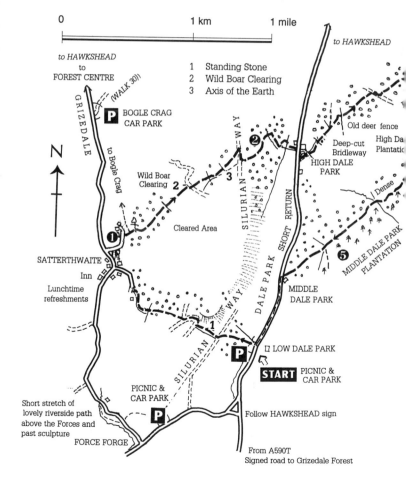

0   1 km   1 mile

to HAWKSHEAD

to HAWKSHEAD

to FOREST CENTRE   (WALK 30)

1   Standing Stone
2   Wild Boar Clearing
3   Axis of the Earth

P BOGLE CRAG CAR PARK

GRIZEDALE

to Bogle Crag

N

SILURIAN WAY

Old deer fence

Deep-cut Bridleway

High Da Plantati

HIGH DALE PARK

Wild Boar Clearing 2

3

Cleared Area

Dense

SHORT RETURN

DALE PARK

❺

MIDDLE DALE PARK PLANTATION

❶

SATTERTHWAITE

Inn

Lunchtime refreshments

SILURIAN WAY

MIDDLE DALE PARK

1

P LOW DALE PARK

START PICNIC & CAR PARK

PICNIC & CAR PARK

P

Short stretch of lovely riverside path above the Forces and past sculpture

FORCE FORGE

Follow HAWKSHEAD sign

From A590T Signed road to Grizedale Forest

The plantation soon gives way to mature deciduous woodland where birds call and oak leaves rustle underfoot. Take care when descending the rock cutting which is both mossy and slippery. Continue down the path which briefly takes to a ridge alongside a trough with a developing stream. Exit from the wood by a stile, to be guided by fences to footbridge and the road at High Dale Park. Turn R.

TO RETURN TO START AT LOW DALE PARK: Follow the road for 1 mile down the tranquil dale passing Middle Dale Park to Low Dale Park.

TO CONTINUE: Walk along the road for 20 yards then turn L, public footpath to Eel House.

Follow the path with the wall to your left. Go over a couple of stiles and on through pasture into the woodland. Ignore an obvious path forking left through a gate. As the path rises a stream has taken over, but the mud is easily avoided on the sidebank. Paths branch off here and there, however, keep beside the flowing way for when a wall is in sight the footpath is dry again. Go through a gateway to a fork and go R (yellow waymark).

Sandwiched between larch and fir the path rises steeply. Pass a gateway with a crossbar stile in a redundant deerfence and a stand of silver birches, then the gradient eases. At the forest road turn R for 30 yards then dive L into the spruce (public footpath sign). Flat going soon brings you over the crest to descend more steeply to a Y junction by a bit of a wall end. Branch L and go steeply down to a cross-track. Turn R to a stile/gate at the forest's edge. Your ears, now tuned to serenity, will cringe as you cross the field to the road. Stay in the field turning R along the roadside hedge to a stile by Eel House.

Turn R along the road for half a mile. Often busy, and with no footpath, care is needed. However the Esthwaite Valley with its water is a pleasure to see as you pass a stream and a small plantation.

Climb the hill and rekindle your appetite for the forest. *This tract of woodland belongs to Graythwaite Estates. Graythwaite Hall was an Elizabethan mansion of the Rawlinson family.*

Now look on the right for a public footpath sign to Middle Dale Park. Set off under a shower of hazel catkins in spring along the narrow rising path. It is a pleasant pull up the hillside through scented teenage spruce to a yew tree clearing. Above the path is a bank where you can rest with a view.

Ignore the gateway in a wall across on the right. Keep ahead on the rising path which bends into another boggy clearing and circles it on the left. Climb out to pass a group of silver birches. (Up on the left is a whaleback of rock. A scramble onto it is rewarded by a view over Windermere and beyond.)

Pass through a wall gateway into a plantation, walking on a soft green carpet in a textured aisle. The descent now begins and as the forest becomes more open the Park Valley appears below. The old path has been attacked in places by streams inflicting muddy wounds where they cross.

Pass a fence with a broken gate then an embanked section where the stream crosses the path and plunges away in an 8-foot waterfall.

The descent is now on a gentle traversing line into the Dale Park Valley. Boggy patches of path can be avoided by taking to the woodland through holes in the wall. At a junction of paths, walls and fences bend right and down a more stony track. The mature oak woodland becomes more open as the road at Middle Dale Park is reached.

Turn L along the road for half a mile to Low Dale Park and the start.

WALK 32: Latterbarrow, Blelham Tarn and Windermere Shore

Latterbarrow summit cairn

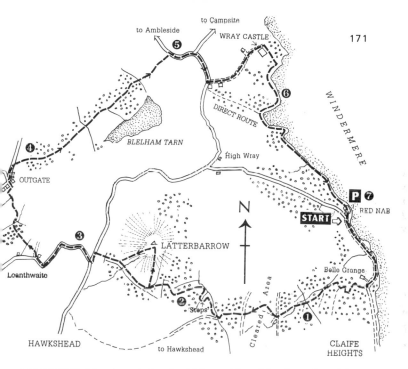

SUMMARY: A lovely varied walk which combines lake shore, forest, tarn, a pretty hamlet and of course the wonderful viewpoint of Latterbarrow.

HOW TO GET THERE AND PARKING: The car park on the west side of Windermere at Red Nab is reached from the B5286 Ambleside to Hawkshead road, through High Wray, then L to Red Nab.

THE WALK: Leave the car park and go through the gate on the continuation of the road, now an unsurfaced track, heading south. For half a mile the midweek pleasure of walking to the rhythmic lap of the water becomes

Distance:	7 miles 11¼ km
Grade:	Moderate
Terrain:	Woodland, forest, low fell, valley
Summit:	Latterbarrow - 803ft (245m)
Map:	OL7

A good walk for a hot summer afternoon.

infected at weekends by the throbbing 'thuds' of the power boats as daring water skiers pursue their sport. (At the moment there are controversial plans to ban power boats from the lake.) Just beyond Belle Grange, the first

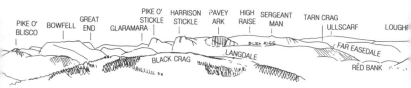

Panorama from Latterbarrow

house on the right, turn R up a stone-paved path which climbs through the wood. The trees are predominantly beech, shading the path as it rises steadily to a junction. To the left an attractive ford has been paved into Belle Grange Beck, its water liberating the true colour of its channelling stone. This is the end of the repaired path.

Keep ahead up the path which is now rough and stony. The angle soon eases causing occasional muddy patches which can be avoided by taking to the bracken. Pass through a glade of mature trees their tops lost in the sky, their trunks wide enough to bring delight to the measuring arms of children. The path rises again then bends by a cross wall which marks the limit of the National Trust Claife Estate. Carry on along the main path. Open boggy areas favoured by orchids enhance the wayside until the main forest haulage road is reached. Cross over the road and go through the gate in the deer fence opposite, signed to Hawkshead. The path now rises through a devastation of newly cleared forest, a few mishapen oaks left behind to mourn their former colleagues. Looking to the left Claife Heights summit lies beneath its forest blanket and the retrospective view of Wansfell and the Troutbeck valley are not enhanced by the foreground. After the gate in the fence cross the forest road and go straight on sign to Hawkshead. Once again the path is shaded by stately trees, the creaking of a half-fallen victim adding an eerie note to the sigh of the breeze high above. When confronted by a wall and gate look for a sign right to Latterbarrow. Go right through a gap in the sidewall and follow the path (white-topped marker poles) downhill with the wall on the right. The path becomes narrow and mounts a setting of steps to bend right round the broken end of an old wall. The path now descends a little then runs level along a forest firebreak between larches. Pass through a gap in the old wall and cross a tiny stream with its grand entourage of mud. The edge of the forest can now be seen. Leave it by a stile with dog flap. The smaller path carries on by the wall, but our way turns R and rises up a wider grassy break through bracken to the summit of Latterbarrow. On reaching the fine stone obelisk it is immediately obvious that this is one of the prime viewpoints of the district so sit on the turf to digest its detail .

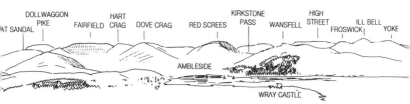

DOLLWAGGON PIKE — HART CRAG — KIRKSTONE PASS — HIGH STREET
AT SANDAL — FAIRFIELD — DOVE CRAG — RED SCREES — WANSFELL — ILL BELL
FROSWICK — YOKE
AMBLESIDE
WRAY CASTLE

The panorama of peaks may be soft in the haze and sails like paper triangles place patterns on shining Windermere. If it is late afternoon, at eye-level watch the aerobatics of swallows skimming the bracken and feeding their young on the wing. A sheer delight.

From the obelisk set off WSW facing Hawkshead and down the slopes, passing a cairn, to join the smaller path by the wall. Turn R along the edge of the wood. Cross a stream and a little wooden bridge then carry on down through an old gateway and pastures until reaching the road.

Turn L and after a few yards turn R into a shady lane. As you stride along do not miss the slate fence, overgrown but still intact. An old barred gate is a curiosity with square holes in the left gatepost and round holes in the right. Pass by a stile which is the footpath to Hawkshead and at Loanthwaite turn R immediately past the farmhouse on the public footpath to Outgate. Now look out for the stile in the left-hand wall which is not very obvious with the track stretching ahead. Go straight across the field to a ladder stile over a section of wall opposite. Keep in line ahead aiming for a lone standing stone. Straight on beneath the oaks a path becomes apparent leading to a stile in a fence. Go over this, turn R along the wall for a few yards and when opposite a spring take a diagonal line L to the field corner and a kissing gate. Cross a paddock to a second kissing gate and proceed through a field, its slate fence straining to hold back the hillside. Another kissing gate leads to the village of Outgate. Turn R at the main road.

The local hostelry 'The Outgate' serves refreshments.

The road is the busy Hawkshead-Ambleside road and needs care as there is no pavement. Ignore the public footpath R by Rose Cottage and take the next public bridleway R into a walled green lane. A pleasing view of Latterbarrow seen over Hale How is available over the wall. Go through a gate and over a brow to enter the National Trust area of Outgate. The bridleway becomes more enclosed, its bramble hedges delicate with pink July flowers full of promise. Suddenly Blelham Tarn comes into view. Go over the stile into the Tarn pasture. The track keeps by the wall but it is a hard person who is not lured from it to sit on an ice-smoothed rocky outcrop and enjoy this beautiful tranquil scene. *As you scan the tarn in its setting let your mind's eye move back in time and picture the stream of ice which branched from the main glacier in the Windermere valley to creep over this side valley and pour* into the Esthwaite valley. The tarn is a kettle hole formed by blocks of ice settling and melting into a hollow. Today trout, pike and perch swim in the water, their smaller relations harrassed by noisy gulls. Grebes and divers are winter visitors.

The track crosses an inflow stream and passes through a delicate birchwood. Presently the wood gives way to more open parkland where a kissing gate leads into open pasture. Follow the track to the lane. Turn R passing by the entrance to Wray Campsite and make your way up the hill. In the left-hand wall an old stone water basin stands almost hidden and disused in the wall at about dog height yet is a point of speculation to ease the tarmac. On reaching the imposing gateway of Wray Castle choose from two alternatives:

a) The direct route to the shore: Just beyond the entrance to Wray Castle turn L into a bridleway signed to Lakeshore and High Wray Bay.

b) Alternative route via Wray Castle: The castle is not open to visitors but it is a worthwhile experience to take advantage of the footpath through the grounds.

Turn L through the gateway and proceed along the drive taking care not to stumble over the sleeping policemen. Pass the Dower House on the left to arrive at the castle. The mock Gothic building is very impressive. Keep L to the car park then walk round on the raised 'battlements' under its massive walls. Go through a gate ahead and down the path into a lakeside pasture. Head for the water then turn R along the shore. A short stroll leads to a boathouse in High Wray Bay. If you are walking on the water's edge move away from the tideline to avoid an area of bog and barbed wire and go over a stile into the bridleway - junction with route a) above.

Go through the slit stile by the second boathouse and along the path to the start.

Blelham Tarn
Blelham Tarn is now used for research purposes by the Freshwater Biological Association. There are remains of a bloomery on the north side of the tarn. The spaghnum bog at the north-west end of the tarn is home of the insect-eating sundew plant.

Wray Castle
This is a mock Gothic structure built in 1840-1847, now owned by the National Trust and used as a College of Marine Electronics. Windermere is at its deepest near here - 219 feet (91 feet below sea level).

Windermere Shore
Yellow balsam grows along Windermere shore - look for the netted carpet butterfly which feeds on it. Herb Paris, quite rare, grows beneath yews along the shore.

WALK 33: **Claife Heights**

Rocky whalebacks on High Pate Crag

SUMMARY: An intricate walk along the densely forested top of Claife Heights is followed by a return past idyllic tarns. The outward route follows a waymarked trail towards Hawkshead. This is Beatrix Potter country for she lived for many years at Near Sawrey. 'Hill Top' is now an international tourist attraction with its memorabilia of her Peter Rabbit books. We gave a lift to two young Japanese girls who were very excited at passing this hallowed place. 'Peter Rabbit very well known in Japan' they said.

HOW TO GET THERE AND PARKING: On the western side of the Bowness ferry take the B5285 towards Hawkshead. A short distance up the road on the right is the Ash Landing car park from which the walk starts.

Distance:	5³/₄ miles 9¹/₄km
Grade:	Moderate
Terrain:	Woodland, forest, low fell
Summit:	High Blind How - 885ft (270m)
Map:	OL7

THE WALK: Leave the car park by a footpath signed Claife

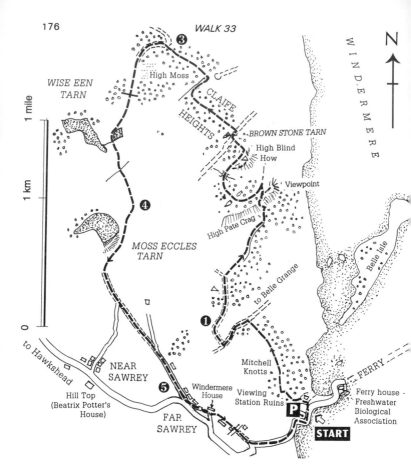

Heights and Hawkshead. There is character in the woodland even as you begin, as an old yew clings jealously to a rock having mutually survived the construction of the parking space. Turn L up a flight of steps (white marker post) to the ruined 'viewing station' seen above. The path passes under the arched wall, but it is worth walking round the angular walls of the remains for a view of the lake. Carry on between a rock and the root boss of an old oak to the now wider path up the hill (white paint waymarks). The wide path climbs steeply. Sprays of King fern spring from beds of sorrel on either side of the path. *If you are here for the view then come in winter when only the minority holly and yew branches retain their leaves, however, in summer the mixture*

The ruined 'viewing station'

of trees is shady yet allowing *sufficient sunbeams through to dance on the ferns.*

At a fence follow the sign R to Hawkshead. The path now levels and runs along the fence-side between the natural woodland and a plantation. Pass a broken wall end where the trees thin and the aspect is lighter. There is a brief view of the lake and Belle Isle with moored yachts pointing your eye to the Fairfield range beyond. *This lake is a series of three deep ice-gouged basins joined by narrow channels at the group of islands. The power of the ice was strengthened by the tongue of ice from Esthwaite which helped deepen the lake further.*

The path descends a little then traverses again past turf coloured with harebells. Pass a huge beech then along between a fence and a wall. Cross a little stream (marker post by an old iron fence) and at a kissing gate turn L, signed Hawkshead and Sawrey.

This bridle path is sheltered by walls and passes through pastures. Turn R up a track, as the wall undulates, Grizedale Forest and Coniston Old Man keep showing their faces to the west. So far views of the onward route have been scarce but now the path winds ahead in full view until being bordered by the forest again at a gate. Occasionally to the east the metropolis of Windermere and Bowness can be seen until cut off by screens of pine and rowan. Continue along more open ground and over a low rise. Ahead is High Pate Crag. Go over a stile by a gate past a varied treescape with the narrowing path becoming more claustrophobic as it bends left and climbs steeply through tropical-sized bracken. Look for a white paint flash on a tree above. (Halfway up the slope is an immaculate view of the Windermere ferry.) Enter dense larches which cut out the light then soon look for a path R which leads through a gap in an old wall onto a rare, but superb viewpoint as the eastern end of Pate Crag thrusts its head from its woody cloak to gaze across the lake.

Return to the main path and continue for about 25 yards to a major path junction. Turn L towards Hawkshead, look for white marker posts, between dark trunks and over roots and rocks. At the next post keep straight on following the waymarks. At a rock hump scramble up (easy) and a grassy track between the rock whalebacks leads to a path junction with signpost. This is a place to pause and let your eyes wander down the shores of the lake past Gummers How and out to sea.

Turn R into the forest tunnel and keep ahead at a cross firebreak. Turn R and drop down to cross a little wooden bridge and into the trees once more. Height is gradually gained and the sigh of the wind and its stormy aftermath of broken trees is ever present. Carry on or take a path branching right which leads to the summit of High Blind How, a mere stonethrow away. This offers a skyscape view where the treetops point to the clouds parading in the west wind.

Return to the main path and descend to a cross path. Turn L and on reaching the forest road turn R for a few yards. By the side of the road is tiny Brown Stone Tarn surrounded by reeds and rushes. Turn L on a small footpath, signpost, and up the rise. Follow the white marker poles into the unknown until bearing R and down into a bog crossed by a log walkway. Carry on discovering the waymarks and enjoying views to the central fells. The path now descends to run alongside the remains of an old wall until it meets the end of the forest road.

Wise Een Tarn with the Langdale valley beyond

Moss Eccles Tarn

At a cairn turn L between the trees onto a waymarked path. Soon you are expected to follow white paint blobs into a boggy hollow but circle it and continue until meeting the bend of a forest road and signpost. Turn L and go towards Sawrey, leaving the white waymarked route. It is a change to be out of the dense forest and making fast progress past High Moss Tarn, more of a moss than a tarn but pretty nevertheless. The road gradually changes to a wide path. Go through a gate/stile at the forest edge.

Strike out now crossing open fell until the path descends to meet one of Lakeland's charming surprises. In the hollow ahead the path runs between two tarns, the first lily-clad with coots dabbling in and out of the rushes. Pass by the dam keeping close under the wall and up the edge of the hollow where a retrospective view tempts you to stop awhile. When you go on there is another rewarding halt a quarter of a mile ahead, with fine retrospective views over Wise Een Tarn to the Langdale Pikes.

Go through a gate and straight along the bridle track. Moss Eccles Tarn is held by a natural rock bar and a small dam. *No-one can pass by and remain untouched by the serene beauty of the tree-fringed water merging into the green folded valley beyond. A scene to sit and savour.*

Continue on the track to a gate and along the enclosed lane. At a fork branch L to Far Sawrey. Cross the footbridge by a ford then across the pasture to join a surfaced lane. Keep ahead over a cattle grid and along the lane to meet the main road.

Turn L and pass the village shop down on the right (*drinks, ice cream etc.*)

and the Sawrey Hotel (*bar lunches and refreshments*) Pass the telephone box then branch L on a rising track with public footpath sign Ferry. At Windermere House go through a kissing gate on the R and keep by the garden fence passing Sawrey Knotts and Tower Cottage. Keep the wall to your left and go down a narrow path by a riding stable with yellow arrow waymark to enter a field by a kissing gate. Keep by the right wall to another kissing gate. Cross the lane and down a walled walkway to the main road. Turn L along the road for 500 yards to the car park and start.

The Viewing Station

Thomas West wrote the first real guidebook to the Lake District in 1778, in which he recommended the best points from which to appreciate the landscape. He advised tourists to stand with their back to the scene and view it through a curved mirror. The Viewing Station on Claife Heights was later the site of a Victorian building a popular venue for dances. The tall windows facing the lake were glazed in different shades which gave impressions of different weather conditions or sunset.

Claife Heights

The iron furnaces of South Lakeland needed copious amounts of charcoal to fuel them and much of the present woodland cover of the area originated in coppice woods of oak and hazel, which were harvested for charcoal or other woodland industries, such as bobbin and swill making. However, in 1799 John Curwen decided to experiment by planting 1,500 acres of spruce and larch on the open common and rough hills above Windermere. It is difficult to imagine Claife Heights now without its forest cover.

The Crier of Claife

Many versions of the tale of the crier are told, reputedly the ghost of a mediaeval monk from Furness Abbey who went mad after being rejected by a lady of ill repute he had rescued. He died crying in anguish on Claife Heights. The ghost was blamed for luring a ferryman one dark, stormy night. The man returned struck with horror and died shortly afterwards. The ghost, however, cannot be blamed for the loss of 47 lives in 1635 when the ferryboat capsized with its overload of guests returning from a wedding at Hawkshead.

WALK 34: Windermere - Lakeside to Bowness (return by steamer)

The motor vessel Teal

SUMMARY: A lovely day out combines a cruise on Windermere with a fine network of woodland and lakeside paths on the lake's western shore. Peaceful little High Dam is a contrast to the vibrant noisy watersports encountered on Windermere. The key passage in the walk is a stretch of permissive path from High Dam which links onto the Windermere shore path. Without this the walk would entail an unpleasant stretch of busy road walking.

HOW TO GET THERE AND PARKING: There are three convenient points from which to begin the circuit.

1) The car park at the station and pier, Lakeside, on the west side of Windermere, one mile north of Newby Bridge.
2) The car park at Ash Landing quarter of a mile from the west bank ferry landing.
3) The car parks at Bowness.

We recommend the first option which allows for the walk to be started in the morning, a picnic lunch along the way, and a review of the walk from the warmth of the ship, relaxing with a cup of tea to hand and a glow on the cheeks. **Note** that you should arrive at Bowness side of the ferry at least 45 minutes before sailing, particularly if your intended boat is the last one! There is a regular steamer service on the lake which should enable you

Distance:	8 miles 13km
Grade:	Moderate
Terrain:	Woodland, valley
Maps:	OL7, PF626

to do this walk between spring and autumn. Check the current timetables.

Lakeside - Cafeteria and toilets at the pier.

THE WALK: Leave the car park at Lakeside and turn R along the road at the Lakeside Hotel. Cross the road and look out for the old bridle track to Finsthwaite which branches L opposite Bucks Yeats North. The rather dank atmosphere of the road is immediately left behind as the path climbs gradually through airy coppiced woodland, once cropped for use in the bobbin mill nearby (see page 192). At a junction keep R and R again at the next junction. The path has levelled off and at the edge of the wood cross over a stile into a pasture. As you cross to the next gate a panorama of roofs and trees appears ahead. So the pretty village of Finsthwaite comes into view, nestling under the wooded brow of Finsthwaite Heights. Go straight through the field to an up-and-over gate and into the school lane. Pass St Peter's church with its solid squat shape enhanced by an elegant lych gate.

Bear L past cottages, each an individual personality, towards the post box on the main road where you turn R for a few yards. Cross and take the footpath L at Plum Green, between the cottages to a stile-gate exit from the village. Straight ahead across the

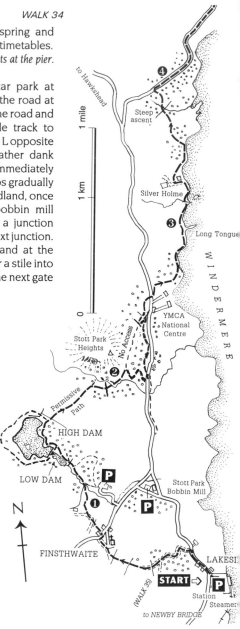

grass is a yellow arrow marker by the wall but as you stroll up to it pause and turn for a last glance at the setting of this peaceful little community. Go over a stile in the wall onto a track but do not follow it left. Keep ahead below the caravan (a smudgy sign to High Dam is painted on a rock) and pass by three mature crab apple trees. To the east Gummer's How 321m rises from its plantation without a hint of the busy road and great Windermere at its feet. The next fence bounds the High Dam National Park Area (See page 190). Go through the gate and over the bridge which crosses the hurrying stream released from the dammed valley. Keep L uphill (the path to the right leads down to the Stott Park Bobbin Mill and the road) to join a better track. Still to the left and uphill by the streamside go straight on, keeping L through a gate to Low Dam. As you mount level with the retaining wall you are met with a flush of light, shade and colour blended into a watery tranquillity. *A Cinderella lake, man-made to work the machines of the bobbin mill and turned into a thing of beauty by the wand of nature.* Leave to the R crossing a bridge and continue up the path to High Dam. Larger and more majestic than its lower workmate, it is worth leaving the route to cross the dam and wander along the path, enjoying its stretch of waters from the pine-clad shore.

Our way continues from the right-hand end of the dam, over the outlet bridge and along the lakeside. *Flocks of Canada geese grace the shallows in autumn*

Finsthwaite Church

undisturbed by walkers on the path which keeps in the trees at a discreet distance from the water.

When a cross wall is seen leave the circuit path and go ahead through a kissing gate at the edge of the High Dam Access area. A wide permissive path lined on one side by silver birches allows an open view of Stott Park Heights before wandering gently down into a little valley. At a path junction by a grand pine bear R. Continue down the valley through a gate in a fence to cross over the stream using a concrete cistern, masquerading as a mantrap, which forms the bridge. *Note the flat area on the right is a pitstead, once used by the charcoal burners.*

Keep ahead through a gap in the wall and through a grove of old yews. The path is naturally paved with slippery Silurian stones for a while. The path ahead now bends back R at a junction and descends, within earshot of the stream, to the road. Turn L for 20 yards and L again on a permissive path shadowing the road to a road gate. Turn L uphill and bend R just before the gate, once more shadowing the road to join it opposite the main YMCA entrance. *At the high point of the path is another pitstead.*

Turn L for 50 yards and opposite is a narrow footpath alongside a plantation. Go R through a wall passing Great Oaks Wood and a planting of birches with pheasants moving in and out of their trunks in frantic haste. Prepare for a sudden change as the path turns abruptly at the waters of Windermere and an arresting view of the Fairfield Horseshoe demands a chocolate bar stop.

Set off L along the water's edge, a path full of interest, tree roots and the occasional puddle. Pass over a bridge, a boat house and a wall end. Mallard and dabchicks enjoy the fragile seclusion offered by Long Tongue's tiny bay, the footfall of walkers being of little consequence when compared to the roar of the foaming skiers. Cross a stream opposite Silver Holme Islet (*so-called because a silver hoard is reputed to be hidden there*) and continue to Silver Holme Cottage. Turn L away from the mere at a stile and go along a fenced walk to a track where you turn R and into woodland, once more moving back to the waters' edge.

Pass a landing stage which doubles as a popular preening perch. Go under a rhododendron arch and past a boathouse where yellow arrows appear. They herald a complete change of scene and gradient as they direct you L up the hillside. Cross a track, following the arrows up a cramped path to a wall end. Cross a small stream and follow the fence uphill to a surfaced lane. Turn R and stride off along the pleasant wooded lane towards Low Cunsey.

It is worthwhile reviewing your day's schedule here, for if you have dawdled too long by the soporific water, now is the time to get a move on. At Low Cunsey pass by the houses and turn R opposite a Z-bend sign. Negotiate an ancient and modern stile combination and with hands held high run the gauntlet of a nettle invaded path to the lakeshore and turn L. Lovely shimmering stretches of water reach back south to Grass Holme but our way is ahead to the oak woods on Rawlinson Nab, another splendid viewpoint. Leave the wood at a stile. The lakeside footpath now passes through an area designated as a wildlife refuge. *It is an important wintering site for goldeneye, tufted duck and pochard. Walkers and mariners are asked to avoid the reedy fringe, although any creature trying to survive the liquidised waterweed soup must be a super-duck.* Piles of chopped weed strew the path to Ling Holme. Cross the bridge over Cunsey Beck, a swift stream fed by Esthwaite Water, and pass two boathouses. Across the lake is the promontory at Storrs Hall. *The tower on the end of its stone jetty is a small summer house known as the Temple of Heroes. It was built to commemorate the Napoleonic Wars and has become a familiar and useful navigation point.* Keep by the shore crossing stiles through two fields to a wallend. Cross the stream at High Cunsey by a gated bridge where the path bends up the fenceside to a stile onto the road at The Bield.

Turn R along the road (for local traffic only) and, with one eye cocked

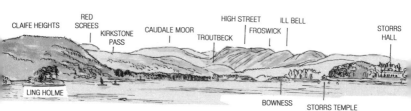

View north over Windermere from Rawlinson Nab

for stray traffic, look skywards with the other to marvel at the trees of Fellborough, giant redwoods of mighty girth, their heads in the clouds. *The sheltered, damp side of Windermere is host to several uncommon foreign trees often in the gardens of fine houses.*

Turn R on a lane, defended by many 'Private' signs to deter motorists. It leads to a neat lakeside track to join the main Hawkshead road. Turn R and cross to the Ash Landing car park. Possible starting point 2.

Walk through the car park and leave on a path into the wood which cuts off a nasty blind bend on the road. On reaching the road again turn L for a few minutes walk to the ferry. (*Refreshments and toilets.*)

Bowness Car Ferry
     8am - 9pm summer   8am - 8pm winter Every 20mins.

On landing walk along the road and turn L into the car park. (*Toilets*) Go straight through then make a L turning into Cockshott Point Park (if you are short of time see map for a more direct route to the ferry) and walk along the lakeside path contemplating that this beautiful park, a favourite spot drawing visitors by the million, was once an aircraft factory where Short Sunderland Flying Boats were built. From the exit gate at Bowness (car park opposite) continue past various shops to the steamer pier (*Refreshments*).

Take the steamer to Lakeside (*Refreshments and bar on board*) .

Cunsey Forge
Half a mile up Cunsey Beck was an important medieval bloomery worked by the monks of Furness Abbey who brought iron ore by packhorse or boat. In 1711 a more productive furnace was built here. Hammer Hole, just south of Rawlinson Nab, was the landing spot for the bloomery.

Char
Windermere is famed for its char and vendace, two fish which arrived in preglacial times and became trapped in the lake.

Storrs
Storrs which is seen across the lake was a grand Italian-style hall. Now it is a hotel.

The Ferry
The ferry is at a natural crossing point where the lake narrows. It has been used for centuries and some of the right of way paths leading to it were important links from Furness to the wool markets at Kendal.

WALK 35: **Finsthwaite Tower and High Dam**

Finsthwaite Tower

SUMMARY: Finsthwaite Tower lies on top of the small hill above Newby Bridge. The tower is almost hidden by dense woodland but a convenient viewpoint allows a fine outlook across the southern reach of Windermere.

Distance:	4³/₄ miles 7km
Grade:	Easy
Terrain:	Woodland, valley
Summit:	The Tower - 607ft (185m)
Map:	PF626

This short walk is useful as a 'filler' on a poor day, or as described it can be combined with a circuit of delectable High Dam.

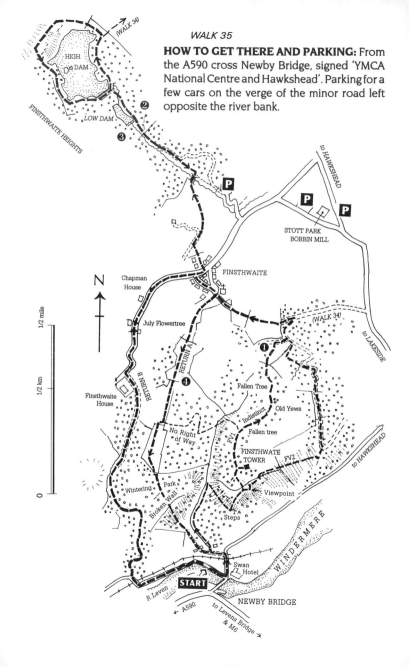

WALK 35

HOW TO GET THERE AND PARKING: From the A590 cross Newby Bridge, signed 'YMCA National Centre and Hawkshead'. Parking for a few cars on the verge of the minor road left opposite the river bank.

THE WALK: From the Swan Hotel take the Hawkshead road towards the Lakeside Steamer Terminal. Cross the railway bridge and turn L along a surfaced track (public footpath sign). In about 50 yards on the R a sign to Finsthwaite Tower points the way over a stile and into a fenced path leading up into the wood. The path begins to climb at once past a cottage to a gate which gives access to Waterside Knott. Freed from its confines the path rises through attractive mixed woodland, where the continual birdsong is punctuated by the occasional puff and whistle of the steam train on the line below.

As it climbs steadily the path runs alongside an old wall arched by shining holly trees and past glades where the summer green is broken by tall foxgloves.

The path bends to the R and the rock underfoot is carved into steps. The trees become thinner with pine and yew hunching their shoulders against the wind. The climb is all but over and the path narrows and levels.

Note a path leading L as you will need to return to this point. This was blocked and partly hidden by a fallen tree at the time of writing.

A window in the trees to the east gives a glimpse over the Leven Valley but do not stop here, a few yards further on is a fine viewpoint.

This platform is an ideal spot from which to study the plantations to the south-east of Windermere, traversed by our Five Tarns Walk No.38, one of Lakeland's shy yet beautiful areas, and in the background the distant folds of the Pennines on a clear day.

Return 30 yards to the point noted and follow the narrow path R. Cross a wall and continue up the bracken slope until the tower looms from its shroud of trees on the R. It is hard to believe that the tower was once the viewpoint.

FV1 - FINSTHWAITE VILLAGE VIA THE WOODLAND PATH

Continue on the path which descends slightly into a little dell with a collection of spiky rocks on the left. 20 yards further is a Y-junction. Fork R, negotiating a fallen tree, and after another 30 yards fork L and descend into a shallow valley. The path now becomes more distinct. Pass under the branches of a beautiful old yew then take care not to lose the line as the path (partly obscured by fallen branches) bends into a larch clearing with a triangular path junction. Turn R where the path is downhill and plain to see. A broken moss-covered wall is to the right. At a T junction turn R through the wall and along the descending path into a shallow vale to reach the main forest road. Turn R to the next junction then L. (FV2 joins here.) The village can now be seen over the meadows. Go L down the track to meet another track. Turn sharp L to a seat and stile in the wall. Cross two fields to the lane by the school and church at Finsthwaite village.

FV2 - FINSTHWAITE VILLAGE VIA THE FOREST ROADS

After examining the tower return to the viewpoint. Go on the path leading past the rock and through a gap in the wall. Turn R and keep by the wallside descending slightly. It is desirable not to overshoot and finish up disappointed on the lakeside road. Large yews line the wall and the path levels. Look for where the wall ends in a rock buttress. Keep on and the wall resumes to the right. Soon another wall meets our wall to make an inverted Y-junction. This is the inconspicuous path we have been looking for. Cross the apex of the Y-walls and traverse the slope rising slightly through firs then down to a T-junction with a forest track in an area of recently felled trees.

Turn L and make your way to the next junction where we go straight on. (Ignore waymark on the pole pointing R.) Walk along the wide forestry road rising a little. At the next junction from the left keep straight on, waymarked, and at a junction from the right keep straight on. A little wall appears to the left. At an S-bend keep ahead where the forest track makes away right to a multi-junction 20 yards on. Ahead again and up by rocks which support a large yew tree. The path now descends to a low wallside and cuts steeply down to join a major track. Turn L and ignoring the path on the right continue to the meadow with view of Finsthwaite village. (FV1 joins here.)

ONWARD ROUTE TO HIGH DAM

Pass St Peter's church with its solid squat shape enhanced by an elegant lych gate.

Bear L up the street towards the the road where you turn R for a few yards. Turn L on the footpath at Plum Green, between the cottages to a stile-gate exit from the village. Straight ahead across the grass is a yellow arrow marker by the wall, a good place for a retrospective glance at the setting of this peaceful little community. Go over a stile in the wall onto a track but do not follow it left. Keep ahead below the caravan (a smudgy sign to High Dam is painted on a rock) and pass by three mature crab apple trees. To the east Gummer's How 321m rises from its plantation without a hint of the busy road and the expanse of Windermere at its foot. The next fence bounds the High Dam National Park Area. Go through the gate and over the bridge which crosses the hurrying stream released from the dammed valley.

Keep L uphill to join a better track (the path to the right leads down to the High Dam car park, the Bobbin Mill and the road). Still to the L and uphill by the streamside go straight on to Low Dam. As you mount level with the retaining wall you are met with a flush of light, shade and colour blended into a watery tranquillity: a Cinderella lake, man-made to work the machines of the bobbin mill and turned into a thing of beauty by nature's

High Dam

wand. Continue up the path to High Dam. This lake is larger and more majestic than its lower workmate. Recent work has made the circuit an easy walk mostly along a gravel path. We prefer to walk round anti-clockwise but the choice is yours. Turn R over the bridge where the path winds between larches and the beauty invites you to stay awhile on the pine-clad shore. On approaching the wall turn L and cross the flat marshy inlet dryshod on a newly raised path which then rises over a heathery bluff and into the woods once more before reaching the dam.

Cross the dam, turn R and retrace the route past Low Dam, not forgetting to go R over the stream to regain Finsthwaite.

Return A - through the fields from Finsthwaite Church.

Return B - by the road and bridle way via Finsthwaite House.

RETURN A - VIA WINTERING PARK

Enter the field opposite the church on a public footpath signed to Newby Bridge. Proceed along a rising trough to a stone stile in a cross wall. Keep ahead over the rise where it is worth turning for a last look over the vale. Carry on to a ladder stile, waymarked, and follow the path along the left wallside through the strip of pasture. At the remains of a wall turn R to a super-slim slit stile standing redundant beneath a holly. Go 'through' and keep ahead past the electricity post to a step stile in the wall ahead, waymarked. Here we enter the Wintering Park woodland. Bend L and continue, level at first, then down more steeply to a stile in a fence. Go ahead along the enclosed pathway which evolves into the track used on the outset. At the road turn R over the railway bridge to the start.

RETURN B - VIA FINSTHWAITE HOUSE

Turn R and follow the road which carries little traffic and gives open views providing a pleasant contrast to the enclosed woodland.

Pass July Flowertree and continue for half a mile. Just before Finsthwaite House turn L onto a public bridleway and along to a gate which gives access to the wood. The bridleway runs through the trees to a second gate and beyond a field to the right allows a view of the secluded hamlet of Town End. Keep on the bridleway which rounds a couple of bends then follows a stream valley to the road. Cross over the railway bridge, turn L and sandwiched between the railway and the River Leven, walk along past the station to the start.

Finsthwaite Tower

Finsthwaite Tower was - 'Erected to honour the officers, seamen, and marines of the Royal Navy who, on defeating fleets of France, Spain and Holland preserved and protected liberty and commerce 1799.' Once known as Penington Lodge Tower it was built by James King of Finsthwaite House to commemorate naval victories at St Vincent, Camperdown and the Nile.

Finsthwaite Churchyard

In the churchyard is a marble cross to the memory of Clementina Johannes Sobieska Douglas of Waterside, 1771, reputedly the illegitimate daughter of Bonnie Prince Charlie. For the full story see 'Lost Lancashire' by A.L.Evans *Cicerone*

Stott Park Bobbin Mill

The mill was opened in 1835. The working mill closed in 1971, but was later re-opened as a working museum where the traditional woodland crafts can be seen. Coppice wood was used for making bobbins, barrel hoops and staves and ships' fenders. Oak bark was used for tanning leather. The demand for bobbins was enormous during the hey-day of Lancashire's cotton industry.

High Dam and Low Dam

Finsthwaite Tarn was dammed in 1835 on the opening of the Stott Park Mill. From High Dam the water was carried by stream and culverts to drive a 32-foot water-wheel which powered the mill's machinery. In 1858 a water turbine replaced the wheel, necessitating constant water pressure, and led to the construction of Low Dam.

The old reservoir on Torver Low Common reflects Coniston Old Man (Walk 25)
The Coniston lakeside path (Walk 27)

Heather-clad fells surrounded the lakes until 1850 when the area was planted with birch and oak to provide coppice woodland for charcoal burning and use by the mill. The tree growth was harvested by cutting regularly to promote growth of long poles from a stump. The poles were then used to make swill baskets, hoops for barrels, charcoal and dyes from the bark.

WALK 36: Leven and Rusland

Finsthwaite Town End

Complete circuit to Newby Bridge
Distance: 10 miles 16km
Grade: Moderate
Terrain: Valley, woodland
Short route - Newby Bridge to Haverthwaite Station
Distance: 6¼ miles 10km
Grade: Easy
Map: PF626

SUMMARY: A gentle attractive lowland walk which starts in the Leven Valley at the foot of Windermere, crossing coppiced woodland into the flats of the Rusland Valley, where the river bank levée makes an easy stroll to its junction with the Leven Estuary. Return along the riverside to Haverthwaite, then an old path over a shoulder of the fells brings a change of character for the last lap into Newby Bridge. A shorter version utilises the steam train.

Delightful woodland walking on the Brantwood Nature Trail (Walk 29)

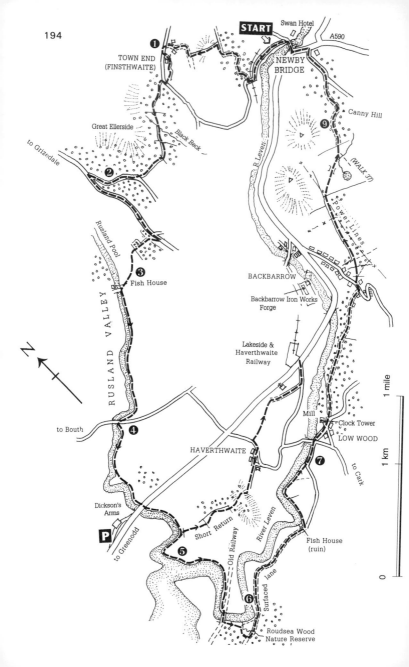

194

START

Swan Hotel

A590

❶

TOWN END
(FINSTHWAITE)

NEWBY
BRIDGE

Canny Hill

❾

Great Ellerside

Black Beck

to Grizedale

❷

(WALK 37)

Rusland Pool

❸ Fish House

R. Leven

Power Lines

BACKBARROW

Backbarrow Iron Works
Forge

RUSLAND VALLEY

Lakeside &
Haverthwaite
Railway

1 mile

to Booth

❹

Mill

Clock Tower

LOW WOOD

HAVERTHWAITE

❼

to Cark

1 km

Dickson's
Arms

P

to Greenodd

❺

Short Return

Old Railway

River Leven

Fish House
(ruin)

Surfaced lane

❻

Roudsea Wood
Nature Reserve

0

HOW TO GET THERE AND PARKING: Newby Bridge lies at the foot of Windermere on the A590. The walk can be done either:

* by parking at Haverthwaite Station and taking the train to Newby Bridge (Easter to October, first train 10.40am).

The 10-minute ride is too brief to enjoy the delights of this scenic old line with its vivified gleaming engines. The Lakeside and Haverthwaite Railway was built in 1872 and re-opened in 1973 and connects with the Windermere steamers at Lakeside.

** by parking at Newby Bridge. Turn L over the bridge and park on roadside opposite the river.

THE WALK: From Newby Bridge Halt turn R on the road bordering the Leven, a stretch of river beloved by canoeists. Downstream the old weir spans the water to take off a leat for the old corn mill (built in 1780), the ruin which can be seen on the far bank. *The skilful and fearless shoot the mill fall, then sport in its turbulence, the novices and faint-hearted descend the longer, tricky but less spectacular 'Staircase' then paddle on their way. (Canoeing is only allowed on certain Sundays during the year and is strictly controlled.)* Turn R over the railway bridge then R again to enter the woodland (Public Bridleway to Finsthwaite). The track winds uphill through old coppiced woodland. At the edge of the wood and junction with a track from the left keep straight on for a few paces to a double gate on the left in a wall. Go through the gate, and turn immediately R to a stile by an old iron gate in the barbed wire fence. The field you are about to cross is a smooth grassy dome, contrasting the woodland setting. Keep by the wallside. This is one of the few elevated viewpoints on the route. To the east is Finsthwaite Tower and Gummer's How rises beyond Windermere. Below the curve of the field to the west appears the secluded hamlet of Finsthwaite Town End. Turn R into a walled green lane which bends uphill to join the surfaced road.

Turn L, and L again almost immediately, sign to Finsyke. Pass in front of the cottage at the end of the lane and climb over a stile disguised as a wall. Cross a stream bed and follow the side of a broken down wall. At the next field bear R towards the wood where a stile leads onto the road. A few yards right on the opposite side of the road a footpath leads into the wood and leaves Town End behind. The way now climbs over the fringe of Great Ellerside, the height gained allowing sight of Bigland Barrow and the breath of the sea. Pass through a plantation of young larches to an iron gate. Cross Black Beck and carry on along the pathway through a second then a third iron gate on the right (ignoring the wooden gate into the field ahead), and down a narrow path. Snug between walls at first the trod then widens to let us look out and recognise Hoad Hill Monument (see page 205) standing proud above the estuary.

The path now descends steeply to a stile and a road. Turn R down the road. The road takes a long U-bend as it winds downhill. At the first stream a slight path can be seen joining the road below, but this is not a right of way and the road must be followed, L at the junction and over the stream once more.

At a rise, pass a barn and a cottage on the left, and take a path R, signed Bouth, down to the flat valley floor bordered by woodland and a deep ditch, fringed with foxgloves. Cross a stile into the field. Keep straight on to the corner of the wood then make your way diagonally L across the meadow through tell-tale tidemarks of last year's hay through a fence gate and immediately R onto the embankment over a stile by the river bank at Fish House bridge. The Fish House over the bridge is a welcome shelter if needed but the path stays on the eastern bank of the water which it follows downstream until interrupted by a small knoll of tree-crowned rock. The stile on the left will allow you to pass over the knoll as the path by the water's edge is long gone. Maintain direction along the river, the stiles being on the left of the fence until you meet the Bouth road. Cross the road and a stile leads onto the river bank again.

The Bouth road crosses the Rusland Pool

The water widens, deepens and meanders. Woven wattle fencing strives to protect the fragile banks from the power of the sea, and soon the main road (A590T) is reached.

Refreshments at the Dicksons Arms just over the bridge.

Continue on the left bank of the river and where it takes a sharp right bend look out for a stile on the left (yellow arrow waymarks).

*If you have parked at Haverthwaite Station take this short return route.

SHORT RETURN TO HAVERTHWAITE: * Cross two fields then rise slightly to a stile at the end of a wall. The path now takes the line of an old track past a stand of old oaks backed by fir. After passing a relatively new plantation, now flattened by a sea-borne gust, enter the oak and yew woodland at a gate. The track now winds over a low ridge, then descends past a pair of old stone gateposts which, in spite of rusting hinges and encroaching moss, cling to their purposeful dignity. The now enclosed pathway narrows and soon the first houses of Haverthwaite come into view.

There was still a working swilling shop in Haverthwaite in 1973. The swill is a coracle-type, handleless basket used for agricultural purposes. Coppiced poles of oak were gently simmered in a boiler until softened. Hazel rods were shaped to form the oval-shaped rims which were then woven about with strips cut from the boiled oak. Sometimes handles were added as used by the cockle pickers of Morecambe Bay.

The cottages are tightly packed. At the surfaced road turn L, then R, then L again past some renovated cottages and down to the main road.

Cross diagonally L. Footpath sign to Haverthwaite Church half a mile. Follow the path through an iron kissing gate, then over a stile into the field. The walk up the rising field must have taken the shine from many best

blacked boots but at least the substantial wall on the right will have provided shelter for the Sunday hat. Ignore the stile in the new wall on the left which leads onto the main road. Exit by a gate ahead to the old road, now only used as a footpath,

Haverthwaite Church

cross the old railway cutting and down the road. Ahead is the church of St Anne's surrounded by neat yews and pinpointed by a towering monkey puzzle tree.

Join the road at the Anglers Arms. Keep L where a footpath leads to the dual carriageway across which lies Haverthwaite Railway Station.

CONTINUATION OF MAIN ROUTE: Keep on the levée to the bracing spot where the Rusland Pool joins the River Leven. The path now changes direction as the levée begins its protective way along the bank of the Leven. Continue until the path drops off the embankment to a riverside stile. At the next stile turn R and cross the river by the old railway bridge. Beware of holes in the trackbed caused more by demolition of the line than collapse of the substantial bridge. Turn L along the river bank. On the right is Roudsea Wood, a reserve belonging to the Nature Conservancy Council with entry by permit only.

The river swings away left on one of its meanders, keep straight on and turn L at the surfaced road. It is worth spending a few moments perusing an information panel about the woodlands before striding out along the road. This is private and belongs to Bigland Hall, an outdoor activity centre. It carries the footpath and permissive cycleway only. The river is approached again and you soon pass by a little wooden hut with a seat. Cross the cattle-grid at the ruins of Fish House then leave the road and turn L over a stream and ladder stile into a field. The river has now lost its sea-borne influence and flows deep and dark. Next is a footbridge under power lines then a ladder stile and at a path junction keep by the water, pass under the power lines and exit carefully from the next field by a stile, almost on the water's edge. Go along the surfaced lane to the road.

* It is possible to turn L over the bridge and take the first R to return to Haverthwaite Station.

Cross the road and take the road opposite signed Low Wood and Bigland Hall.

To the left is the impressive building of the Clock Tower, an old gunpowder factory. It has had a dramatic change of use and now houses a craft centre where a crystal engraver nurtures his delicate art. Well worth a visit. At the end of the last garden in the village turn L on a pleasant woodland way.

This path is comfortable and we ponder how many folk have tramped this way, side by side chatting in the morning light, then wearied by the day's toll, drawn ease from harmony with plants and trees as they made their way home. This old footpath connecting the villages is more than a path, it was a way of life.

The old mill leat can be seen down to the left and, as the path rises, the noise of the river, fretting down its rapids, can be heard. Leave the woods at a gate. The path is now in a tunnel of trees. Pass through a slit stile and continue by a high wall then pass through a gate onto a surfaced road. The next little community is at the brink of Backbarrow. *Across the river in the main valley can be seen a large derelict area with crumbling buildings. This is the site of the renowned Backbarrow Forge*

The clock tower of the old Low Wood Gunpowder Works

powered by water from the weir. Turn L down the road for 25 yards, then R taking the footpath through the children's playground (*picnic table*).

A gate gives access onto the fell. Ignore the most obvious track which goes R. Keep straight on by the fence. Cross a stream and enter woodland again. Keep beside the fence, then a wall passing more open heathland and holding the same direction, between the wall and the power line, towards the gap in the hills ahead. Ignore a ladder stile on the left to carry on to a ladder stile in a cross wall. The path now leaves the wallside and its companion power line and rises diagonally R to cross over a low col.

On the col the short bright grass gives way to bracken and heather. Take a break on the rocks just above the col for there is an outlook over the Staveley valley to Gummers How and the forested hills of Walk 38. The path now descends. At the first stream and path junction turn L towards a wall and by a step stile or gate enter the fenced track beyond.

The track goes downhill passing tiny plantations, keep ahead where another track joins from the right. Bend L onto a surfaced road which leads down to the main road at Newby Bridge. Turn L, cross the road and R over the Leven bridge to the Swan Hotel and the starting point.

Hay Bridge Deer Conservation Centre
This is a reserve a little further up the Rusland Valley. It was established in 1971 as a memorial to Major Herbert Fook. Visitors by appointment.

Bouth
Bouth is a small village on the west of the Rusland Valley, famed for the Black Beck Gunpowder Works which was active from 1860 to 1929. It was closed after the second of two major explosions. It is now a caravan site.

The River Leven
This is an important salmon and sea trout river.

Roudsea Wood
Roudsea Wood is a National Nature Reserve - a woodland on a raised bog. Animals include roe deer, red squirrel, stoat and weasel. Access is by permit only from the Nature Conservancy Council in Windermere.

Low Wood Gunpowder Works
Founded in 1799, it was busy until the 1920s but suffered from several fatal accidents and explosions. Now the Clock Tower is a popular craft centre. Basket weaving (swills) was an important local craft until the 1970s. There was a thriving charcoal burning industry in the local woods, for iron smelting. Ash was the favourite wood for charcoal used for gunpowder.

Backbarrow Iron Works
This furnace was the largest of the Lakeland iron furnaces, founded in 1711, the last place where charcoal was used for smelting, until 1920. It closed in 1967. The buildings are now derelict, but worth investigating with care. It is a site crying out for restoration, especially the old furnace. Here, John Wilkinson, the inventor of iron ships, perfected the blast furnace.

GUMMER'S HOW

WINDERMERE

WALK 37: **Bigland Barrow and the Tarns beyond**

Newby Bridge over the River Leven

SUMMARY: The low hills south of Newby Bridge above the Leven valley are easily overlooked, yet they provide a pleasant walk in typical South Lakeland terrain - miniature fell country with a colourful blend of bracken, trees and sparkling tarns. The park-like grounds of Bigland Hall, with its serene lake, makes a gentle interlude. Views at first lie over the densely wooded hills around Windermere backed by the Coniston Fells, and later over the broad flats of the Leven Estuary with glinting sands and a breath of the sea. The stretch of quiet lane walking does not detract unduly from the route.

HOW TO GET THERE AND PARKING: Newby Bridge lies at the foot of Windermere on the A590.Cross the bridge and turn L to park on the righthand verge of the riverside lane.

THE WALK: Cross the bridge over the River Leven. *This is the most dangerous part of the walk. There are no pavements and if it is necessary to take refuge in the alcoves*

Distance:	8 miles 12³/₄km
Grade:	Moderate
Terrain:	Low fell, woodland, valley
Summit:	Bigland Barrow - 630ft (192m)
Map:	PF626

from the traffic there are compensations. Upstream the tail of Windermere transforms itself into the River Leven and slides past the Swan Hotel before passing under the bridge and over the weir. Turn L, cross the main road and look for a sign to Canny Hill, a narrow road on the right. The road rises passing several residences, their gardens won from the rough, rocky hillside by tender care. Take a bridle path branching R, sign to Hillside Beechwood. The track continues uphill and views to the east show the fells above Staveley. To the west the slopes of Old Backbarrow display a scattering of shapely old pines.

Branch L along a less prominent path identified a short way on by a split stone. Ahead the dark geometrical shape of Hoggarth's Plantation upsets the delicate hue of the moorland. Cross over a

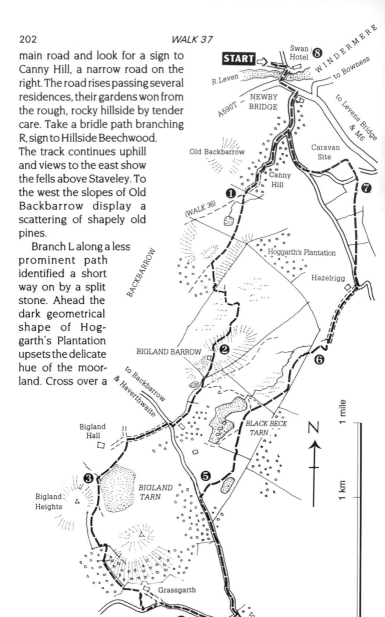

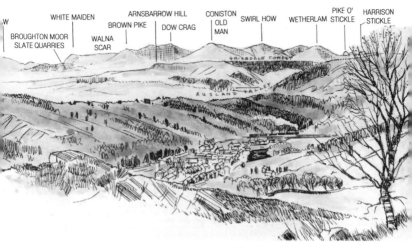

W · BROUGHTON MOOR SLATE QUARRIES · WHITE MAIDEN · WALNA SCAR · BROWN PIKE · ARNSBARROW HILL · DOW CRAG · CONISTON OLD MAN · SWIRL HOW · WETHERLAM · PIKE O' STICKLE · HARRISON STICKLE

GRIZEDALE FOREST

RUSLAND VALLEY

View over Backbarrow to the Coniston Fells

path and go straight on up the moor on the green path between the bracken. The reservoir on the right provides a tranquil foreground for a view of Old Back Barrow and the Coniston Fells on the far horizon. Go through a gate in the wall and continue in the same direction. A gap in the moor on the right unveils a tantalizing glimpse of the Leven Estuary and the finger of Hoad Hill Monument above Ulverston. The path now follows a flat shelf. Where this ends do not descend. Pass between hawthorns then fork L on a narrow trod traversing the hillside (ignore the wider path going ahead down the valley). On arriving at a high wall look right for a stile and climb over to enter the Bigland Allotment. Bigland Barrow with its strange summit structure is now in view. Go straight on to meet a prominent path then turn R along it heading for the top. (Not a right of way. The old right of way path officially goes straight on but it has become lost in time and use of the well worn paths is permitted.) The path winds about and is somewhat horsy in places as it is used by and belongs to the riding centre at Bigland Hall. The summit has a pleasing aspect and you may be tempted to climb onto the wartime relic to improve your vantage point. Be careful, the iron ladder is not very stable. *An elderly resident of Backbarrow recounted with pleasure how the local children would visit the summit as their annual trip to see Blackpool Illuminations.*

To the south lies Black Beck Tarn. *The addition of a small dam has transformed the boggy hollow into a lovely stretch of water, now stocked with fish, for the pleasure of angler and walker alike.* Take the path in its direction and descend to go through a gate in a cross wall. The tarn is in a tranquil setting with clumps of birch and larch carpeted by heather. Turn R and walk past a small pond with bulrushes. Pass on towards High Gate ignoring a stile. (Direction over the stile is to High Brow Edge, Haverthwaite and Backbarrow.)

Go through a gateway in the next wall and pass to the right of an alien gas installation, fenced and barbed, to reach a gate onto the road. (See map for alternative short return.) Sign to Bigland Hall Country Sports. Cross the road and go up the drive opposite. At the cattle-grid turn L to Bigland Tarn. Keep L on the wide gravel path which skirts the peaceful tarn. A seat by the water's edge is a good place to spend a few minutes rest. Go through an iron kissing gate and continue on the tarnside path. Soon it rises, keep by the wall as the path bends away from the tarn. Yellow direction arrows now show the route, towards a low col between Grassgarth and Bigland Heights. The way takes on its moorland character once more with shining views over the Leven Estuary. The path now leaves the wall, bends left and passes wind-bent hawthorns to meet another wall with a gate on the left. Go through the gate and into the coppiced-oaks of High Stribers Wood. At the edge of the woodland go through a gate and turn L towards Grassgarth Cottage. Turn R to join a surfaced road. Turn L along the road. There is little traffic and the road is not unattractive as it passes by Outley Mosses and rocky outcrops golden with gorse. It was once the old drove road between Lindale and Haverthwaite. At the junction turn sharp L and continue for about 1km then look out for a footpath sign, gate and stile on the right. Take this track which leads past a man-made tarn, its stillness belied by noisome shooting butts. Cross the inlet stream and at the sign on the right follow the way straight on to Hazelrigg. Keep ahead where the track bends right and go through a gate in the wall and onto the open moor. Black Beck Tarn lies below to the left and ahead on the distant horizon stand Ill Bell, Froswick and Harter Fell.

As you continue notice that the last bay of the tarn has a small island. Opposite here we turn R down a shallow valley with a white topped stone, to a gate and wall with footpath sign. (The main path, well used by fishermen, circles the tarn. If you miss the previous R turn, go to the outlet stream below the dam, turn R to the wall then turn R again to reach the gate and footpath sign.) Go through a gate to Hazelrigg. Ahead is the boggy hollow of Black Beck.

At the gate in the intake wall go straight on for 25m then, either, keep to the left of the wall and make a wet traverse of the grass sods and footstones, or, go though a slit stile in the wall, turn L and scramble over the rough ground on its right to join the wet path at a gate. Leaving the wall bear R across the field and descend to join Palace Lane where you turn L.

Bigland Barrow from Black Beck Tarn

Cross a stream and cattle-grid into Hazelrigg Lane.

Look for a footpath leaving the lane on the right signed Newby Bridge. The path marked on the map but invisible on the ground leads in an almost direct line across the fields to Crook Hill which is a somewhat vague point on the northern scene. Go diagonally L and under the power line halfway between the poles. Keep the same direction between clumps of gorse crossing a little stream and trackless grass to a stile in the next cross wall. Pass under the next set of wires and make for the lowest corner of the wood ahead. A wooden stile hiding by a beech tree gives access onto a road. Turn R down the hill for a few metres then L at the footpath which takes a signed route through the Newby Bridge Caravan Site. A 'Welcome' sign for the caravanners may give an adverse feeling to walkers, but not so. The path is clearly signed with yellow arrows and the traverse through the neatly gardened plots in attractive woodland then over the rustic bridge of Crook Moss Beck is pleasant and to be enjoyed. At the lane turn R and continue until meeting the main road at Newby Bridge. Turn L then R over the river bridge to the Swan Hotel at the start.

Hoad Hill Monument

This prominent tower in the form of a lighthouse was built as a monument to Sir John Barrow, who travelled extensively and encouraged exploration particularly in the Arctic. The Barrow Straits bear his name. He was one of the founder members of The Royal Geographical Society.

WALK 38: **Raven's Barrow and The Five Tarns**

Middle Tarn

SUMMARY: A varied walk which begins in the forest above the southern end of Windermere and bursts into a mixture of pasture, woodland and tarns overlooking the Winster Valley. The low fell arm of Raven's Barrow (Cartmel Fell) is a worthy goal and an expansive viewpoint from the Kent Estuary and the Pennines to Lakeland's eastern fells.

The return is an interesting linkage of woodland paths along the valley side, before a stiff climb onto the open fell of Hare Hill leads back into the forest and down to the start.

The walking is easy yet steep in a few places. The paths have occasional very boggy spots on the forest section but are otherwise sound and easy to follow. Fingerposts and direction arrows are placed throughout the route.

Distance:	8½ miles 13½km
Grade:	Moderate
Terrain:	Low fell, forest, valley
Summits:	Near Simpson Ground Reservoir - 656ft (200m)
	Raven's Barrow - 525ft (160m)
Maps:	PF626, PF627

HOW TO GET THERE AND PARKING: Leave the A590T at the sign to Staveley. In 250 yards turn R up the forest road, parking on the right before the forest gate.

THE WALK: Go through the gate and walk up the forest road. As the forest road bends left look for a yellow waymark on the R indicating a small path. Follow it, at first shadowing the line of the road until it bends left, then keep parallel to an old wall. This ascent of Barrow Bank is short. Pass by a low cliff on the right then bend R through an old gateway gap in the wall, waymark. (The left fork follows the wall to the forest road which is visible below.) Keep straight ahead on a narrow path. Airy larches soon give way to a dark evergreen tunnel. At what appears to be a firebreak, but is actually the route of the right of way path from Hare Hill and Simpson's Ground to Staveley, turn L and join the forest road in 25 yards. (Footpath sign towards Staveley village, blue waymark.)

Turn R along the forest road for 100 yards then turn L on a footpath, yellow waymark. The woodland is light and attractive. Pass through a clearing edged with silver birch to meet a path coming up from Staveley. Bear R on the rising path beside a lively little stream and on to meet the forest road again. Turn L where copses of larch, birch and sycamore herald a change in gradient which occurs at a junction. Go straight on for 100 yards then where the main track veers left keep straight on, waymark. Follow the narrowing pathway and cross a boggy area as best you may to reach a dell of old birches.

On the right is Simpson Ground Reservoir. Turn aside to spend a few minutes beside this man-made mere, a delightful experience where the reflections rival the realities and the silence is profound.

Retrace your steps to the little footpath and carry on R crossing a small brook. Join a wider path, which comes from the reservoir dam. Turn L and pass over the bed of a captured stream, step over the next one and proceed until stopped by the forest boundary wall.

SHORT RETURN VIA THE DAM

At the forest boundary wall turn R. *It is well worth looking over the wall before you move off. The Leven Estuary and Whitbarrow acting as a foreground for the distant Pennines provides an interesting identification exercise from this unusual viewpoint.* Keep on a path parallel to the wall then cross Way Beck using a concrete dam. The path now gradually bends R away from the wall passing through an open glade and just managing to avoid its mire. At the dam of the Simpson Ground Reservoir turn L and walk along the base of the embankment to its end. Cop o' Cow Hill peeps above the forest to the west. Continue along the access track for 100yards then turn R (Bridleway sign). At 20yards keep ahead on the major path (ignore wheel tracks off to the left). The forest allows shafts of afternoon sunlight through its delicate branches to delight your way but progress will now depend upon the previous week's rainfall. The track encloses puddles which grow into boot-top depth pools forcing forays into the forest. A section to delight children and dismay mum and dad. At the forest road turn L. Go down the hill to a bend by a small quarry, look for a bridleway sign to turn R. Continue until joining a major path and the longer route at a three-way junction.

TO CONTINUE THE ROUTE: An arrow sign L indicates a path parallel to the wall. Follow this curbing your enthusiasm for the enticing view, as the path gains height the .eastern panorama can be fully enjoyed. A stiled gateway leads onto the open fell of Foxfield Allotment.

The path now circles a rocky knoll on its left and descends to a wallside and farm track. (Fingerpost pointing back.) Turn L through the gate towards Sow How Farm. Just before the farmyard a signpost right points across a field and through a gate to Sow How Tarn. The path skirts below the tarn crossing the outlet bridge and rises up the field, from where the tarn may be appreciated in its delicate setting. At the wall is a gate with waymarks on its gateposts. Ignore the blue and white bridleway arrows. Turn L by the wall and follow the waymarked route across the field making towards a patch of evergreens in the larch forest well to the R of an obvious gate. Enter the wood at the right of the pine clump, yellow arrow.

The path soon tiptoes along the edge of Middle Tarn then through a rhododendron arch to join a bridleway. Keep L and pass through a gate, blue arrow, and through a field to a track bending sharp R to Heights Cottage. Now L, arrow on the cottage gable wall, and down the track to the gate which opens the way onto Raven's Barrow.

The green track straight ahead is the right of way (which soon branches left and circles the ridge on the north). Keep on the good track along the ridge winding and undulating between rocky platforms to the cairn monument at the end of the ridge. What a view! By thrusting out into the Winster Valley this 155m seat captures a tableau worthy of a mountain. Make a steep descent east from the monument to the wall corner and continue down by the wall to meet a footpath traversing the hillside.

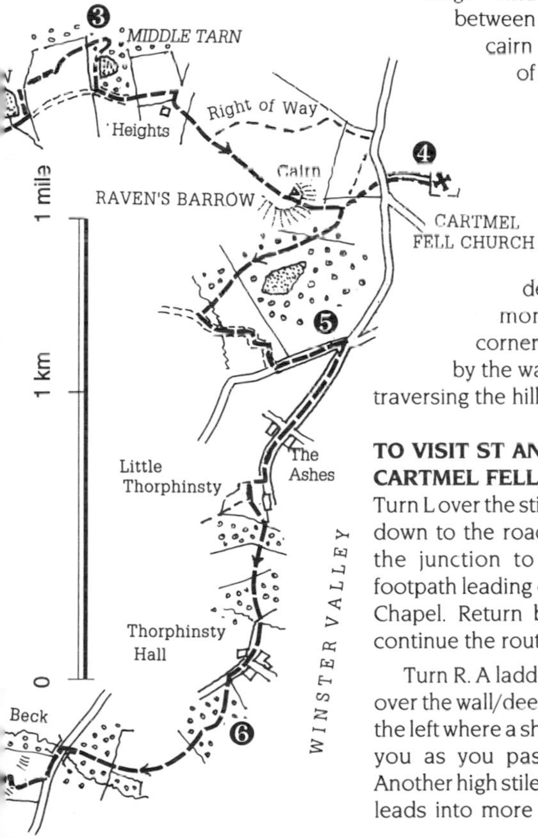

TO VISIT ST ANTHONY'S CHAPEL, CARTMEL FELL (30mins)

Turn L over the stile and follow the path down to the road. Go straight across the junction to the narrow signed footpath leading down to St Anthony's Chapel. Return by the same way to continue the route.

Turn R. A ladder stile takes the path over the wall/deer fence. Look down to the left where a shy little tarn will please you as you pass its shady hollow. Another high stile, with flap for animals, leads into more open heathland and down into a shallow valley. Turn sharp L along a pony track overlooked by an attractive parapet of pines until a gate gives access onto a surfaced road. Turn L for 100m then sharp R at the crossroads, fingerpost by a cattle-grid. Pass The Ashes and after crossing a bridge take the public footpath on the R. The path passes behind Little Thorphinsty and through a gate. Cross the field diagonally L to a stile in the bottom corner. (Don't make the mistake of following the other path to the top corner!) The path is well waymarked as it crosses the woodland ahead. Straight ahead through a slit stile in a low wall, cross a field, then a ladder stile gives access to woodland again. Exit by a gateway using the stile. Ford a shallow stream and pass to the right of the barn. This leads to a farm track and road at Thorphinsty Hall.

Turn R up the hill passing a cottage with typical Lakeland round chimneys. Look for the footpath on the left, very high ladder stile, and cross the woodland, yellow arrows, to exit by another ladder stile. Cross the next field diagonally R to discover a stile hidden behind a crab apple tree. More yellow arrows direct the way through a new hardwood plantation to a stile in the fence. The path now begins to climb between an old fence and a small new plantation to enter mature forest by a stile. The steep gradient soon eases and a stile leads out onto the road. Turn L, cross a bridge and go over the next stile on the R. follow yellow waymark poles steeply up the hill heading for the left-hand electricity post on the skyline. Behind this post a stile in the wall reveals the flatter felltop. Keep ahead, waymarks, roughly parallel to the wires to gain a farm track. Turn R and

Heights

St Anthony's Chapel

go along to a new stile to the left of a gate. Follow the recently designated path along the wall/fence to the open fell of Hare Hill. Cross a ladder stile and skirt rough ground to reach another ladder stile. Keep along the wall on the right until a gate is passed and so onto a road. Simpson Ground Farm can be seen nestling in the valley to the north. Cross the road and go through a gate opening onto the moor.

The track leads straight to the forest but a fan of tractor tracks may be confusing. Cross a stream on the way. Enter the forest at an old gate where a narrow but distinct path, the right of way path to Staveley, leads on. A balancing act on branches may be necessary to cross the depression of Bog End Moss but it's fun as long as someone else falls in. At a junction with a forest road keep straight ahead. A small tarn on the left is passed. It is bigger than it looks from the road and is an ideal place for a break. When the road begins to rise and bend right look out for an arrow sign on the left. Fork L here on the continuation of the R of W path to Staveley. At the next 3-way sign keep straight on.

SHORT RETURN JOINS HERE
The path now begins to descend more steeply and soon joins the forest road. Turn L and continue down to the road to the forest gate and the starting point.

Cartmel Fell Chapel

The simple fell chapel of St Anthony was built in 1504, and contains old box pews and fifteenth-century stained glass from Cartmel Priory.

Heights

Once a barn, it was used by the Quakers as a Friends' Meeting House from the seventeenth century to the 1920s.

WALK 39:   Gummer's How

Gummer's How

SUMMARY: In a commanding position overlooking the southern reaches of Windermere, the conical peak of Gummer's How rises from a cloak of woods. A road (to Bowland Bridge) climbs steeply from Fell Foot near the foot of the lake, and crosses a low col south of the summit cone. From a large car park in the woods, the walk is simple and short, for unfortunately the right of way goes only to the summit.

It is a justly popular stroll, an ideal peak for youngsters, offering the flavour of the hills without a great deal of effort.

Distance:	1½ miles 2½km
Grade:	Easy
Terrain:	Low fell
Summit:	Gummer's How - 1052ft (321m)
Map:	PF626

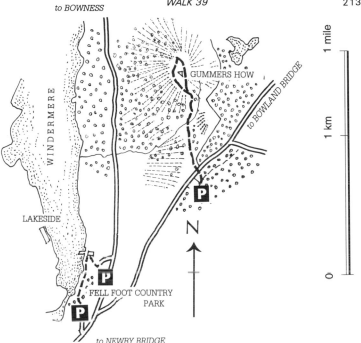

HOW TO GET THERE AND PARKING: Start from the car park which is on the right just before the highest point of the road when approaching from Fell Foot.

THE WALK: A short path forks left through the woods to cross the road and continue on the other side, at first almost level, towards the steeper slopes of the summit cone. Here there are many paths - a recommended route is to keep L along a high balcony with grandstand views of the lake dotted with flimsy white sails. The balcony path arrives round the end of the ridge where the summit triangulation point is gained.

Windermere is spread out below, with the Leven snaking away to the sea, between a buckled swathe of tree-clothed hills. If you have done some of the other walks in this book you will delight in spotting their whereabouts - Finsthwaite Tower, High Dam, Bigland Barrow and of course the Windermere Shore. You can see the old glacial terminal moraine at Newby Bridge, where the ice which gouged the lake turned to grind the broad flat valley which leads to the sea near Cartmel.

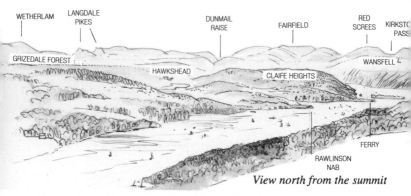

WETHERLAM LANGDALE PIKES DUNMAIL RAISE FAIRFIELD RED SCREES KIRKSTONE PASS

GRIZEDALE FOREST WANSFELL

HAWKSHEAD CLAIFE HEIGHTS

FERRY

RAWLINSON NAB

View north from the summit

Return down the steep, well trodden path to the car.

A visit to Gummer's How could be combined with a look around Fell Foot Park at the foot of Windermere. There are large car parks, a cafe, a multitude of short paths both by the lake shore and through tunnels amongst the dense rhododendrons. Mature beech and stately oak add a grandeur to the scene. It is a very popular spot in summer for the numerous visitors to potter about by the lake and enjoy the water. Sail boats and sail boards vie with the resident ducks.

View south-west across Windermere from the summit

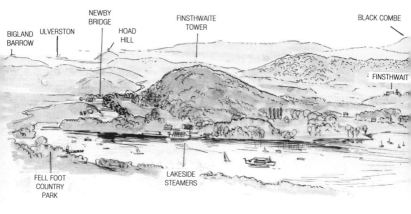

BIGLAND BARROW ULVERSTON NEWBY BRIDGE HOAD HILL FINSTHWAITE TOWER BLACK COMBE

FINSTHWAITE

FELL FOOT COUNTRY PARK LAKESIDE STEAMERS

WALK 40: The Winster Valley and Rosthwaite Heights

Birk's Bridge and ford over the River Winster

SUMMARY: The Winster Valley is noted for its attractive scattered houses in a pastoral setting. This walk takes a look at the valley and its gentle surroundings, with a visit to the viewpoint of Rosthwaite Heights which overlooks Windermere. You will certainly meet cows, and possibly horses, on this walk, but not many pepole. You can easily split the walk to make two shorter ones. Enjoy it in spring when the blossom and flowers are at their best, yet the colourful shades of autumn have their attractions too.

HOW TO GET THERE AND PARKING:

1) At Winster village. Parking is somewhat sparse but there are spaces to the north of the village by the junction of the A5074 and the lane to Kendal, and room for two or three cars opposite the

Distance:	8¹⁄₂ miles 13¹⁄₂km
Grade:	Moderate
Terrain:	Valley, woodland
Summit:	Rosthwaite Heights - 443ft (135m)
Map:	OL7

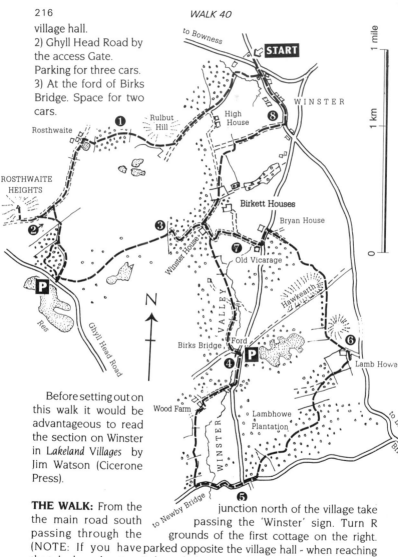

village hall.
2) Ghyll Head Road by the access Gate. Parking for three cars.
3) At the ford of Birks Bridge. Space for two cars.

Before setting out on this walk it would be advantageous to read the section on Winster in *Lakeland Villages* by Jim Watson (Cicerone Press).

THE WALK: From the the main road south passing through the junction north of the village take passing the 'Winster' sign. Turn R grounds of the first cottage on the right. (NOTE: If you have parked opposite the village hall - when reaching the telephone box turn L through the gate at the next cottage on the left.) There is no footpath sign and you appear to be entering someone's private garden (if you reach a road junction sign and the telephone box you have gone too far), but all is well, a gate leads into an old enclosed footpath, little used and replete with rural charm. A raised causeway by the infant River Winster leads to a two-span clapper bridge. Cross the bridge and take the right of two gates ahead. Continue by the wall/fence which soon bends rightwards and becomes delapidated. Keep to the line of the wall passing to the L of a tree-crowned rock outcrop. The path by the wall becomes engulfed by water and its attendant mud and rushes but the general line is easy to follow dryshod on the fell until it is walkable again. As height is gained you appreciate the peaceful Winster Valley in contrast to its vibrating neighbour Windermere. Go through a gate and join the track from High House Farm. Keep ahead and uphill passing a spring on the right. The track becomes a pleasant balcony. At a fork keep R (yellow footpath arrow) passing a fine yew as the path rises up the slopes of Rulbutt Hill. On reaching the brow Gummer's How can be seen to the south while the intervening fellside is a variety show of rocky knolls, supported by trees of multiple shapes and colours on a backcloth of heath.

Continue to a wall and go through the gate into a larch plantation. The path may have large puddles which are easily skirted and soon Rosthwaite Farm is reached.

Turn L on the surfaced lane. As you pass the farm look at the unusual yard gates, the work of a craftsman - I say no more rather than spoil your pleasure. A stile by a gate leads to the track onto the open fell. Continue to a dip where the stream is crossed by easy stepping-stones. The track now rises and on reaching a 3-way dwarf signpost note the direction left to Ghyll Head Road. Do not take it, but go on past a lone oak to the corner of the wood (electric wire post). Turn R to the summit cairn on Rosthwaite Heights from which there is a grandstand view of the southern half of Windermere and its bounding forest-clad fells.

Return to the lone oak and turn R to a stile in the wall ahead (as indicated by the signpost). Stay along the woodside fence to another stile. Here the route splits for a short distance.

Path 1) Keep ahead by the fence. The path passes a boggy area where duckboards have been laid. At the next gateway the alternative Path 2 joins from the Ghyll Head Road which is 50 yards ahead.

Path 2) Go over the stile on the right into the National Park Access Area. A rooty path winds amongst silver birches until bounded on the right by a rock slab attractively hung with ferns, lichens, mosses and ling. White arrows keep you to the way although they point in the reverse direction. The narrow path gradually bends leftwards and soon Ghyll Head Reservoir is seen over the road to the right. At the roadgate is a small parking area.

Winster House barn

Turn Immediately L through a gate signed 'Footpath to Winster'. In 50 yards join the alternative Path 1 and bear R along the green path through the open pastures of Birkett Houses Allotment. The path is visible well ahead. After the first boggy level a small trod branches right. It leads onto a slight knoll which is hiding a pretty tarn, man-made to attract wildfowl to its double-barrelled sanctuary.

The path undulates across the allotment to a high wall. Either, turn L, then R through a gate into a lane, or, climb the stile, cross the wood corner and climb another stile into the lane.

The lane bends right revealing a descent into the Winster valley. Reach Winster House, a Georgian house with a great barn.

SHORT RETURN: Turn L into a walled lane overhung with beeches which passes to the rear of Birkett Houses, a medieval manor house worth seeing from the front. A kissing gate gives access to a field. Cross to a gateway in the wall and take a diagonal line to the far opposite corner of the next large field. Go through the gateway and keep by the wallside bending left to a gate into a lane. Turn R and cross the valley floor passing Mid Winster House to the main road.

Turn L and walk through the scattered village to the start.

TO CONTINUE: Turn R passing in front of Winster House to a kissing gate on the right. Go through and continue with the low hedge/wall to your left allowing a view of the stilted River Winster banked by formal sheep-mown meadows and the valley beyond. The field on the right is a display of daffodils if visited in March. At a Y-junction keep L and level and from the next gate head across the middle of the field to a gap in the facing wall with a stream, Lowhouse Beck, flowing before it. After negotiating the water, which may be a trickle or a few yards splash, cross the limekiln field to join a major track by the electricity wires. Minor paths branch off to the left towards the river, however continue ahead on the main track leading down the valley. The river is now accelerating and the springtime daffodils peep through a russet mat of last year's bracken. Pass a ruin and make for a kissing gate in a wall corner where the track enters the wood. The track, now enclosed, leads to a surfaced lane. Turn L to a ford and Birks Bridge, an attractive raised causeway leading to the road. Turn R at the road ignoring the various footpath signs hereabouts. Pass a cottage on the right, its garden noisy with the cascading river, and take the next track right to Wood Farm.

Cross the river again (blue arrow bridleway sign) and carry on to the farm. The first main building is a fine stone barn. A slate propped against the window directs a L turn to Strawberry Bank and Hartbarrow, this is the way. Go R at the end of the barn into a green lane along the side of the orchard. When confronted with two gates go through the L-hand one and cross the field to a gate under the electric wires then continue along the line of the wires crossing a small stream to a gate almost hidden from view but pinpointed in the field corner at a three-wall junction by a wood.

Enter a walled lane, which only extends a dozen yards, as the right wall swings away keep on course by the broken down left wall passing under wires to a gate in a cross wall. Continue along the lane to the road. Turn L and cross the river bridge.

It is now time to leave the valley floor and climb the wooded slopes of Lambhowe. The road rises steeply for 300 yards. At a left junction keep straight on signed to Kendal and Bowland Bridge. In 100 yards is another junction from the right. Keep straight on to Kendal via Crosthwaite and in another 100 yards locate and take a footpath on the L to Lamb Howe.

The track/path leads into coppiced birch with stands of oak, a delightful little-visited wood. Do not be put off at the sight of the desolate quagmire neighbouring the road. Near the gate is a sheltered feeding place for animals, the soft spots are easily negotiated and the footpath is well signed with yellow arrows. Cross the stile in the fence and go ahead, if the fallen tree has been removed, onto a small waymarked path. Keep R of a ribbon of water crossing a boggy patch on laid branches. The path now begins to rise onto a small rocky knoll and the way becomes drier. Go under yew trees keeping an eye out for the guiding mini-stick waymarks. Stride over a cowboy-style fence and bear L and continue as the forest becomes denser through a stand of fir, to a stile in a wall. Go straight ahead down the field parallel to the wall away on the left past a great oak, devastated by wind and weather, its great limbs broken, but its budding fingers grasping for life. Go over a ladder stile in the wall and continue on the path ahead. A path joins from the left. Keep ahead (no waymark) to a stile in the wall at the edge of the wood. From this stile note the direction of Lamb Howe Farm for which we are heading. There is a gate with a waymark which can soon be seen when you make your way over the field in the direction of the white farmhouse. Go through the gate and follow the garden wall when it bends L. From here is a lovely open view across the Lyth valley its gentle landscape a series of hillocks with trees of graceful silhouette, patterned by hedge and wall.

Go through two gates and cross the surfaced lane (ignore the sign right to the main road A5074 at 150 yards). A great iron cauldron acts as a water butt for the barn, a fine example, its great wooden beam over the door still intact. Turn L and go up the rising lane behind the barn and through the gate into a field. Keep close along the hedge passing Lamb Howe Hill on the right. At a waymarked ladder stile cross into an enclosed pathway alongside a new plantation. Take a look over and beyond the young trees to the west. A beautiful wooded valley with a lake laying in its folds and unrecorded by the O.S., will be screened into secrecy by the passing years. Enjoy it while you may.

Cross over the R-hand wall by a stile then continue in the same direction with the wall on the left. Gradually rise to the upper field corner where, at the last minute when you think there is no way out, a stile made of protruding stones climbs the two high walls onto the gorse strewn slopes of Hawkearth Bank. (Care is needed at this stile as the stones are very slippery in wet weather.) From the stile go straight ahead on a level line between clumps of gorse towards a clump of trees. After a hundred yards or so the path becomes clearer and over a rise a track and broken wall remains appear. Cross a spring and keep on the track through empty gateposts. At an area of track junctions keep ahead. Soon another track joins in from the left and at a gate our way underfoot becomes more businesslike. The walls also are standing and where the left-hand one turns away the Winster Valley can once more be seen. A gate leads into a walled lane. Turn L (blue arrow) to the road.

You could go directly back to your car by turning R along the road, but if time allows it is more pleasing to complete the figure of eight circuit. Turn L and almost immediately R into a lane which passes the Old Vicarage. Note the fine crest on the stone gateposts. The lane passes the private drive to Birkett Houses to reach Winster House and a junction with the outward route. Follow the **Short Return** back to the car.

Crest on the stone gatepost of the Old Vicarage

The Winster Valley

The valley was formed by a branch of the glacier which flowed down Windermere. Now it is famed for its damson and apple blossom from late March to mid-May.

Bryant House

This was the home of Jonas Barber from 1682 to 1720 a famous clockmaker. His sons carried on the tradition, making fine grandfather clocks.

WALK 41:   **Lord's Lot**

Lord's Lot from above Crosthwaite

SUMMARY: If you fancy a short peaceful walk on the fringe of Lakeland, then this will suit. You may meet a few cows and sheep, see some of the local inhabitants going about their daily tasks, but few if any walkers, in marked contrast to the busy paths of central Lakeland. Almost all the paths are barely visible and much of the walking is over grass.

In early spring the rough slopes of Lord's Lot are a blaze of yellow gorse. Don't underestimate the walk, it is difficult to locate the correct route in clear weather, keep away in mist. The stark ruined tower of St Catherine's will attract the curious but please don't go inside!

HOW TO GET THERE AND PARKING: Midway between the A590 and Bowness on the A5074 turn at a sharp right-angled bend to Crosthwaite, a quiet little village. Turn L in the village, signed Starnthwaite, Crook, keep straight on at junction and in 200 yards park at the entrance to a wide footpath on the R. There is just room for three cars without impeding the farmer.

Distance:	4¼ miles 6¾km
	5¾ miles 9¼km (with the extension to St Catherine's Tower)
Grade:	Easy
Terrain:	Low fell
Summit:	Lord's Lot - 686ft (209m)
Map:	OL7

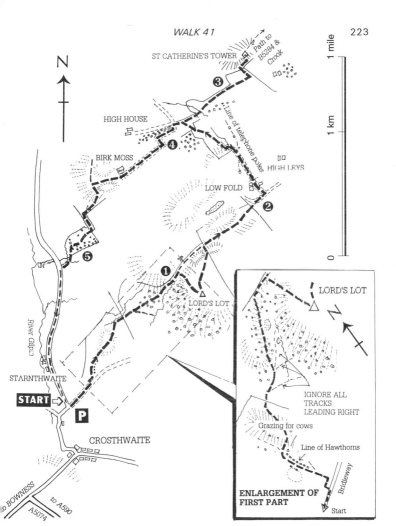

THE WALK: Follow the stony ash-hung bridle path uphill for 250 yards to a yellow arrow waymark on a gate on the left. From here the path is not obvious, but is an old way invaded by plants and sapling which provide a habitat for the peacock butterfly. From the gate turn R then angle L away from the wall. Do not go right into the field but go below a line of hawthorns on a slight path, above a patch of gorse. Pass a spring and where the

St Catherine's Tower in 1994

tractor marks go straight on, bear R, on gorse-dotted turf over the brow. *The hillside is so little disturbed that rabbits stand and gaze in surprise before moving, not too hurriedly, away.*

Over the rise you see a wall with a waymarked stile. A path is now visible ahead rising towards the gorse-covered flanks of Lord's Lot. To the right the cairned-summit is Tarn Hill. Ignore the track which swings away right after 100 yards. Head straight for the gap in the skyline hills.

At the entrance to a little valley don't keep to the valley floor but go up the hillside slightly L. A faint path is visible, which soon improves and keeps L of a boggy area. You can see the gap we are heading for straight ahead. A wall appears, keep it on your left and follow it to the gap.

Turn R and make your way up the rocky slope to the summit of Lord's Lot. The view is not spectacular but gentle and interesting in its rural detail. Either return to the gap and continue along the intermittent path just above the wall; or better, stay on the higher ground parallel with the gap, to reach a cross wall just before another little hillock. Turn L by the wall and descend to a stile at a junction with the wall followed on the direct gap route.

Over the stile go straight ahead down a shallow valley between the folds of the hillside and on down a slight trough to a ladder stile on the L just before Low Fold Farm. Join the farm track ahead and in 50 yards turn L into the farmyard. Keep straight between barns through the gate ahead on a definite track. Progress through a couple of fields and go through a wall gap on the hill crest. St Catherine's Tower can be seen on the hillock ahead.

High Dam is delightful in all seasons (Walks 34 and 35)
View across the Winster Valley to Whitbarrow Scar (Walk 38)

Bear L away from the telephone poles through another wall gap. As the track descends follow the yellow waymarked route to a stile. Cross the field to join a lower wall at a signpost.

TO VISIT ST CATHERINE'S TOWER
Turn R along the wallside on a barely visible green track. This leads along the base of a slight valley, across a small stream then by the wallside again to a cross wall below the hill which is topped by the tower. Turn L and through a stile in the top corner to reach the tower. It is ruinous and must not be entered.

Only the tower remains of the original church which was used from 1516 to 1887 when it was abandoned. It was restored in 1993 by English Heritage.

Return the same way.

TO CONTINUE THE WALK: Follow the wallside to join a surfaced farm lane. Turn L over a cattle-grid, sign Birk Moss, on a rough lane beside a strip of woods. Keep on the lane round a bend to Birk Moss Farm which is bypassed by a signed diversion of the bridleway. Past the farm a blue waymark points the way straight on over the grassy rise. One hundred yards down the hill an old green bridleway crosses our route. Note that this may not be easily recognised. Clues are the edging stones and hoof marks! Bend L along the bridleway which then curves downhill by a wall to a gate in the corner. Turn L into an overgrown walled section to a gate at its end. Go diagonally L down the rough pasture, through the remnants of a hawthorn hedge to go through a gateway just above the stream. Cross the field to the road.

Turn L and along half a mile of quiet country lane, passing Starnthwaite Ghyll School, to the start.

Kentmere valley, with its reborn lake, seen from the Garburn road (Walk 48). Walk 43 comes along the right hand side of the lake and passes Kentmere Hall, in the foreground.

CHAPTER 3

The Eastern Fells and Dales

Lakeland's eastern fells dominate long straight valleys, the upper regions of which are comprised of hard volcanic rock whilst the more southerly reaches are in the Silurian, which creates a dramatic change of scenery from craggy mountain to more gentle ice smoothed moorland. The walks chosen here provide a contrast between the two types of scenery - combined with the more sylvan charms of the valley floors.

The Borrowdale walk is the most easterly in Lakeland, separated from the Howgills and The Pennines by the Lune Gorge.

Apart from the villages of Troutbeck and Kentmere you won't find crowds in this area - even on Bank Holidays!

Troutbeck Tongue lies cradled by the higher fells at the head of the Troutbeck Valley. Viewed from the Garburn Pass (Walk 48)

RED SCREES   KIRKSTONE PASS   STONY COVE PIKE

WALK 42:
Troutbeck Valley -
A walk round Troutbeck Tongue

SUMMARY: A walk of contrasts. Starting close to the highly commercialised, busy campsite of Limefitt Park, a pleasant stroll along a quiet lane through flat meadows to Troutbeck Park Farm is followed by a short climb through attractive woods of alder into the secluded and lonely upper valley of Troutbeck. This is little walked and the path is slight - with evidence here and there of a broad track used in distant times. The slate bridge poses questions. Why is it such a solid, broad construction, obviously designed to carry laden carts, when there is no evidence of quarrying higher up the valley?

Distance:	7½ miles 12km
Grade:	Easy
Terrain:	Valley
Summit:	Neck of Troutbeck Tongue - 984ft (300m)
Map:	OL7

Return is across the low neck of Troutbeck Tongue to join the quarry track along the base of the parallel valley of Hagg Gill.

THORNTHWAITE   THORNTHWAITE   FROSWICK   ILL BELL   YOKE
TH   CRAG

This makes a gentle descent along the base of the steep slopes which form the eastern side of the Troutbeck Valley, following the line of the Roman road.

HOW TO GET THERE AND PARKING: Start on the A592 Kirkstone Pass road, two and a half miles north of Troutbeck Bridge. Parking places 50 yards before and after the entrance to Limefitt Park Campsite.

THE WALK: Set off northwards up the road for 200 yards then turn R down a signed bridle path. Although called a bridle path it is a pleasant hazel-arched footpath gently descending to the valley and only the smallest pony would find it comfortable. Views across to the sweeping flanks over which the Garburn Pass track rises, give a feeling of great space, where scale is difficult to assess.

Pass by a left fork to Town Head and continue until meeting a road. Turn R and walk along with ease as, other than to the farms, no vehicular access is allowed. This gives a chance to study the glacial U-shaped formation of the Troutbeck Valley. Cross Trout Beck at Ing Bridge and keep straight on

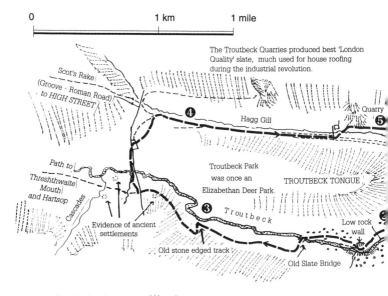

The Troutbeck Quarries produced best 'London Quality' slate, much used for house roofing during the industrial revolution.

Scot's Rake
(Groove - Roman Road)
to HIGH STREET

Quarry

Hagg Gill

Path to
Threshthwaite Mouth and Hartsop

Cascades

Troutbeck Park was once an Elizabethan Deer Park.

TROUTBECK TONGUE

Evidence of ancient settlements

Old stone edged track

Troutbeck

Low rock wall

Old Slate Bridge

Note: Fording the stream could be dangerous in high water.

at the ensuing junction to Long Green Head. The centre of the valley is now occupied by the steep end of The Tongue (once separating the two arms of a glacier) with Troutbeck Park Farm nestling in its lee and a variety of trees adding a picturesque setting. Cross the stream at Hagg Bridge and follow the public footpath sign to Threshthwaite. The way through the farmyard is signed to the exit gate (please close) and the pasture beyond. The climb up Trout Beck now begins as the footpath narrows and steepens through scrubby outliers of Hird Wood. Carry on through the gate in a wall. The hillsides close in and become rougher. At a winter feeding station for the sheep, trods fan in all direction, keep parallel to and above the wall. The footpath soon becomes clearer as it heads into the jaws of the valley. At the end of a low wall of rock on the right, fork R. (The path straight on gradually dissolves in a streamside wallow.) In the crease of the valley below the Trout Beck frets through cascades and deep pools in its confined bed. The path traverses above the marshy area to emerge into the wilderness of the upper valley. Cross the Trout Beck by a sturdy stone slab bridge. *Could this have carried the old valley road onto Kirkstone Pass? From a distance the line of an old road is visible slanting diagonally up the hillside into Woundale, where another similar bridge is located.*

Keep ahead across a spongy area before turning R up the valley once more. The path is intermittent but always keeps above the reeds and rushes. Flat areas hereabouts are the sites of ancient settlements. A harsh spot to live with the north wind funnelling

Iagg Gill is a tiny stream in a deep U-shaped valley. In glacial times ice gouged out the two valleys and left the low promontory of The Tongue. Moraines are evident in the upper reaches of Troutbeck.

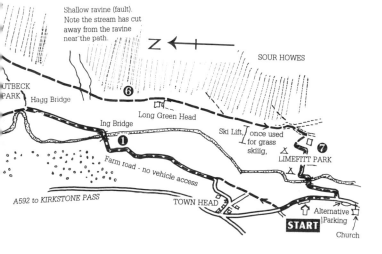

Shallow ravine (fault). Note the stream has cut away from the ravine near the path.

N ←

SOUR HOWES

UTBECK PARK
Hagg Bridge

Long Green Head
Ing Bridge

Ski Lift, once used for grass skiing
LIMEFITT PARK

Farm road - no vehicle access

A592 to KIRKSTONE PASS

TOWN HEAD

Alternative Parking

START

Church

The stone bridge in upper Troutbeck

between Threshthwaite Crag and Stonycove Mouth Pike and whistling down the valley. Pass a boulder with a small cairn on top and the remains of a sheepfold. A line of large stones by the way hints at an old trackway. Keep on it up to the left, to a rocky outcrop then continue to traverse the bracken slopes. Pass a boulder - dropped and split by ice, then go over a stile in the next crosswall. Beyond the wall a side stream (Sadgill) rushes down from Pike How in a series of waterfalls. A fine incentive to take this walk in wet weather. Turn R not directly beside the wall, but circle and follow an avenue of grass between the bracken alongside a tributary stream to where the main stream meets the wall. Now you must cross Trout Beck. Normally the wide stream is just a quick sole-deep splash. (*If the flow is intimidating go further upstream or turn back to Troutbeck Park Farm.**)

Continue up the fellside to join a track. Turn R through a gate in the wall into the sheepfold. Turn L and exit through an upper gate. Above looms the vast slopes of Park Fell. A slanting green line is the way of the Roman road, now the footpath from High Street, descending to the Hagg Gill valley. Cross the neck of The Tongue and join this path - now a track, and turn R. The track descends gently for a mile or so. Go through a gate in a fence and proceed until near a fine barn. Take the National Trust bridleway (-> sign), fork L and cross the gill by ford or bridge then fork R on a green track down the valley. *The quarries above were renowned for the fine quality of the slate, which was used particularly for roofing during the Industrial Revolution.* At a cross wall with two gates go through the left upper one. The path is now narrow traversing between the woods which line the gill and the bracken-clad slopes of Lowther Brow. Continue past a gate and barn, and a rocky gill with attractive cascades. Go through a fine old iron gate with a scrolled latch, typical of south Lakeland smiths. Pass a track turning down to Ing Bridge. Our path has graduated to a surfaced track, but not for long. It is interesting to note the streams on the hillside hereabouts - fault lines running SW/NE have been used, then deserted by the gravitating water.

At Long Green Head keep L of the buildings. The Trout Beck below is now captured between levées on the flat valley floor. Our path climbs a little giving a chance to look back at the route and admire the glaciated shape of the valley as a whole. Beyond the next gate is the top of a forlorn ski tow, the muscle of a grass skiing project which never really took off. Keep on beside a deer fence which protects a new plantation. A short cut down from the Garburn Pass road joins in on the left. Go ahead, then branch R, keeping beside the deer fence, down to a gate where you enter the Limefitt Park Campsite a few yards from the door of the Haybarn Inn. It is a very large campsite with many access avenues for the campers, but there is a right of way through. From the Inn keep on the path to the central road. Turn L and follow it as it bends and after passing reception buildings and crossing the Beck Bridge, rise to join the Kirkstone Pass road near the start. A little further up the road past the layby is The Queen's Head (*Refreshments*).

Unusual stile at the furthest point of the walk

WALK 43: Kentmere and Hollow Moor

Kentmere Hall

SUMMARY: This approaches Kentmere by a gentle walk past a reedy mere where the rugged setting of the village can be appreciated to the full. Return is made over the grassy top of Hollow Moor, perhaps the finest viewpoint into the ring of steep fells which blocks the head of the valley. A lonely tract of moorland completes the circuit.

HOW TO GET THERE AND PARKING: On the Kentmere road, 2 miles north of Staveley there is roadside parking (space only for three cars) by a turning to Ullthwaite Bridge. The route can be joined at Kentmere village from the car park there, but it is recommended and described from Ullthwaite Bridge to savour the gentle lower valley before seeing the formal mountain setting which dominates the head of Kentmere.

THE WALK: Go down the lane and onto the bridge over the River Kent.

Distance:	7 miles 11¼km
Grade:	Moderate
Terrain:	Valley, low fell
Summit:	Hollow Moor - 1397ft (426m)
Map:	OL7

Unfortunately it is impossible to see this sturdy old seventeenth-century bridge without a trespass into the adjacent meadow or woods but the sight of the dipper, busy about the shallow water, from its jagged parapet may compensate.

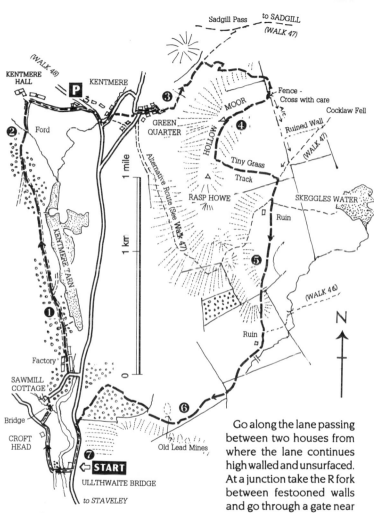

Go along the lane passing between two houses from where the lane continues high walled and unsurfaced. At a junction take the R fork between festooned walls and go through a gate near Sawmill Cottage. Turn L on the waterside path and over a narrow footbridge spanning the mill stream. Cross the lawns ahead to the road at the old sawmill, now a pottery studio, in a perfect setting of rural charm.

Turn R and go along the road to the gate of the Hepworth Mineral and

Chemical Company at the sign of the smiling camel. The footpath now goes ahead through the factory yard and emerges alongside a fence made of old sleepers, its end not quite terminating our brush with industry for today. Keep on the track ahead which returns to its rural aspect briefly. Turn R on a small path to enjoy a few tranquil moments on the quay by Kentmere Tarn .

The substantial quayside complete with bollards may look somewhat out of place but the metal pegs protruding from the quay show the site of the aerial ropeway, used to transport diatomite from its source in the gravels of Kentmere to the factory. Its extraction extended and improved the face of the boggy mere into the tranquil waters we see today from the quay.

Return to the path and at the next fork keep L on the upper path to a ladder stile. *As we can now look out over Kentmere Tarn, the broad expanse of Green Quarter Fell beyond gives true scale to the mere pools in their reedy beds, and near at hand the turf holds a haze of bluebells in the spring.* Go through the next gate where the open view is brief as another gate leads into a once coppiced woodland. At a cross junction angle R, descending gently to a gate at the woodland's edge. Ahead the valley is blocked by the appropriately named Crag Quarter, with the line of the ancient packhorse way from Troutbeck to Longsleddale via the Garburn Pass on its flanks and the village of Kentmere clinging to its foot. Its prominence however is usurped by the intriguing Kentmere Hall Farm. Approach by going through two gates, over a ford and through another gate which will bring you to the position where you can take a better look at the Pele tower.

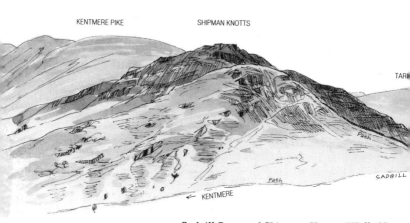

Sadgill Pass and Shipman Knotts (Walk 45)
from the ascent of Hollow Moor

Turn R along the lane to Kentmere village. (*Car park, telephone* up the road on the left)

At the main road bear R down the hill for 200 yards until crossing the bridge over the River Kent.

(For a **short return** the road can be followed down the valley for 1³/₄ miles to the start.)

The field by the bridge is often used as a temporary overflow car park at busy weekends in the summer season.

Turn L past Bridge End House up the rising lane (ignore the first public footpath on the right) and cross Kill Gill at Low Holme. Take a steep footpath R up the side of the Gill, signed Longsleddale via Green Quarter. The character of the walk changes abruptly as the verdant valley is left behind and you head for the open fell. Mount the pasture to a stile left of the gate in the far wall, turn L into the hamlet of Green Quarter. Follow the public footpath sign left to Longsleddale and allow the many yellow arrows to hustle you along the short stretch of road (*teas at Maggs Howe on the right at the top of the hamlet*). Opposite the Old Forge go through a gate on the R by a sheepfold (to Longsleddale and Sadgill) and along the track onto the open fell.

This is a good place to stop and to look out over the valley. The view expands to the north and west, enough to whet the appetite for the Kentmere Horseshoe walk which can be traced on the horizon, and to pick out the line of the old pony track from Kentmere to Longsleddale.

Where the track levels leave the main path and branch right, climbing again. The track becomes little used but its foundation can be followed as it winds up the hillside to a leaning gate in a rickety fence. The track now bends R uphill keeping in line, but at a safe distance, from the fence. As Hollow Moor spreads to the right Longsleddale deepens away to the left. The track finally evaporates and the way approaches the fence.

It is now time to decide on one of two routes. If the weather is fine and visibility good take route **a)**, if it looks ominous with mist or low cloud follow route **b)**.

a). Move into virgin territory and immediately experience the feeling of isolation which inhabits this lonely upland area. Cross the fence with care on the R at its highest point and set off at 90° across the multicoloured moor keeping on the ridge. If you are an habitual path walker it is a good rule to keep off the yellowish-pale-green patches. It is sphagnum moss which grows in the wet boggy places. In a few hundred yards a slight sheeptrod appears leading SW to the summit of Hollow Moor. The trod

Skeggles Water, surrounded by bog and drumlins, is a lonely place

strengthens to a path as it reaches a five-holed stone, a forlorn finger on the featureless summit, a pointer which indicates the way to take along the ridge top. The views are extensive yet strangely dominated by sober Skeggles Water, set amid the heather. It lies, captive in its bleak basin, but beyond there are signs of planting which will in course of time restore purpose to the desolate Sleddale Forest. The path now begins to descend. It is narrow yet easy to follow until suddenly, on reaching a shallow saddle, it disappears in an area of rushes. Leave the line of the ridge and turn L as though heading for Skeggles Water, SE, on the hint of a long-gone pathway to join route b) as it cuts the corner where the converging fell walls join. Turn right onto the footpath.

b). If you dislike the idea of climbing the fence, continue to follow the line of the fence, keep straight on at the delapidated cross wall southward until you meet a more distinct path coming in on the left from Longsleddale. Go through the gate on the right diagonally crossing the moor corner where route a) from the summit of Hollow Moor rejoins.

Carry on to the gate in the wall. The path is now wide and heads towards a dejected ruin. At a major path junction keep straight across passing well below the ruin. The way underfoot requires attention for, like the building it serviced, it has fallen into disuse and in places has sunk into miry oblivion, but after passing through a gateway in a wall things begin to look up. A patch of forest to the right, Birk Rigg, pinpoints progress and the aspect becomes open and pleasant and we begin to return towards

Kentmere. The path descends gradually passing a little ruin to the right, then a cairn. After an area of boulders a footbridge will be seen crossing the Skeggleswater Dike. This is a red herring, keep straight on to a gate in a wall. Go through the gate on the L and cut across the field corner through a gate in the wall on the R. Proceed straight along the green track parallel to the wall. Cross a path which comes from a gate left and keep by the wall. Soon the wall begins to climb Millrigg Knot but our path swings obligingly right to contour towards the H. P. Plantation.

Note the disused lead mines on the left. Pass a ruin R and spoil heaps on the line of the vein to meet the next wall. Go through the gate and down the broad path beside the forest which gradually descends between two plantations, Philipson's wood being on the right. Keep by the side of the left hand wood passing into it for a short way. Turn L at the new plantation and through two gates where your arrival in Kentmere at the road is almost unexpected. Turn L along the valley road for 250 yards to the Ullthwaite Bridge road junction at the start.

Kentmere
The old marshy mere was drained in 1840 and its diatomite deposits mined until recently. Diatomite, minute vegetable organisms in a silica case, was used in fireproof cement and insulation material, and before that, as absorbent in explosives. During the digging, in 1955 a tenth-century wooden boat was found, now in the National Maritime Museum.

Now the re-flooded diggings form the new Kentmere, an attractive lake once more.

Kentmere Hall
Kentmere Hall, one of many pele towers in the area built in the fourteenth century as defence against Scottish raiders, was the home of Bernard Gilpin (b.1517). He became a well known reformer and later the Archbishop of Durham. Spot the original long drop loo in the pele tower.

The Quarters
These were holdings, each of which had to provide a man to serve against raiders in medieval times.

Sawmill Cottage
This was built in 1840 as a sawmill which provided timber for the construction of the Windermere railway, it is now Gordon Fox's pottery studio.

WALK 44:
Upper Kentmere and The Ullstone

The Ullstone

SUMMARY: Anyone who visits The Ullstone will be impressed by its commanding presence over its valley. The name means 'Owlstone'. Was it named by the people who lived in the Iron Age settlements just over the 'tongue'?

The rest of the walk is dominated by the steep craggy fells which encircle the old reservoir at the head of Kentmere. There is a short descent of a steep grassy trackless slope to reach the reservoir. Boots recommended.

Distance:	5³⁄₄ miles 9¹⁄₄km
Grade:	Moderate
Terrain:	Valley, low fell
Summit:	The Ullstone - 1542ft (470m)
Map:	OL7

HOW TO GET THERE AND PARKING: From Staveley village on the A591 take the minor road up the Kentmere valley. Half a mile before Kentmere village turn

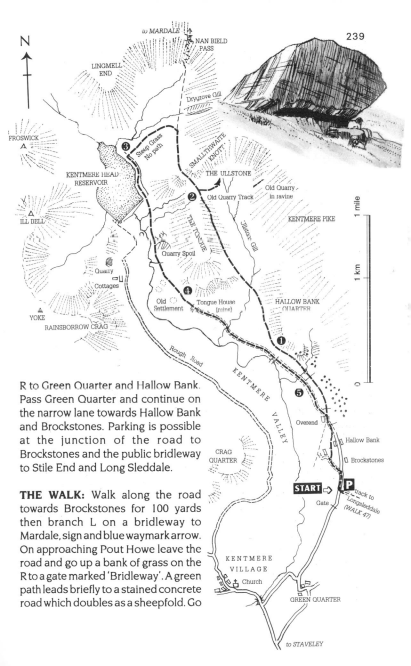

N

to MARDALE

NAN BIELD
PASS

LINGMELL
END

Drygtove Gill

FROSWICK

③

Steep Grass
No path

SMALLTHWAITE
KNOTT

THE ULLSTONE

KENTMERE HEAD
RESERVOIR

②

Old Quarry Track

Old Quarry
in ravine

ILL BELL

KENTMERE PIKE

Quarry Spoil

THE TONGUE

Jillgot Gill

Quarry

Cottages

④

Tongue House
(ruins)

Old
Settlement

HALLOW BANK
QUARTER

YOKE

RAINSBORROW CRAG

①

KENTMERE VALLEY

Rough Road

⑤

R to Green Quarter and Hallow Bank.
Pass Green Quarter and continue on
the narrow lane towards Hallow Bank
and Brockstones. Parking is possible
at the junction of the road to
Brockstones and the public bridleway
to Stile End and Long Sleddale.

Overend

Hallow Bank

CRAG
QUARTER

Brockstones

THE WALK: Walk along the road
towards Brockstones for 100 yards
then branch L on a bridleway to
Mardale, sign and blue waymark arrow.
On approaching Pout Howe leave the
road and go up a bank of grass on the
R to a gate marked 'Bridleway'. A green
path leads briefly to a stained concrete
road which doubles as a sheepfold. Go

START ➡

P Track to
Longsleddale
(WALK 47)

Gate

KENTMERE
VILLAGE

Church

GREEN QUARTER

to STAVELEY

1 mile

1 km

through its gates and along the issuing walled lane to a group of cottages (Overend). At a midget three-way signpost bend R on the bridle path to Mardale and the Nan Bield Pass.

The path, now inviting, passes through fell pasture, running high enough above the flat valley floor to give splendid views opposite, of Crag Quarter and the rugged face of Rainsborrow Crag, and reveals the weathering quarry scars. Beside the path pass a majestic sycamore which almost demands to be congratulated having withstood the harsh gales of many winters. Continue for a mile past a gate, hop over a stream until the path is hemmed in between the wall and the rocky foot of Hallow Bank Quarter. Beyond the next gate the path ahead can be seen threading its way up the hillside between Tongue Scar and the tributary valley of Ullstone Gill. Begin the climb and cross a stream, which blossoms into a gushing fall from almost under the bridleway to enter a small ferny gorge. Continue for 20 yards up onto a grass bank then ahead beside the wall again. Cross Ullstone Gill and through the waymarked gate. The climb is steeper now. Follow the cairned path up the rushy fellside to the top of a rise which is just the place to turn around for the valley view. *The glacial deposits create rich emerald water meadows which contrast with the ice-shorn U-shaped valley sides in their darker wooded shades.* Keep uphill on the cairned path ignoring a branch R. When the gradient eases a grassy recess in the great flank of the valley side reveals the Ullstone, the large boulder edged by a dark overhung shadow and to the right the deep gash of a quarry.

Keep on the cairned path which bends slightly leftwards away from the Ullstone, until an easy rightward traverse can be made across the fell, on an almost extinct path, to the Ullstone. Do not be disappointed at its insignificant appearance from the path. When you have arrived under its shadow, unseated the sovereign sheep from its throne and settled there yourself you will, weather permitting, have a royal view. Return to the path well pleased.

Continue on the path which is now narrow and makes its way round the shoulder of Smallthwaite Knott. Turn up your collar for on rounding the this shoulder you step out suddenly on to a different stage. The upper reaches of the valley bore into a circle of mountains - atmospheric and bleak - its twin arms sucking the wind round Lingmell End to beat upon the waters of the reservoir below. Contour the hillside on the narrow path passing a scree slope and some spiky rocks. The path can be traced across the open slopes to the horizon and (ball-shaped) boulder in the cup of the Nan Bield pass, but we leave it well before then.

Keep an eye on the slopes above and to the right, for there is no mistaking the curious trough of Drygrove Gill cut out of the fellside. When below this gill leave the path to turn L down grass slopes and follow the flow of the stream. The grass steepens but the descent is easy. Head for one of the many broken sections in the wall below and gain the Kentmere Head Reservoir side. From here the fine peaks of the Kentmere Horseshoe look daunting, their summits remote behind craggy buttresses. Turn L along the waterside path to reach the dam. Do not cross it but go straight over, then turn L through a gap and cross the overflow channel. Turn R down the valley on a meagre path and turn your attention to things of interest close at hand. At the foot of the dam is a simple edifice and pool where the River Kent is dismissed from captivity. Next pass Whether Fold - a circular sheepfold.

Quarries dominate the foot of Rainsborrow Crag opposite, and the Tongue Scar Quarries on our side of the river. Ignore a ford, pass straight on to a wall and high ladder stile. The mounds in the field right are sites of ancient settlements.

On reaching Tongue House - now in ruins - go through the gate and round the back of the house. The gate L opens onto the continuing path, now a track. Cross Ullstone Gill, its old clapper stone still functioning under its tomb of concrete, to a ladder stile with waymark. The pastures now give way to hay meadows and the track is relaxing. The river meandering quietly nudges the track against a bank of spring bluebells before going under a lovely old arched bridge and curving on its way. Pass on through gates and a pasture past a rusty barn and on to the cottages at Overend by the midget three-way signpost. Re-trace the outward route to Hallow Bank, remembering to bend R after passing the road/sheepfold, onto the green path toward Pout Howe to the start.

Kentmere Head Reservoir

The reservoir was built in 1845 to supply a regular flow of water for the numerous mills lower down the valley, especially the paper mill at Burneside and Cowen Head. Other mills were at Low Bridge Kentmere (corn), bobbin and wood turning mills at Staveley. The reservoir was built by Irish labourers whose revelling caused the Low Bridge Inn at Kentmere to have its licence revoked. Kentmere is one of the few Lakeland villages without a public house. Other reservoirs were planned in adjoining valleys, but money ran out and the need for water-power diminished.

Rainsborrow Crag

The huge rambling crags of Rainsborrow attracted nesting eagles when they returned to the Lake District, whilst peregrines nest in the upper reaches of the valley.

Tongue House Settlement

The ancient British village near Tongue House was discovered in 1969, similar to others in the valley, notably Millrigg. Another lies on the opposite side of the stream below the southern slopes of Rainsborrow. The remains show a large circular settlement with field enclosures, a platform where the house stood, and signs of an old track.

WALK 45: Upper Longsleddale (Wren Gill Quarries) and Kentmere Pike

The old quarry road at the head of Longsleddale

SUMMARY: The most popular walk from Sadgill is along the valley to Gatesgarth Pass then an exhilarating high but easy ridge route back to Sadgill. The paths are easy to follow and views are extensive. Our recommended route is slightly shorter and includes the dramatic scenery of Wren Gill Quarry, one of the earliest to be worked in Lakeland. Thus we get a contrast between the well walked valley and ridge, and the lonely trackless approach to the ridge from the quarries. Route finding is easy but

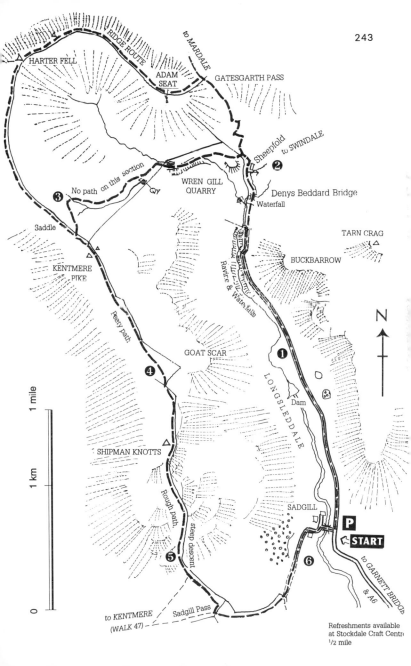

HARTER FELL

RIDGE ROUTE

to MARDALE

ADAM SEAT

GATESGARTH PASS

Sheepfold

to SWINDALE

❷

No path on this section

Qy

WREN GILL QUARRY

Denys Beddard Bridge

Waterfall

❸

Saddle

KENTMERE PIKE

TARN CRAG

BUCKBARROW

Ravire & Waterfalls

Peaty path

GOAT SCAR

❶

N

LONGSLEDDALE

Dam

1 mile

1 km

❹

SHIPMAN KNOTTS

Rough path

steep descent

SADGILL

❺

P

START

❻

to GARNETT BRIDGE & A6

to KENTMERE (WALK 47)

Sadgill Pass

Refreshments available at Stockdale Craft Centre ½ mile

Distance:	6¼ miles 10km
Grade:	Strenuous
Terrain:	Valley, high fell
Summits:	Kentmere Pike - 2394ft (730m)
	Shipman Knotts - 1925ft (587m)

Gatesgarth Pass Route

Distance:	7¾ miles 12km
Summits:	Adam Seat - 2184ft (666m)
	Harter Fell - 2551ft (778m)
Map:	OL7

unrewarding to walk it in mist. Boots recommended.

HOW TO GET THERE AND PARKING: From the A6 north of Kendal take the road to Garnett Bridge and park at Sadgill, the end of the surfaced, narrow lane up Longsleddale. It is amazing how many cars can squeeze into the limited parking on a busy day!

THE WALK: Set off up the rough valley road. *Note the terminal moraine just above Sadgill where the river has cut through glacial debris. Above is a flatter area, once a glacial lake, where the stream has been straightened. Just below the cascades, below Buckbarrow Crag there is a gravel trap which helps to keep the pastures clear. There was a workmen's camp here, built during the construction of a water pipeline in the 1930s from Haweswater. A reservoir was proposed in 1845, to regulate flow for the numerous mills lower down the valley, but the neighbouring Kentmere Head Reservoir cost so much nothing came of the plan.*

The valley was an important packhorse route connecting with Swindale and Mardale. Once a major route from Kendal to Penrith before the opening of the A6 over Shap. It was considered as a possible route for the M6. The deepset glacial valley is subject to the changing moods of the weather. The road was most recently used as an access to Wren Gill Quarries which we pass through later.

After a mile the valley sides close in and become craggy with Buckbarrow Crag - used by rock climbers - on the right and the formidable slopes of Goat Scar and Raven Crag on the left. The road steepens in zigzags, still partly paved with pitched stones. It is well worth diverting through a gate L where the infant River Sprint makes a lively descent down cascades and waterfalls which are hidden, though heard, from the road. From here too is an impressive view down the length of the valley. *When approaching the top of the steep rise a broken wall descends the western hillside. By the stream is a discarded rusting tub with wheels, the first relic of the quarrying, moving further downvalley with every flood.* Go through a gate and over the Denys Beddard bridge. At a two-way signpost Public Bridleway, follow Mardale via Gatesgarth, the other direction shows Swindale Head and Stack House. Pass quarry workings up on the left, a gate and sheepfolds. (A path can be seen climbing the hillside ahead to the Gatesgarth Pass.)

THE WREN GILL QUARRY ROUTE

About 150 yards past the sheepfolds go over a ladder stile on the L which

The waterfall in Wren Gill Quarries

gives access to the quarry workings.

OLD QUARRY WORKINGS ARE DANGEROUS, STAY STRICTLY ON THE PATH, CLOSE SUPERVISION OF CHILDREN.

Make your way up the old incline, now a grassy path. The high wall ahead carried a race pipe over the stream. At the top of the incline pass a row of ruined buildings and the remains of a mighty engine its strength spent.

The path ahead is narrow, a bit exposed, but founded on the bed rock, just take care. (You can make your way to the right by the wall but this

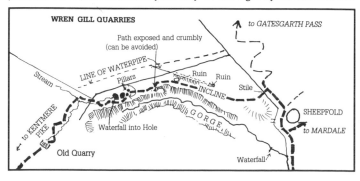

misses out the best bit.) Gain the raised path and approach two stone
pillars. **Do not pass the pillars to admire the waterfall** but go L just
before the left-hand pillar and onto the raised path. A fine waterfall drops
into the black hole on the right to vanish into an underground chasm and
appear in the main quarry which is to the left. (Look back to the pillars and
see why it was prudent not to go past! It is very impressive.) Carry on to the
streamside and find a suitable place to cross. Keep up the right side of the
stream to a stile in the wall. About 20 yards upstream cross back over and
go up the right-hand side of a tributary stream and head for the next quarry
workings above. Encounter an old track with its tiny slab bridge, which
leads to a ruined building. The access into the quarry is safe, so go under
the arch and listen to the eerie echoes in the flooded cave. **DO NOT
ENTER FURTHER, THE WATER MAY HIDE PLUNGING SHELVES**.
Back outside behind the ruin cross the stream onto its right bank. Keep an
eye on the wall to the left which is a good guideline to the ridge just short
of the summit of Kentmere Pike. Wander up the pathless turf to the valley
head bearing L (SW) near the top to meet the ridgetop fence and path at
its lowest point (small cairn and stile). * Junction with Gatesgarth Pass
route.

GATESGARTH PASS ROUTE
Continue on the pony road, now narrowed to a footpath. The next section
was badly eroded but is being repaired in the traditional style. The path
winds up the western side of the upper bowl. The views are limited, the
sweep of moor grass is broken only by the hint of a forgotten path to old
quarry rids and the silence is held in place by the trills and chirps of pippets
and skylarks. The crease in the eastern skyline marks a pass over an ice
overflow channel, the way to Swindale Head via Mosedale, a solitary spot
indeed. Our path is cairned and climbs steadily. As the gradient eases a
sliver of the High Street Range peeps up and Gatesgarth Pass (580m) is
attained.

Go through the gate in the fence and turn L through a peaty wallow to
a clean dry path rising diagonally up the fellside. *The pony path goes ahead
making a steep descent to Mardale and the head of Hawes Water. The little village of
Mardale Green and its surrounding farming community fell victim to Manchester's cry
for more water in 1937 when the valley was dammed and the water level raised.* The
outlook improves with every step. To the left is the fingerlike cairn on
Adam's Seat and to the right wonderful views down Haweswater, across
the Eden valley to the Pennines beyond.

The path is now on a broad ridge with a fence to your left. (This fence, or
lengths of wall, is a guideline over Harter Fell, Kentmere Pike and Shipman
Knotts then down to the Garburn Pass in case of sudden mist.) Keep by

*Bleawater lies in a craggy hollow below High Street.
Viewed looking north from Harter Fell*

the fence passing an area of spiky rocks in a dip which gives a dramatic birds-eye picture of Haweswater below. If you look carefully at the valley side, across the water from the wooded promontory, the line of the old corpse road from Mardale to Swindale can be seen . Stay by the fence as it turns a right angle left. The High Street ridge and Bleawater are down to the right. The first summit of Harter Fell is a strange affair. Two cairns arrayed with ironmongery. Pass an H boundary stone to the main summit with another strange cairn plus iron fence remains The unmistakeable hump of Great Gable is visible on the skyline to the west with the Scafell Range, and the Coniston mountains on its left.

Keep to the fence bending L and downhill now along the broad ridge freewheeling along towards the distant horizon, Windermere, the sea, the Pennines and not a habitation in sight. The fence is replaced by a wall and at the lowest point the route from Wren Gill Quarry joins at the stile.

*Junction of Wren Gill Quarry and Gatesgarth Pass Routes.

The way is now straightforward - just follow the path L along the crest of the ridge, keep the wall on your left. At first the breadth of the ridge obscures the view into Kentmere but soon the wall bends and an extended horizon is exposed. The fence turns away left, keep straight on the path to the summit of Kentmere Pike 730m. Continue in the same direction, descending now to a cross wall. (At a cairn a minor path leaves to the right for Kentmere.) Cross over a ladder stile in the wall and keep the same direction, cairns. Climb gently over Shipman Knotts and hold the same direction as you make the steep, rocky descent. Keep by the wall passing a few cross walls to reach an area of bog and rushes. After another steep rocky section,cairned, keep by the wall to meet the pony road at the Garburn Pass.

Go L through the gate and follow the rough road downhill to Sadgill and the start.

Wren Gill Quarries

Well named - look for wrens! The quarries produced excellent slate and was one of the earliest to be exploited. Work ceased suddenly in 1945 when the Italian prisoners of war who worked there were repatriated. The remains of the terrace of cottages and a light railway can still be seen.

Walls

The many stone walls which are a feature of the Lakeland fells were a result of the Enclosure of Commons between 1760 and 1800. They often run along the fell top, a sure navigation guide for today's walkers, with side walls dropping steeply in improbable places. Small openings, hog holes were incorporated to allow passage for sheep. 'Throughs' were large stones going through the wall to stabilise it. These are often used as makeshift stiles by walkers.

WALK 46: Longsleddale, Skeggles Water and Brunt Knott

Distance:	10 miles 16km
Grade:	Strenuous
Terrain:	Valley, low fell
Summits:	Above Skeggleswater - 1050ft (320m)
	Brunt Knott - 1400ft (427m)
	(additional 1/2 mile)
Map:	OL7

SUMMARY: The richly wooded valley of central Longsleddale makes a pleasing contrast to the lonely moorland encountered on the rest of the walk.

HOW TO GET THERE AND PARKING: Longsleddale is approached from the A6 north of Kendal, by a very narrow lane past Garnett Bridge. In early summer the colourful display of the hedgerows compensate for the slow drive up the valley. There is parking opposite St Mary's Church, Longsleddale. *Telephone and toilets.*

THE WALK: Start at the church (which is situated on a glacial moraine above the general level of the valley floor). Take the narrow road north for quarter of a mile up the valley, the tight hedgerows patriotic with campion, white stitchwort and blue speedwell. *The valley, fashioned by glaciers, is flat-floored, once occupied by a lake and now supporting rich meadows as its legacy.* As you

walk along look up at the western valley side. Clothed with rich woodland, a plantation of larch breaks the swell of foliage, and, with the exception of this short stretch of road, hides a fine skein of waterfalls from view.

Turn L at the bridle way to Low Millrigg (in the Kentmere valley). Cross the bridge over the River Sprint then follow the blue arrow way-mark R following the wallside and field to a barn. *The glaciated upper Longsleddale valley*

Looking over Docker Nook to the ancient woodland of central Longsleddale shows its U-shape to perfection and with a change of rock from Silurian slates and grits to the Borrowdale Volcanics above Sadgill, the richly-wooded slopes give way to crags and mountains of the upper valley.

Turn L and go through waymarked gates onto a rising stony track. Pass along the upper edge of Spring Wood to the corner of a larch plantation. *Only the sound of the waterfalls are heard. No sighting escapes the disciplined ranks of branches.* Go through a gate by a ruin (with hints at restoration) and continue ahead by a wall on a green track to a waymarked kissing gate and on over a rise. The arrival on the moor top is greeted by a fine view of the Kentmere Fells to the north and the heathery slopes of Sleddale Forest to the south. On each side of the path stone shooting butts stand like relics of ancient worship - memorials to wildlife gone. When the wall bends away left keep straight on and in 100 yards meet a cross track. Turn L now on a wide green path which passes a trio of isosceles-shaped rocks with a cairn on top. To the right Skeggles Water sits in its peaty hollow skewered with new drainage ditches. Does this forecast a forest? Watch this space. The bulk of Green Quarter Fell lies beyond.

The wider vehicle track rises over a 'barrow-like' mound with pools to the left and right. A footpath goes round the right-hand side between the mound and the pool. Take your choice as they run parallel to reach a gap in the broken down boundary wall. I prefer the footpath which passes another pool and is easier underfoot. Keep ahead for quarter of a mile still on a good path through the heather towards an horizon formed by the

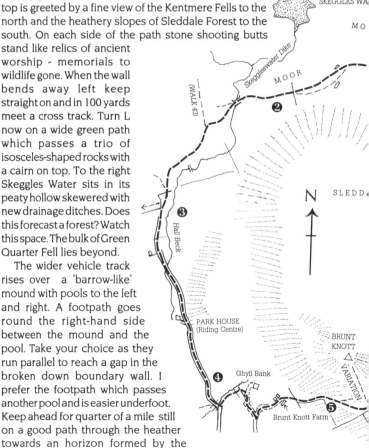

Coniston Fells. At waymarked posts cross a sleeper bridge over the Skeggleswater Dike and follow retrospective waymarks forking left downstream to a gate in a wall. Keep ahead for 100 yards to cross a boggy spring in a 'causeway' of stones, then fork L. Descend to join a main path by a cairn and a small ruin. Bend L. Ignore the bridge over Hall Beck and keep through the cutting. The path now commands an absorbing scene over the pleasant little Park valley with the beck tumbling in cascades alongside. Just the spot to take a break before the next brush with civilisation. Go through a gate and keep on the track beside the wall through pastures and gates to a walled lane. There is now a three-quarter mile road walk, but the valley is pleasant and something interesting is sure to catch your eye: a tiny barn with a sycamore umbrella; Park House, a riding school; prolific hedgerows contrasting the stiff bistort with the outspread wild geranium; and a hog hole of which any wall builder could be proud.

Ignore a stile right (public footpath to Elfhowe) and after crossing a stream, turn L at once, over a stile, public footpath to Ghyll Bank, with

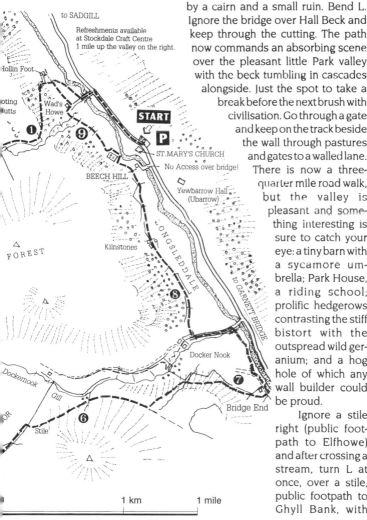

yellow waymarkers. Follow the stream uphill to a stile in a fence. Continue up the stream bank to a gap in the wall. Go over a stile in the fence right to the surfaced track by Ghyll Bank. Turn R 25 yards to a gate and the continuing track leads to a road. Turn L to Brunt Knott Farm. The uphill climb continues. At the farm go between the farmhouse and the barn through gates onto a track which winds diagonally right up the hillside. As you gain height the view right of the lower Kent valley extends to encompass a hint of the Kent Estuary and Arnside Knott beyond. Go over a ladder stile in the intake wall and on the track clearly ahead. Ignore two vehicle tracks branching left and carry on to meet a wallside. Follow the wall to the crest of the hill. (If you wish to visit the summit of Brunt Knott turn L here and go up the hill for a quarter of a mile.)

Still using the wall as a guideline pass a pond and bear L to cross a stile in a fence and continue close to the wallside through wet patches to a high ladder stile over the wall on the right. The path is faint but leads straight on along a slight crest before dropping towards the stream. The track now traverses the hillside and is heading down Longsleddale. Make sure you turn L along a smooth green path through the bracken to descend a steep spur towards the intake wall. Just before a wall corner cross a tiny stream and the path continues to traverse above the wall, descending into a rough lane. Through a gate cross the field L to join the farm lane at Bridge End.

Turn L in front of the cottage and in a few yards take a riverside path on the R. This crosses the meadows, veering away from the stream to join the Docker Nook farm lane. L along this and through a gate before you reach the farm turn R along the fence towards a wall end and take the right-hand gateway. Keep straight on to

Across Longsleddale Whiteside Pike is a landmark

a gate giving access to a path along the base of the Dockernook Wood and Kilnstones Wood. When Kilnstones is in sight, go through the facing gate into the field and along to the front of the farmhouse. Two interesting carved stones are set into the wall. Keep ahead through a gate between the barns, over a clapper bridge and on across the field keeping by the wall. When the wall bends away left keep straight on across to a gate with blue arrow waymarks. Pass the next house, follow waymarks turning R down the bank then L by the wall to a gate. Cross three fields then turn R into the access lane to Wads House. There is no right of way down the 50 yards to the River Sprint bridge. The public footpath turns through the gate on the L to cross the field to the barn. Turn R and return on the outward route to the bridge. Cross the bridge, turn R and on the road for quarter of a mile to the start.

Longsleddale Woods
Remnants of the primeval mixed oak forest which once covered large parts of the Lake District, still dot the valley sides in the central part of the valley. On the west side are oak woodlands, on the east a mix of oak and ash.

Ubarrow Hall
The hall has a gabled pele tower, currently being renovated, attached to a seventeenth-century house.

Kilnstones
This was a sixteenth-century farm, once used as a hostel for packmen. Earlier there was a thirteenth-century corn mill here. Note the carved stones in the wall by the path.

Sleddale Forest
The forest is a relic of the medieval hunting grounds, belonging to the Barony of Kendal.

Docker Nook Gill
This was the site of a fourteenth-century fulling mill where Fuller's Earth, a type of clay, was used to clean and thicken cloth.

The Drove Road Complete - Sadgill to Ambleside

The start of the The Drove Road at Sadgill

SUMMARY: Centuries ago this was a road used by wheeled carriages and before that a drove route - note the 'byeway' sign at Sadgill. Now it is popular with walkers, but wheels are once again making an impression, for the Garburn Pass at least is one of the favourite crossings of mountain bikers and trail riders.

To walk a linear route is most satisfying and if you can arrange to be dropped off at Sadgill and met at Ambleside it makes a fine day's walk across two low passes and around the shoulder of Wansfell.

Distance:	9¼ miles 15km
Grade:	Strenuous
Terrain:	Valley, low fell

Alternatively you can do the walk in parts by taking the suggested alternative returns described as the next three walks. The circuits each visit lonely moorland, a nice contrast to the outgoing drove road, and the expansive view from Sour Howes is especially recommended.

WALK 47: The Drove Road Section 1: LONGSLEDDALE TO KENTMERE

HOW TO GET THERE AND PARKING: At Sadgill, Longsleddale. Approach from the A6 north of Kendal. Limited parking at the end of the surfaced road.

THE WALK: The Sadgill Pass drove road begins by crossing the River Sprint. The old stone bridge built in 1717 and since widened stands beside the ford and wrens flit about the walls which line the road to the little community. It is a picturesque starting point.

Cross the bridge and turn L to pass behind the cottages to a gate, signed Byeway to Kentmere. Notice the 'wee house' on the right at a discreet distance from the dwellings. The way begins to climb immediately and a little progress is rewarded by a lovely view of the shapely ice-carved valley. Go through a gate leaving the enclosed lane for the open pasture and straight on through the next gate.

Note If you return to Sadgill, Route **B**, the track to the L is where you rejoin the outward route at this point.

Keep on the road as it winds up a shallow valley and eases into the pass between Shipman Knotts and Cocklaw Fell. Pass the cairn and through gate (where the intake wall angles away right with the path up Shipman Knotts and Kentmere Pike). A stile on the left indicates a footpath leading direct to Green Quarter and Kentmere, but we continue through the gate along the drove road to leave the moor at Stile End. From here is an excellent panorama of the upper Kentmere valley lying in its horseshoe of mountains. Continue down the road to a gate beside a stand of trees and into High Lane. Turn L along the surfaced and gated lane for 100 yards. After the first gate look for a public footpath sign on the R. Climb a high stone-stepped stile over the wall and follow a smooth green path through the field leading down to a gateway. Cross Low Lane to go through a gate opposite and down the path into the rapidly narrowing valley and the River Kent. Cross by the wooden

Distance:	6¼ miles 10km
Grade:	Moderate
Terrain:	Valley, low fell
Summit:	Sadgill Pass - 1148ft (350m)
Map:	OL7

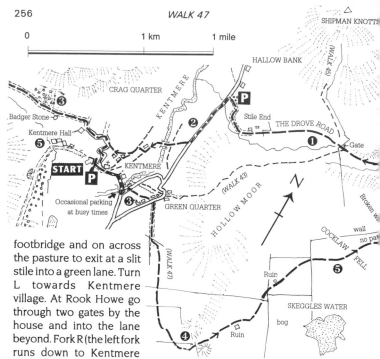

footbridge and on across
the pasture to exit at a slit
stile into a green lane. Turn
L towards Kentmere
village. At Rook Howe go
through two gates by the
house and into the lane
beyond. Fork R (the left fork
runs down to Kentmere
church) and through a gate into a wall-enclosed track. The elevated
position allows a direct view down the valley, its flat bed of watermeadows
enclosing Kentmere Tarn and its sides rising in unison to the moors above.
At a huge four-trunked sycamore fork R and along to the trackway beyond.
The walls overshadow as the path becomes narrower, then pass through
an iron gate to pass picturesque Heads Cottage, in beautiful surroundings,
and on its access track to the road.

A. TO CONTINUE TO THE GARBURN PASS:
Turn R (Continue on Walk 48)

B. TO RETURN TO SADGILL: Turn L.

B. Walk down the road which makes an S-bend round the village hall
(*telephone & parking*) and the church and down to the next section of the
village. At the road junction turn L just over the bridge to Green Quarter
(*Sign to Maggs Howe - teas, up the hill in Green Quarter hamlet*).

Look carefully on the right for a signpost public footpath which may be partly obscured by bushes as also may be its stile in the wall. Go up the steeply rising field to a gate to Low Fold and over a signed low wall to the road. (*If you want refreshments continue along the road to the hamlet and the tea shop is the highest house on the right.*) Turn L, then after 30 yards turn R on the bridleway signed Longsleddale via Cocklaw Fell. The track makes its way gently up the hillside passing two gates to a fork. Keep L where there is a small footpath sign, and begin to climb more steeply. *From here there is a fine retrospective view of the Garburn Pass track shining white as it snakes its way over to Troutbeck. The pele tower of Kentmere Hall is prominent.*

Pass through a sheepfold then carry on. As height is gained more gently now, the views expand. After a gate the path levels and by degrees turns away from the Kentmere valley to reach an iron gate in a crosswall. Carry on along the rutted track to another gateway (Evergreen plantation away to the right.) Follow the track over the brow you are looking down onto the flat desolate hollow of Skeggles Water.

If you want to bag a summit, the hill to the left, Rasp Howe is really the end of the ridge descending from the dome of Hollow Moor 426m to the NW.

Our track does not go to the ruin but circles the hillside above it. (A track

The head of Kentmere from Stile End

off to the right, used by Walk No.43, leads to Park House, lower Kentmere and Staveley.) Keep straight on and look out for a prominent rock. Just beyond it turn L on a path to a gateway in a wall. The bridle path underfoot has gradually diminished but the line can be determined with a bit of walkers' eye and faith. Go ahead on the green path between the stiff grassy bristles and bog to a gate. Now on over the shoulder of Cocklaw Fell, passing another little ruin on the way, taking a rising diagonal line through bog to the wall corner and a stile beside a gate. Continue on a narrow path over the moor. Shining Skeggles Water is left behind and the new plantation beyond, on the southern horizon of Sleddale forest, waits for time to fulfill its name. As Longsleddale comes into view the path becomes faint amongst the rushes and thistles, both avoidable, but runs parallel to a wall/fence on the left for a short distance, then turns right down the hillside to a gate. If you reach the shaly remains of a broken down cross wall you have missed the path as we did. Just turn R down the line of the wall to the gate to rejoin the bridle path.

Go through the gate and carry on with a wall on the right until the way steepens and a small quarry hole is on the right. Here the path bends left and its line is clear. *From here is a lovely view of Sadgill and the upper valley of Longsleddale softened by a foreground of mature trees.* Walk on, descending gently, to an iron gate in a crosswall. Continue traversing, ignoring a gate R, to ford a gill, ignore the ladder stile, and join the outward drove road. Turn L and retrace the outward route to the start.

Picturesque Heads Cottage at Kentmere

The Drove Road

The road follows a line of weakness over the Sadgill and Garburn Passes, created by a soft thin band of Coniston Limestone which separates the older volcanic rocks to the north from the Silurian rocks to the south. Both cols were formed where the weakness was attacked by ice erosion.

Packhorses were used until the end of the eighteenth century.

WALK 48: The Drove Road Section 2: KENTMERE TO TROUTBECK

View back to Kentmere from the way up the Garburn Pass

SUMMARY: The Garburn Pass is a popular crossing for walkers and bikers, although it is deeply rutted on the Troutbeck side. If you prefer grass beneath your feet then the diversion over the extensive viewpoint of Sour Howes will please, and this is included in the circuit.

HOW TO GET THERE AND PARKING: Kentmere village is approached from the A591 at Staveley.

Distance:	6¼ miles 10km
Grade:	Moderate
Terrain:	Valley, low fell
Summits:	Garburn Pass - 1476ft (450m)
	Sour Howes - 1584ft (483m)
Map:	OL7

THE WALK: START 1 - AT KENTMERE VILLAGE Park by the church and village hall. Walk up the road towards Crag Quarter and the Garburn Pass. After a few minutes the access

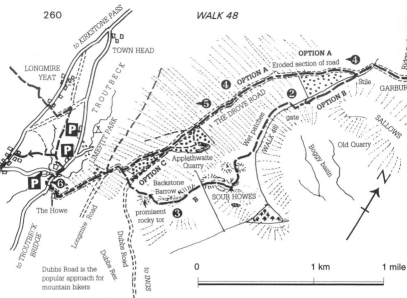

to KIRKSTONE PASS

TOWN HEAD

LONGMIRE YEAT

TROUTBECK

OPTION A
Eroded section of road ❹

OPTION A
❹

❺ THE DROVE ROAD ❷ **OPTION B**

Stile

GARBURN

Ridge

SALLOWS

LIMEFITT PARK

P

P

P ❻

The Howe

to TROUTBECK BRIDGE

Applethwaite Quarry

Backstone Barrow

SOUR HOWES

prominent rocky tor ❸

Wet patches

(WALK 48)

gate

Boggy basin

Old Quarry

N

B

OPTION C

Longmire Road

Dubbs Road

Dubbs Res.

to INGS

Dubbs Road is the popular approach for mountain bikers

0   1 km   1 mile

track to Heads Cottage comes in from the right. This is the junction with the drove road from Longsleddale and the Sadgill Pass (Walk 47).

A. THE DROVE ROAD - Turn R up the road. Three ways now turn off to the right. Pass the first which is signed to Hartrigg Farm. Pass the second which is the footpath to upper Kentmere. Opposite The Nook (*mugs of tea*), take the third way to the right signed 'To Troutbeck and Garburn Pass'. Mount the stony way which now looks more like an old drove road until the gradient levels and it makes a traverse below Goat House Scar, passing the Badger Stone, a landmark in a field to the left. Although walls enclose the road make a point of looking over for from here the pele tower at Kentmere Hall is well seen. The next gate gives access to the open fell. Continue along the slopes of Crabtree Brow, a wilderness of bracken interspersed with patches of reeds and rushes, and into a flat basin. Cross the stream. After this brief respite the road climbs once more. When the gradient eases look back across the Kentmere valley to Green Quarter, amazingly green, tucked under Hollow Moor, to Sadgill Pass. Go through a gate and straight on. (A path to the right is the ridge-top path leading round the Kentmere horseshoe.) Our road bends left and a new prospect shows the Troutbeck valley and the snaking road to the Kirkstone Pass. Pass through a gap in wall ends and in a few yards a right bend is reached.*

A. The Drove Road continued Keep on the drove road towards

Troutbeck. Only recommended if you are walking the whole way to Ambleside and may be short on time. Remember to keep R at the fork just past Applethwaite Quarry. The diversion described below joins soon afterwards.

B. DIVERSION VIA SOUR HOWES.* NB. Inadvisable in mist.

This is our recommended route whether you are walking the length of the Drove road or returning to Kentmere.

At the bend is a new plantation. Go over a stile in the left-hand wall. Turn R and follow the wallside trod. The plantation contains a variety of trees, some struggling to survive in this inclement spot. Still by the wall progress round the shoulder of Sallows until without warning you come over a rise to gaze across the boggy basin of Kentmere Park and ahead, the ridge of Sour Howes. (If you want to bag an extra summit Sallows 516m is a couple of minutes away on the left.) Cross a stile in a fenced gap in the wall on the R. Keep on in the same direction with the wall now on the left along the almost level ridge around the head of the combe. At the lowest point the narrow path forks. Go on the R fork which gradually angles away from the wall and along the

The summit of Sour Howes is amongst glaciated knolls

grassy crest to the hummocky tops of Sour Howes. The first knoll, to the right of the narrow path, with a little cairn offers a 270° view to the north, whilst 100 yards further on the main summit 483m takes in the southern aspect. The vistas are superb.

Do not go towards Windermere, its silvery length so splendidly visible, but descend 20ft to gain a narrow level on the R, (SW). An identifying feature is a tiny pool in the level - not the larger pool below the summit cone. A path winds through and over hummocky knolls to a wall with a stile set in a wooden fence. Go over and on to what appears to be the ridge end, but is not. It is a good point to assess the onward route before admiring again the view over southern Lakeland to the sea. If you are not returning to Kentmere, note also the church tower down to the west in the Troutbeck valley, our destination. A slight path descends the ridge, Backstone Barrow, in a series of undulations. In parts the upended strata of the rock has weathered into naturally cleaved slates. The path passes to the left of slabs to join another track which heads L towards Dubbs Reservoir. Follow it through bracken for 100 yards then branch R past a knoll to a prow, the true ridge end, with its crown of triangular rocks. Descend on the R of this to a stile onto Dubbs Road.

C. RETURN TO KENTMERE VILLAGE

Turn R along Dubbs Road above a plantation and soon join the Garburn Road. You could return completely by the road but just before a gate a stile on the R leads into the abandoned Applethwaite Quarries, now an attractive larch plantation with rowans fringing the quarry hollows. Trail bikers' tracks in unbelievable places hint at its present use. Regain the road near the end of the plantation.

The climb to the top of the pass allows time to admire the head of Troutbeck. You can see the present Kirkstone road slanting across the hillside, but try to pick out the line of the older road in the woods below. Join the outward route near the top of the pass and retrace your steps to Kentmere.

B. Continued

After descending Backstone Barrow to the Dubbs Road, go over another stile across a field to the left of the plantation to join the Garburn Road.

A Continued

Continue down the road passing a track which bends back sharp right to the campsite. At the next Y-junction keep R. (The left fork is the Longmire road.) Go down more steeply now between moss and fern-decked walls to The Howe which sports an unusual clock and fine weather vane. A gate leads onto the last steep and shaly section of the road to reach the A592 at Troutbeck. Turn R, cross a footbridge over the Trout Beck and pass the church.

WALK 49: The Drove Road Section 3: TROUTBECK TO AMBLESIDE (Wansfell)

SUMMARY: The final leg of the Drove Road curves gently round the end of Wansfell on a track which may be the line of the Roman Road from High Street to Galava Fort, past the renowned viewpoint of Jenkin Crag to reach

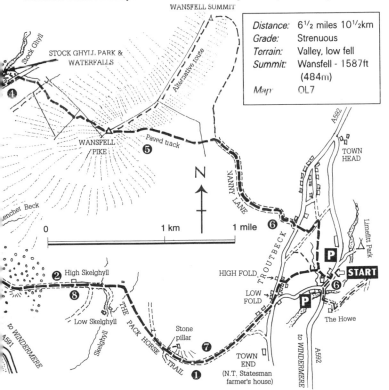

Distance:	6½ miles 10½km
Grade:	Strenuous
Terrain:	Valley, low fell
Summit:	Wansfell - 1587ft (484m)
Map:	OL7

Ambleside. The circuit visits Stock Ghyll waterfalls then makes a strenuous climb up the steep slopes of Wansfell Pike, another worthy viewpoint.

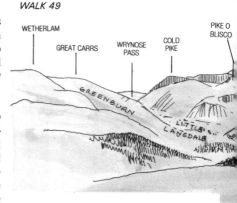

HOW TO GET THERE AND PARKING: Start near Troutbeck church on the A592 Kirkstone Pass road. Limited roadside parking north of the church and also on the same verge beyond the entrance to Limefitt Park. Another parking area lies close to the stream - turn off the main road by the bridge.

By the church is an old drinking trough dated V1887R restored by the Friends of the Lake District in 1989. It has no tap. The one opposite (1898) has a tap but it is not working.

THE WALK: Start along the bridleway between the church and the trough, ignore the path branching right, which is the return route, and cross the stream. Go through a gate and straight on up a stony path under vaults of edging hazel with the red berries of 'parson-in-the-pulpit' (*wild arum*) along the verges. The hazels thin and the remains of a slate fence allow a peep down the valley before arriving at Low Fold and the road. Turn L past seventeenth-century cottages to a triangular road junction with a gossip seat under a shady tree, a telephone and post office (*selling cups of tea/coffee, ice-cream etc.*).

Turn R at the post office into Robin Lane, a bridleway signed to Ambleside. It is a pleasant sheltered track with occasional views through gates in the high side walls, yet it is not worth stopping to look yet, as there is a seat a bit further on with a lovely view south along Windermere. (A pillar up on the right can be reached by going over a stile in the side wall. It is a good viewpoint on the end of a ridge.)

Keep on over the brow to the highest point of the drove road (250m). The track levels and to the north the expanse of Wansfell and Wansfell Pike dominates the horizon. At a branch take the L fork to Skelghyll, Jenkin Crag and Ambleside (the track right is the 'Hundreds road' to the higher fells).

Our way now begins to descend gently and, as you move along, acts as a viewing platform to the west - note Blelham Tarn (gouged by an ice overflow from the main Windermere glacier) and Wray Castle (see p.174).

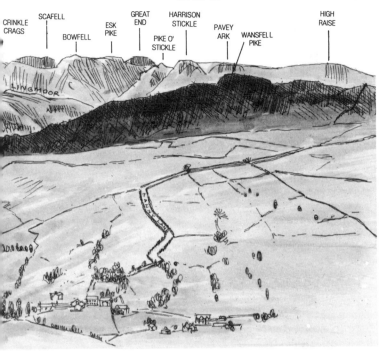

CRINKLE CRAGS · SCAFELL · BOWFELL · ESK PIKE · GREAT END · PIKE O' STICKLE · HARRISON STICKLE · PAVEY ARK · WANSFELL PIKE · HIGH RAISE

LINGMOOR

*Wansfell makes an attractive foreground to the central fells,
seen from Sour Howes*

Keep on through a gate, the old road now more of a green path, to a ford and slab bridge over a pretty cascading gill. Pass a ruin and descend more steeply to Skelghyll. At the surfaced lane turn R over the bridge and wind up to Skelghyll Farm. Arrows direct the way straight through the farmyard with gates and out onto the level track beyond. We have now reached National Trust Skelghyll Woods, an area of mixed woodland containing the well known viewpoint of Jenkin Crag, one of Thomas West's viewing stations described in his first guide to the Lakes, 1799. A paved path to the L leads to the crag, from which the view over Windermere shows not only the landscape, but a mobile skyscape mirrored in the water.

Keep along the track, ignoring a stony shortcut, which descends in easy curves crossing Stencher Beck. At a backward left fork keep ahead past Skelgarth and Broad Jugs. The track surface gradually becomes more civilised and descends into Ambleside. (*Refreshments etc.*)

There is a convenient car park opposite Hayes Garden World, if you have arranged to be picked up here, if doing the linear walk from Sadgill.

TO RETURN TO TROUTBECK : At the road turn R (Mountain Rescue Post). At the next junction go ahead along Lower Gale Road to its end. Descend the first flight of steps to the L and on down the snicket to meet the road near the town centre.Turn R, signed Stockghyll and Wansfell Pike, and Waterfalls ½. [If you divert to the main street for refreshments leave between the bank and the market hall, where there is a sign on the bend - Waterfalls ½ (to the left)]. The lane climbs steadily, it has no footpath, however, the local traffic is minimal, and it overlooks the attractive ghyll with its re-designated water mills.

When opposite the mill weir fork L into the woodland walk, where you can stroll under the beech boughs and enjoy the falls. Choose your own way - there are many paths, seats and picnic tables. All the time you will be acquiring height as an easy bonus. (At a DANGER notice a walkway branches L for a better view of the main fall.) Keep up the stepped path. The fall thunders yet from here it is barely visible in its cloak of foliage. Turn R just after a picnic table, on a major path to a formidable turnstile with access to the lane once more.

Turn L (sign Kirkstone 3½) for 200 yards then look right for an iron ladder and stile signed Troutbeck. This is the prominent path to Wansfell Pike summit and straight on down the other side to Nanny Lane. It is very easy to follow - even in mist, but here are a few landmarks to define progress for extra confidence. Follow the streamside path up to a ladder stile over a wall. Straight up through the scattered woodland until the stream becomes a trickle. Go through broken ends of an old cross wall and bend L to a great cairn - the halfway stage. Keep on up the eroded path through a gap in a wall, which has supplied stones for two cairns, and up to the summit wall and ladder stile. The waysign is carved into the top rung 'Nanny Lane and Troutbeck.' Go over the stile to the summit cairn of Wansfell Pike, a mere gesture away. Go straight on down the newly repaired path for quarter of a mile across the moor, negotiating two awkward iron gates on the way, to Nanny Lane. Turn R along the green walled lane for half a mile to meet the road at Lanefoot Farmhouse and we are back in Troutbeck. Turn L for a few yards (continue along the road if you need refreshment at the Mortal Man Inn), then turn R down a public bridleway. Cross the stream and next turn R at the cross junction towards the church along a green track. A gate gives egress from the track to continue along a narrow path which crosses the fields. It is tightly fenced, but at least it is safe from bulls. Go through two kissing gates and the church is in sight. Pass a section where the path has just about been saved from erosion and go to the stile. This leads back onto the outward bridleway. Turn L to the church and the start.

Jesus Church, Troutbeck.
A stone above the tower doorway is dated 1736. Fine stained glass windows.

Statesmen's Farms
A typical Lakeland scene includes a sixteenth/seventeenth-century white rough cast, long farmhouse with a stone or slate roof and often with cylindrical chimneys. The house was whitewashed, the adjoining barn left in stone. Sometimes the house had a spinning galley. There are many fine examples in Troutbeck village, the most important being Town End, now owned by the National Trust and open to the public.

Troutbeck
Troutbeck is a typical Lakeland seventeenth-century village, a string of hamlets based on a line of wells. The Mortal Man Inn was named after a comic verse on the original inn sign.

> 'Oh Mortal man that lives by bread,
> What is it makes thy nose so red?
> Thou silly fool that lookst so pale,
> Tis drinking Sally Birkett's ale.'

Town End dates from 1626 and is well worth a visit. There is a fine bank barn opposite - where cattle feed at ground level, the hay being taken in at the higher floor level.

Stock Ghyll Falls
A slender but attractive 70-foot fall in a verdant ravine. Water from Stock Ghyll powered five mills in Ambleside. Local industries were wool carding and fulling, linen, bobbin making, paper, saw and corn mills.

Cottages on Robin Lane, Troutbeck

WALK 50: The River Kent and Tarns of Potter Fell

Bowston Weir on the River Kent

SUMMARY: A walk for late summer when the heather is in bloom around Gurnal Dubs, or after rain when the river is in spate. The riverside path along the Kent is most attractive, especially the stretch 'The Dales Way' misses out by the little ravine at Cowen Head. The paper making industry is very evident on this walk, for the factory of James Cropper plc dominates Burneside whilst Bowston and Cowen Head both had mills until relatively recently. The upland tarns visited on the walk still supply water to Cropper's mill, which is now renowned for its high quality speciality papers.

Distance:	8¼ miles 13km
Grade:	Moderate
Terrain:	Valley and low fell
Summit:	Above Gurnal Dubs - 984ft (300m)
Map:	OL7

The return route is the most interesting of several possible alternatives and incorporates the attractive little ravine of Emanuel's Ghyll, formed by the action of fast-flowing ice melt water. Smooth, rounded drumlin hills which edge the base

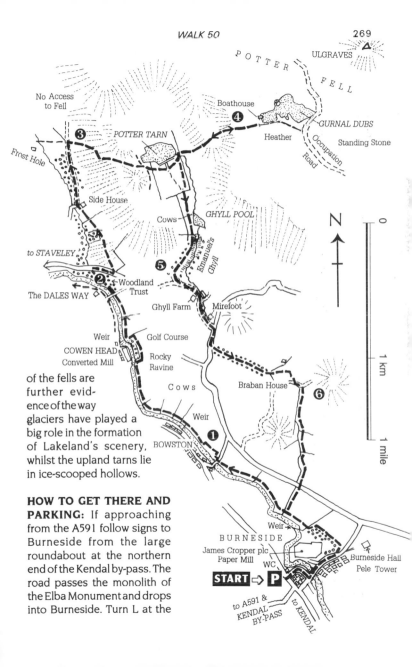

ULGRAVES

POTTER FELL

No Access
to Fell

Boathouse

4

GURNAL DUBS

3 POTTER TARN

Heather

Standing Stone

Frost Hole

Occupation
Road

Side House

Cows

GHYLL POOL

N

0

to STAVELEY

5

Emmitt's Ghyll

2 Woodland
Trust

The DALES WAY

Ghyll Farm

Mirefoot

Weir

Golf Course

COWEN HEAD
Converted Mill

Rocky
Ravine

1 km

Braban House

6

of the fells are
further evid-
ence of the way
glaciers have played a
big role in the formation
of Lakeland's scenery,
whilst the upland tarns lie
in ice-scooped hollows.

C o w s

Weir

1

BOWSTON

1 mile

**HOW TO GET THERE AND
PARKING:** If approaching
from the A591 follow signs to
Burneside from the large
roundabout at the northern
end of the Kendal by-pass. The
road passes the monolith of
the Elba Monument and drops
into Burneside. Turn L at the

Weir

BURNESIDE

James Cropper plc
Paper Mill

START ⇨ **P**

WC

Burneside Hall
Pele Tower

to A591 &
KENDAL
BY-PASS

to KENDAL

crossroads in the centre of the village and park by the WC on the L. The large private car park belongs to James Cropper plc. and may be used by walkers.

THE WALK: The walk begins with a 'tour' of the paper factory. Cross the road and take the lane which follows the riverside to join New Street. Turn L and after a few houses, the name changes to Hall Road. Pass three factory gates (which indicates the dominant role of the industry to the village). At the edge of the village the Dales Way crosses the road on its way from Ilkley in Wharfedale to Bowness. On the right is Burneside Hall with its pele tower, now in ruins, but imposing nevertheless. Turn L on the Dales Way to Bowston. The path runs close along the side of the factory, then L through a kissing gate into a hedged path along its back. Turn R over a stile which brings you onto the bank of the River Kent. Ahead over a rural patchwork of fields rises Brunt Knott and the moorland of Potter Fell. Keep on the pleasant riverside path to a stream and iron ladder stile then straight across the next field to rejoin the meandering river. Cross a stream and continue to a flight of steps leading onto the road at Bowston Bridge. The Dales Way goes left through Bowston, we turn R for 25 yards then L over an iron plate bridge where the track is barred by a lethal-looking gate. Keep the same direction by popping over a stile in the right-hand hedge and continue to meet the thundering river. *An ugly concrete weir with two opposing fish ladders has succeeded in transforming the black placid water into a myriad of sparkling triangles intricately woven into an eye-catching display.* Continue and climb a stile over the next wall with care. Alder, willow and marsh marigolds border the river. Pass three fields and stiles to reach Cowen Head. *A huge tree stump makes a good seat from which to view the river gorge, the restored mill, the leat water returned to the river via a pretty watergarden and waterfall and the single arch bridge, all now part of the Cowen Head Mill residential complex.* Yellow waymarks guide through the golf course, along the wallside and over a rise to a five-barred gate into the next field. Keep on along the river bank. Go quietly; you may see a kingfisher as we did, and other water fowl.

Go through a kissing gate and straight across the track at Hagg House Farm bridge. Here we enter a stretch of woodland by courtesy of The Woodland Trust. The trees provide a welcome contrast but all too soon the road is reached and the riverside left behind. Turn R for 200 yards then L

Gurnal Dubs backed by Potter Fell and Ulgraves

at a finger post to Frost Hole. Go diagonally L (as indicated by the finger post) across the field and pass L of a lone hawthorn to the wall enclosing a beech wood. Keep along the top corner of the wood to a five-barred gate. Straight on now to Side House which is seen ahead. Pass the house on its left and go ahead up the track beside a waterfall. At the next gate the track becomes walled and rises gently, so we leave the valley behind. Keep on until two notices appear. One denies access ahead. The second points the direction of Potter Tarn right.

The levels marked on the O.S.map were lead mines.

Go R up the green path (opposite the hogghole, 10 yards before the notice) which leads up the fell and bears R to a gap in the right-hand wall. Keep on the path which leads through the cross wall on the L. Continue ahead at first then bend to the R aiming for the low point in the ridge. *Turn to look at the view as you climb. The line of the River Kent, although secreted in the folds of its valley, can by traced from its source to the sea, and the white limestone ridges of Whitbarrow and Cunswick wear a green disguise.*

Arrive suddenly at Potter Tarn which, though occupying a bleak weather-beaten spot, looks drought-stricken, since its retaining dam became weakened and necessitated the lowering of the water level. The ugly scars on its banks are healing gradually as it settles into its new format. Continue along the south side of the tarn to a stile where you turn L and walk below the dam, crossing the outlet, a mere trickle as the water is still used by the paper mill at Burneside. Continue along the dam to a stile over the wall by the redundant overflow**.

Note: The return route is from this point.

To continue cross the bed of the dry overflow and jump the merrily flowing Emanuel's Ghyll. A pleasant green path leads up the bracken slope to a high wall with a ladder stile. Over the other side lies Gurnal Dubs, a picturesque tarn lying in a hollow surrounded by green rock-capped knolls. A tree-decked island and heather-clad shores with a handsome stone boathouse completes the picture. Go down to the dam and outlet then walk along the continuing footpath from which you can enjoy the tarn.

Note: The track round the tarn is not a right of way.

Before damming enlarged the tarn there were two small 'dubs'. A tiny island is protected from sheep by a boggy moat allowing trees to flourish there.

Return to the high wall with the ladder stile. From here is an extensive view of the Lakeland fells from Black Combe in the west to the Coniston Fells, Crinkle Crags, with the Scafells behind, and the Langdale Pikes.

Return to the stile** by the Potter Tarn overflow. Turn L over the stile beside the wall and follow the green path down the pasture. Cross the meagre trickle from the tarn and go over a stile by a gate. As you walk on to the next wall gap the valley to the left deepens. *This was an ice overflow channel in glacial times into which Emanuel's Ghyll now cuts its own groove.* Pass Ghyll Pool where the waters from the two tarns collect to enter the high pressure main which supplies the mill. After the next gate the path becomes a track and takes an S-bend to run beside the Ghyll. The cascades in their tree-lined defile will encourage you to linger. Go on to a stile by an iron gate. The track is now high above the stream and on leaving the sidewall the site of Cowen Head Mill is seen down by the River Kent. Pass a guarded building with clover leaf bosses. This is on the aqueduct from Thirlmere to Manchester. At Ghyll Farm the track becomes partly surfaced. Keep straight on to cross the Ghyll and pass Mirefoot to the road.

Turn R for 200 yards then L into the bridleway, Carlbank Lane, hardly a lane but a hedged and walled green pathway which leads almost straight to a gate near Braban House. Cross the grass to a track, turn L and go through a gate and almost immediately turn into the gravelled drive to pass L in front of the house. Continue past buildings and a cottage to a T-junction. Turn L along a lane for 50 yards to a bend. Go through the gate ahead (ruin to left), and take the green pathway which branches R around the hillside. Continue ahead when the path disappears, to a gate in the wall under power lines. Keep in line across the next field where a tiny stream hosts golden marsh marigolds on your right. Keep ahead to a stile in the field corner then on still by the gold-lined stream to its ignominious end in a muddy sump where you go over a stile onto the road. Cross the road to a stile opposite. Go straight by the wallside to join the outward route at the River Kent weir(see map). [1] Turn L and retrace your way to the start.

[1] **Note** In the future a footbridge over the river may be erected at this point allowing a shorter return to the start.

WALK 51: Low Borrowdale and the Lune

Low Borrowdale

SUMMARY: This walk links the deep valleys of Borrowdale and the Lune by an old track over a grassy fell. There is river scenery and woodland, whilst the moorland crossing gives a breath of fresh air and distant views. The Lune Valley is an important highway - the Romans came this way and now the narrow valley buzzes to the sound of motorway traffic, and the occasional train.

HOW TO GET THERE AND PARKING: Leave the M6 at Junction 38 Tebay. Take the A685 Kendal road, through Tebay and shortly after it crosses the motorway you reach the end of Borrowdale. Turn R into the dale to a parking area.

THE WALK: A bridleway signed to High and Low Borrowdale Farms leads up the valley westward. At first the narrow valley is clothed in woodland,

Distance:	7 1/2 miles 12km
Grade:	Moderate
Terrain:	Valley, low fell
Summit:	Belt Howe - 1338ft (408m)
Maps:	OL7, PF617 or
	Landranger 91 1:50,000

mainly alder, near the valley bottom but planted to fuel the Whinfell Beacon. Progress is swift along the surfaced lane. The glacial V-shaped upper valley gradually opens with a pleasant aspect of the surrounding fells of Whinfell on the left and

View over Jeffrey's Mount to the Howgill Fells from the ridge of Belt Howe, with the M6 in the Lune Gorge

Casterfell Hill (Castle Fell) on the right. *Close at hand the walls contain granite erratics, carried by ice, and dropped and used locally alongside the native Silurian slates and shales - and look out for gritstones too.*

Cross the Borrow Beck bridge and continue up the valley. A bend in the valley reveals Belt Howe 408m with our intended path rising across its slopes. Continue past two cattle-grids (there may be cows and a bull grazing here), to Low Borrowdale Farm. Go through the farmyard and turn sharp R on a path rising behind the house. In 25 yards bend L through a gate to go up the hill track, to another gate giving access onto the open fell. Proceed along the rising traverse line we saw far below. The farmer uses large wide-wheeled motor bikes for his work so you must keep alert to stay on the true old path. The path makes a zigzag then heads for the gap between Roundthwaite Common and Belt Howe. Keep R at a junction and where the double track ends keep ahead towards the gap. (From here a diversion can be made to the domed summit of Belt Howe 408m. This is not a right of way but the narrow path leading to the summit suggests that you will be allowed there to enjoy the splendid view over the Lune Valley to the Howgills and the Pennines.)

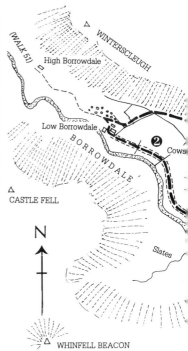

From the gap the descent looks inhospitably vague. Descend the grass following the left-hand side of a shallow rushy valley. (Ignore the sheep trod off to the left.) At prominent stones the path becomes comfortingly more distinct as it descends a lonely place. Keep on a slight rise on the left-hand side following the line of the valley in which the Burn Gill has begun to flow. Drop down to cross the stream by a ruin and proceed along the ongoing track. The next mile is quite straight-forward along the intake wallside on a good track. When the M6 is within earshot go through a gate and descend slightly R to the road ahead at Roundthwaite.

Turn R to join a surfaced lane. Erase the M6 from your mind and enjoy the beautiful Lune Valley. Speedwell, violet and silverweed abound on the verges, and kestrels hover above. At the junction turn L towards Tebay A685 and cross the bridge. Stop in the centre for an amazing view is beneath your feet. The old bridge and the gorge of the River Lune are well

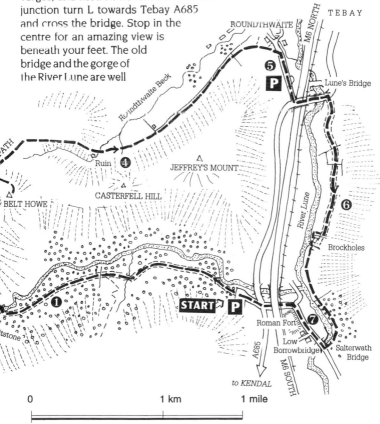

MABBIN CRAG   ASHSTEAD FELL   ILL   KENTMERE   HARTER
                                           BELL   PIKE   FELL
                                                FROSWICK   SHAP ROAD

NEW FORESTRY

LOW
BORROWDALE

*Looking up Borrowdale from the pony track over to the Lune Valley.
The Ashstead Fell-Whinfell Beacon ridge seen on the left skyline is a very
popular walk but not a right-of-way, hence its exclusion from this book*

worth craning your neck for. Over the bridge turn R through a gate to
Brockholes Farm. *As you progress look at the rock-cuttings made for the M6, in
Jeffrey's Mount. Problems awaited the engineers. The rock strata is a series of small
anticlines and synclines - a mere 20 feet across and dipping towards the Lune. To stop
the beds of rock sliding the rock is pinned and constantly monitored for movement.*

At Brockholes Farm the right-of-way goes round the back of the farm
(can be muddy) and into a meadow beyond. Turn R until level with the
building then L using a trod on the bank top above the fence. Keep by the
fence then go through a gate into a lonely waterside meadow. Cross the
grass to a gate, wired against flood but easy to stride over, and enter a
small wood. In springtime a carpet of bluebells screens the scented path,
which leads to Salterwath Bridge, an old stone bridge. Turn R and walk up
the surfaced lane to Low Borrowdale. Keep R on the road. *The earth bank,
topped with a wall, which rises on the left is the side of the Roman parade ground,
belonging to the fort of Borrow. The fort was on the main military route from Manchester
to Carlisle and housed an infantry battalion of 500 men (better seen from above).*

Go under the viaduct and the motorway bridge. The latter serves well
a threefold purpose. It carries the M6, shelters cattle and is a haven for
many birds. Cross the A685 diagonally R and reach the High and Low
Borrowdale lane and start.

CHAPTER 4
The Limestone Fringe

Between the Lakeland hills and Morecambe Bay lies an interesting area of limestone scarps and shelving plateaux which forms a complete contrast to the walking elsewhere in the region. Here we have close-cropped turf, woodland of birch, ash, whitebeam and yew, and a rich rock garden of limestone-loving plants.

Walk easily along the tops of long grey ribbons of limestone scars, or enjoy the beautiful woodlands. Look north and west to the distant high fells of Lakeland - look south-west onto the glittering expanse of Morecambe Bay. There are no high summits here, yet the tops bring a feel of space and an enrichment of spirit. This is still South Lakeland, yet quite different in character from the other areas described in this book. The paths are generally drier underfoot than in Central Lakeland but remember wet limestone can be slippery.

Delicate tracery of silver birches on Yewbarrow

WALK 52: Cunswick Scar and Scout Scar

The 'Mushroom' indicator on Scout Scar

SUMMARY: The limestone scars above Kendal give easy walking with panoramic views to the fells of the Lake District and The Pennines. This walk drops off the escarpment to explore the quiet farmland and woods along its base.

HOW TO GET THERE AND PARKING: Take the minor road from the middle of Kendal to Underbarrow and park on the right at the hill top by the radio station access track, or over the brow in the Scout Scar Car Park.

THE WALK: From the car park take the transmitting station access track in a northerly direction to enter a larch wood. After passing the station keep the wall to your right and go through a kissing gate in the wall corner. Permissive footpath sign to Cunswick Fell. Follow the signed path along the fell wall turning R in the next corner (arrowed signpost) and keeping the wall to your left. At a cross track, Gamblesmire Lane (which we use lower down), go straight across then angle left at the wall end, sign, across open

Distance:	6¾ miles 11km
Grade:	Moderate
Terrain:	Woodland, low fell
Summit:	Cunswick Scar - 679ft (207m)
	Scout Scar - 770ft (235m)
Map:	OL7

fell. The path crosses upland pasture, through an area of smooth cropped turf textured with overgrown molehills and hardy hawthorns. Cross a stile in a fence and descend into a shallow depression. (The path ahead rises gently to the summit of Cunswick Scar.)

At the lowest point of the depression cross the fence by a kissing gate L (sign) and enter the wood on a narrow path. The path uses a break in the scar to descend. Remember that the rock is limestone and very slippery when wet. Go straight across a track and down through the wood. In winter glimpses of Cunswick Tarn can be seen through the trees but if it is summer enjoy the pleasant woodland. At a fence cross a stile R and continue along the edge of the wood until a stile and slit L give access to a field. Go across aiming for the L-hand edge of the woodland opposite. There is a retrospective view of the tarn in its hollow below the wooded face of the Scar. Enter the wood by a slit and follow the path to exit on a farm track at the other side. Turn L and continue by the side of the wall (pillow mounds in the field over the wall), ignoring a stile into a stand of trees, to reach

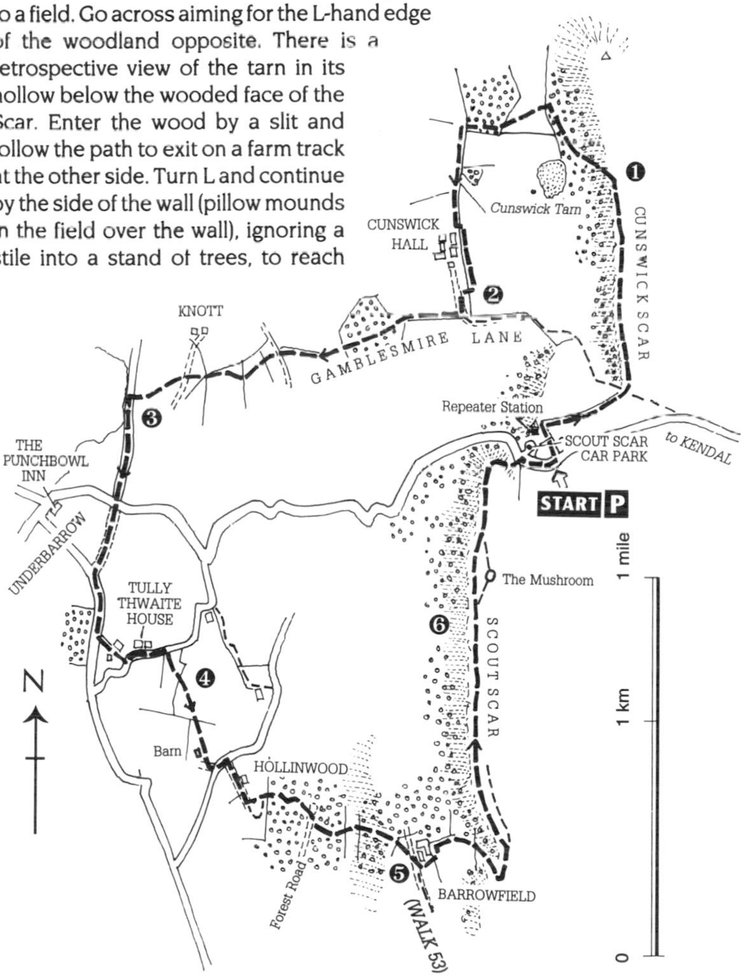

KENTMERE   SHIPMAN   CUNSWICK
PIKE   KNOTTS   HILLS ABOVE LONGSLEDDALE   SCAR

                                            CUNSWICK   CUNSWICK
                                            TARN   SCAR

STAVELEY

CUNSWICK
HALL

View from the northern end of Scout Scar

Cunswick Farm. Opposite a fine group of old yew trees by the first house
is a waymarked stile up on the left. Go over and few metres through the
mud is a kissing gate on the right. Keep close to the wall on the right and
continue up the field to a stile on the right near the top. Go through and
turn L up the track to reach Gamblesmire Lane.

SHORT RETURN TO CAR PARK: Turn L and keep on the track. The next
gateway has a kissing gate for walkers, but beware its jaws as it has a
massive counterweight. The track now gradually rises up the escarpment
to give excellent views along the Scar, over the Tarn and the undulating
chequered pattern of walled fields of the Lyth Valley. As the angle eases
the lane arrives at the wall and cross ways passed on the outward journey.

Turn right and follow the wall round the field edge to enter the wood at
the kissing gate and past the transmitting station to the car park and start.
Turn R for the Scout Scar car park.

TO CONTINUE THE WALK: Turn R along the green indent of the lane
which runs along the wallside to enter a wood, in company with a wet-
weather stream, at a gate. The stream soon goes its own way leaving the

lane more user-friendly. At the edge of the woodland the lane reaches a low point which holds a quagmire but its sound foundation allows a reasonable passage. Carry on along the lane now narrowed by claustrophobic vegetation and emerge into an open limestone pasture at a road. Go straight across the road, public footpath sign, and go ahead as directed by the finger post, (avoid a small rock-step immediately in your way) to reach a stile and gate, Yellow waymark, bear leftwards to the next waymarked stile/gate then fork R. Pass a waymarked post then guess the way to the bottom right-hand corner of the pasture to a kissing gate. Ahead is a broken wall, from its end turn half right following yellow arrows on electricity posts to a kissing gate and surfaced lane near a bridge over the Underbarrow Beck. Turn L and continue. The lane runs beside the beck and gives pleasant views over the fields to undulating wood-dappled folds of Barrowfield Lot and Scout Scar. At the crossroads go straight on into the green lane. (If you need refreshment turn R to Underbarrow village and The Punchbowl.)

The green lane makes a shortcut to the next road. Fork L along the road for 250 yards where there is a public footpath sign and stile on the left. Go up the brambly path beside a little stream to a white cottage, Rockyfield. It is necessary to pass the cottage and go down its drive so a quiet passage would surely be appreciated. Turn L on the surfaced lane past Tullythwaite House . Continue over the brow to a public footpath on the R. Go through the slit stile and proceed across the middle of the field towards Tanyard Beck. This is crossed by a grassed over bridge and keep the direction to a step-stile in a wall. Continue straight up the brow to a step-stile beside a gate. In this pasture is an isolated barn on a knoll. Keep along the right hedgeside to a gate behind the barn. Turn L down the surfaced lane for 50 yards then turn R on the public footpath to Scout Scar and Kendal. Pass a couple of cottages at Hollincrag and turn L at the bottom of the garden,

The isolated barn on a knoll

(or keep on the green track which circles easily to the same spot) to the waymarked access gate to the forest. There is now a climb to gain the top of the Scar. Go up the waymarked path through the forest to meet a forest road. Turn R for 10 yards then fork L back into the trees again. The forest path is delightful, especially in autumn. Cross a strip field by waymarked stiles and enter the forest again. A stony path leads up through lighter woodland to a pasture at Barrowfield Farm. As you leave the woods the next signpost is up to the right. Turn L to Scout Scar and Kendal.

At Barrowfield Farm, sign to Scout Crag and Kendal, go between the small orchards then signs show the way to a track leading up the hill between a wall and a fence to Scout Crag. At the field gate enter the woodland. A yellow arrow points up a well used path. Climb up steeply and take a well-earned rest at a platform to enjoy a map-like view of the Lyth valley. Circle L to join the main path north along the crag edge. Note that the cairn marked on the map is back from the edge and although close at hand is not visible from this point. The path keeps to the cliff edge, but there is also another velvet trod running alongside about 15m from the edge where no one need feel exposed and can still enjoy the bird's eye panorama. At the end of an old wall pass the prominent buttress Hodgson's Leap and carry on until the mushroom shelter on the summit comes into sight. *An outline of the principle surrounding fells is painted on the inside edge of the canopy. It is novel to lean on the cross wall of the wind shelter and to identify the hills with their names above them.*

Set off again along the cliff edge path still in the same direction (north) for quarter of a mile to reach the end of the Scout Scar ridge.

There is a good view of Cunswick Scar from here. Turn R and descend to the ancient iron kissing gate at the road. Turn R and the parking is a short distance up the road.

Kendal Green

In medieval times Kendal was famed for its cloth, dyed to a distinctive colour known as Kendal Green. This was used as uniform for archers. The dye was made by mixing blue and yellow colouring obtained from plants. The yellow colouring was obtained from weld (dyers' rocket) and dyers' broomweed, both found in abundance on Scout Scar.

WALK 53: Brigsteer Woods and Scout Scar

Barrowfield under Scout Scar

SUMMARY: Underbarrow Scar, with Scout Scar the highest point of its northern tip, is a limestone ridge between the Lyth Valley on the west and the Kent Valley on the east. Its sides support mixed woodlands, renowned for a wide variety of trees and plants. Its western edge rises in scenic crags which give extensive views over the Lakeland fells, the Kent Estuary and the Pennines.

This walk approaches the scar by way of Brigsteer Woods, famed for its spring daffodils. The walking is easy and on good paths with one steep pull of short duration onto the plateau edge. The return passes the stately home of Sizergh Castle. It is possible to split the walk into two shorter ones, which would allow time to visit the castle.

HOW TO GET THERE AND PARKING: From Junction 36 of the M6 take the A590, turning off at the Milnthorpe and Barrow junction for 1km. Do

Distance:	8¼ miles 13km
Grade:	Moderate
Terrain:	Woodland, low fell
Summit:	Scout Scar - 770ft (235m)
Map:	OL7, PF627

not take the first turn R signed Sizergh Castle, but the one immediately afterwards signed Sizergh. Fork L signed Levens and drive uphill over the brow of the hill. Park on the verge near Middle Wood

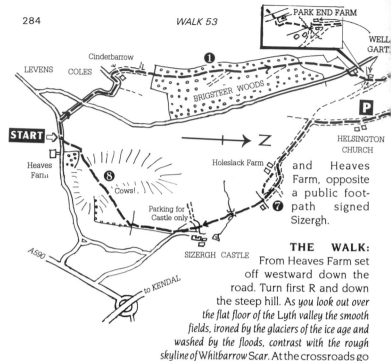

THE WALK:
From Heaves Farm set off westward down the road. Turn first R and down the steep hill. *As you look out over the flat floor of the Lyth valley the smooth fields, ironed by the glaciers of the ice age and washed by the floods, contrast with the rough skyline of Whitbarrow Scar.* At the crossroads go diagonally across, signed Cinderbarrow and down the Z-bends past Cinderbarrow Farm. Immediately past the farm turn R into a lane, signed 50 yards down, to Park End.

Enter the National Trust Conservation Area of Brigsteer Woods by a stile. In a few metres look on the left of the path for an information board which will quickly convince you that this is indeed a walk for all seasons. A path joins in from the right but keep ahead, past a bubbling spring. The path is narrower for a while, then joins a wider track. Keep in the same direction until leaving the wood at a ladder stile. There is no sign of a path; however the right of way crosses the field diagonally right heading uphill to a gate by the side of Park End Farm. (The line of the path has changed from that marked on the 1:25,000 map.) Cross the road and go through the farmyard. The next waymark is on the first electricity post, pointing left to the top left-hand corner of the field to a gate. The way is barred by a tumbling stream at Wells Garth. Either step over the low fence, cross the stone slab and squeeze through a slit stile, or go through a little wicket gate and cross an iron bridge. A lane leads between two cottages, each wall a

hanging garden, to join a bridle path. (Signpost to
Levens and Weather Bank.) Keep straight on until the lane
rises to join a surfaced road (sign to Brigsteer).

Turn R up the hill for 25m where the walk continues by turning L to
Barrowfield. If you want to make a shorter circuit continue up the road to
join the return path where the lane to Helsington church turns off to the R.

A short way along the farm track is a seat with a view. The track now rises
gradually beneath Burnbarrow Scar until coming to a gateway with an
arresting view of Scout Scar. As you approach the gateway look for a small
path branching down to the L into Honeybee Wood. Keep on this narrow
path which shadows the wall. Two paths join in from the left and one from
the right as you progress, but when a wall seems to bar the way the path
swings R to rejoin the farm track. Turn L to a stile and cattle-grid, then
follow the track round R to Barrowfield Farm, sign to Scout Crag and
Kendal. Go between the small orchards then signs left show the way to a
track leading up the hill between a wall and a fence to Scout Crag. At the
field gate enter the woodland. A yellow arrow points up a well used path.
Climb up steeply and take a well-earned rest at a platform to enjoy a map-
like view of the Lyth valley. Circle L to join the main path north along the
crag edge. Note that the cairn marked on the map is back from the edge
and although close at hand is not visible from this point. The path keeps
to the cliff edge, but there is also another velvet trod running alongside
about 15m from the edge where no-one need feel exposed and can still
enjoy the bird's eye panorama. At the end of an old wall pass the
prominent buttress Hodgson's Leap and carry on until the mushroom
shelter on the summit comes into sight. *An outline of the principal surrounding
fells is painted on the inside edge of the canopy. It is novel to lean on the cross wall of the
wind shelter and to identify the hills with their names above them.*

Before starting the return journey look at the indicator - aim to set off
half way between Ingleborough and the south pole, about 20 degrees left

Scout Scar

of your approach line. Go towards white barked ash trees and a stone wall. At an old iron kissing gate do not go through but keep the wall on your left. The path leads to a broken gap in the wall which marks the Lake District National Park Boundary. Go through, triangulation point on the right, then angle L towards five ash trees and along the plateau top to pass a large cairn on its left. Straight on at the junction with a major path and past a walled larch plantation on the left. A path from the wallside joins in on the left. The path now descends into a heathery dell and climbs up the other side. Still keeping by the wall and now descending another path joins in from the right. Turn L through a gate just before the wall corner to enter the National Trust area of Helsington Barrows. A wide track leads past a large heap of stones and some shapely old pines to the road. Turn R down the hill then L at the bend towards Helsington Church.

The shorter circuit joins the route at this point.

Pause to read the poem by the gateway. Wordsworth's words from his *Tour of the Continent* written in 1820 have been beautifully illustrated by Marion D'Aumaret on the altar wall of the church. Past the church ignore the first turn left to Holeslack. Keep straight on and bear L at a sign Kendal Road. Go through the gate and down to Holeslack Farm, straight past its farmyard and take a waymarked path R to join a track by a barn. Or reach the same point by continuing down the lane from the farm. (Ignore the old track to Kendal which leaves to the left.)

Keep straight across the next field on a good dry track and through another field offering an appetising view of Sizergh Castle. To visit the castle turn L, to carry on turn R.

Cross the car park and leave by a stile in the far left corner. Keep along

WALK 54: WHITBARROW NORTH

(The circuit of Township Allotment)

The route from The Row to the wood has become difficult due to re-fencing and planting. The following is recommended and provides a straightforward and scenic alternative.

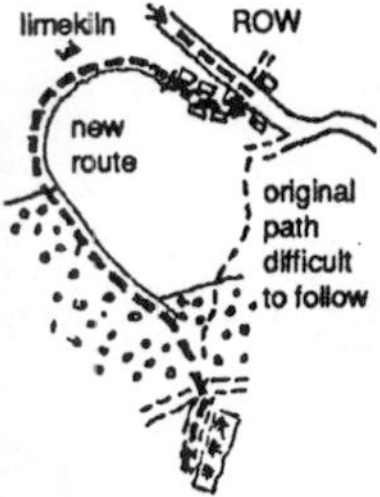

Page 288 The Walk paragraph 1 line 11 '...tunnel of birdsong to Row. As you approach the hamlet of Row spy a limekiln in the field on the right. Our onward route takes a path through this pasture.

At the lane junction bend back sharp right across the front of Row Farm and up the unsurfaced track between the cottages. Go through the gate ahead. Follow the left-hand wall round the damson orchard and, still by the wall side, look across to the limekiln which is in an excellent state of preservation. Ignore the facing gates which form angles in the wall. As you gain height there is an undulating view north-east to Scout Scar and east over Kendal and the Kent valley to the Pennines. The wall itself is interesting being built of round sandstone cobbles stabilised with flat limestone thins.

At the woodland gate go through and take the signed path ahead still shadowing the wall. Keep on the level main path, edged with violets in spring, through once-coppiced ash, birch and sycamore.

Page 288 paragraph 2 line 3 - '... a wider track etc....

limekiln

ROW

new route

original path difficult to follow

the wall side to reach a stile by two gates. Make your way diagonally R aiming for a low col which appears as a slight dip on the skyline. Pass through a line of trees growing on the remains of an old wall and over the brow of the hill. Cross a stile and keeping the wood on the left go down to a gate in a wall. Then turn L on a vehicle track towards Heaves Farm. A stile to the R of the gate in the shade of a holly bush brings you onto the road at the start.

Brigsteer Woods
An ancient wood of coppiced ash, oak birch and yew. Look for lily-of-the-valley, butterfly orchids - and of course in profusion bluebells and dwarf daffodils.

Sizergh Castle
Owned by the National Trust and open to the public, Sizergh Castle has been the home of the Strickland family for over 700 years. A fourteenth-century pele tower, built to withstand Scottish raiders, is incorporated into the later Elizabethan buildings. It is renowned for its wealth of Elizabethan wood carving and panelling.

St John's Church, Helsington
Dates from 1726 but was rebuilt in 1845 with a school alongside. The school was closed in 1965.

WALK 54: Whitbarrow North (The circuit of Township Allotment)

Cairns on Township Allotment

Distance:	4¹/₂ miles 7km
Grade:	Easy
Terrain:	Woodland low fell
Summit:	574ft (175m)
Map:	PF627

SUMMARY: Whitbarrow is a broad limestone ridge rising between the Winster and Lyth valleys. It is edged west and south by steep crags and fringed with mixed forest.

Limekiln at the start of walk

This short walk circles the northern third of the ridge on old green lanes or woodland tracks, returning over the plateau and visiting cairned viewpoints on the summit. A rewarding walk for autumn.

HOW TO GET THERE AND PARKING: Leave the A590 at Gilpin Bridge, and follow the A5074, signed 'Bowness and Windermere', for almost 4 miles. Turn L signed 'Cartmel', and after three-quarters of a mile park on the left by the side of a limekiln.

THE WALK: Pass in front of the fine limekiln and take a green lane which leads uphill and bends right towards the limestone edge and woodland fringe. A backwards glance reveals the Cartmel fells over the flat Winster valley. At the intake wall turn L into a hazel walk. Go through a gate and continue on the level lane enjoying a view into the upper Lyth valley. The lane soon begins to rise into woodland. Where the trees end and the track swings away to the right towards the Township Allotment pastures, keep straight ahead by the side of the wall, through a gate to the continuation of the hazel-clad lane. Through the leafy arches to the north the tiny rock summits of Lord's Lot can be seen. The lane descends gently through a tunnel of birdsong to Row, and at the first house the road becomes surfaced. As you pass through the village look out for an old mounting step on the left and, a little further on, an arrow sign directing you straight on for 75 yards. Next look for a finger post on the R pointing back sharp R for a few yards, then a yellow waymark L. Go between the buildings and enter into a rising green lane. After a gate turn right crossing the wire barrier by a stile. The hedged path rises gently and another stile has to be climbed. Stand here a moment and look for the next objective. It is a stone slit stile by an empty gateway. Slant diagonally L up the field and pass through the gap. Keep walking diagonally L through a long abandoned orchard to enter the next area of woodland by a slit stile in the wall.

The path is narrow but clear and rises gently. Keep L at a junction and after passing an area of limestone pavement on the right the path meets a wider track coming in from the left. Cross this track taking the L fork. The path now follows the side of a young fir plantation and rises over a

shoulder to descend into a more densely wooded valley. A high wall is
crossed by a stile-cum-wicket gate then the path passes pleasantly through
a contrast of mature silver birch and young cypress trees to a junction with
a major track. Turn R here. The track rises gently for a while then more
steeply. Now look for a smaller level path to the R between two large oak
trees (cairn). This path follows the valley and threads its
way through bracken, passing a lone stone gatepost
and a few overgrown remains of the boundary
wall of Horse Pasture Wood. Pass under
an ancient yew then rise steeply
but briefly. The woodland
ends and the bare slopes
of the fell top can be
seen over the wall.
The way bends L
parallel to this wall
and crosses it by a
ladder stile. The
fenced boggy area

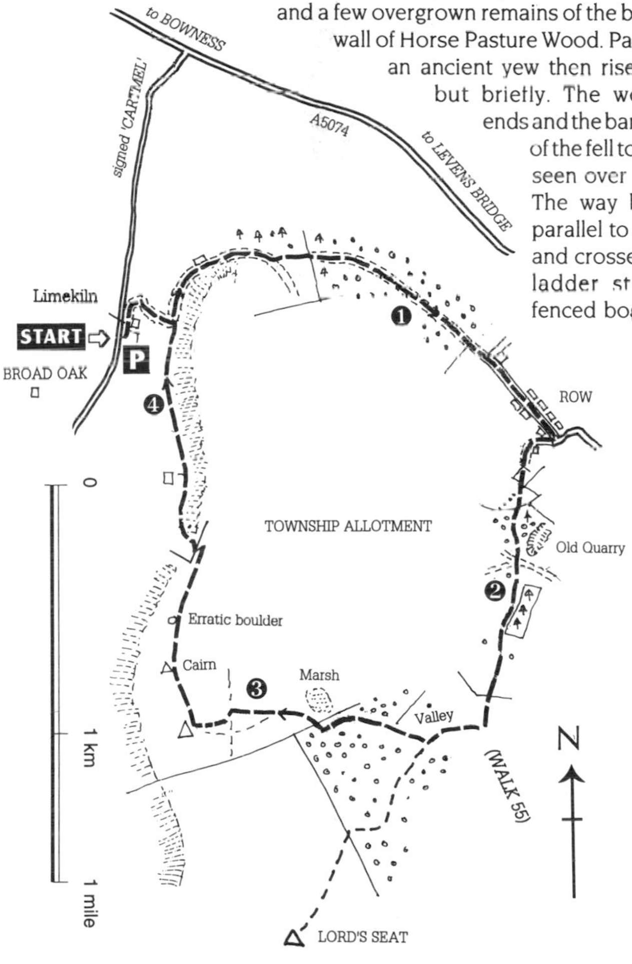

The northern end of Township Allotment

to your right is, or was, Toby Tarn. The crossing and descent from the plateau lies directly NW from this point. We will make a short yet worthwhile diversion. From the stile pass a clump of stunted hawthorns at your R and swing L keeping wind-bent larches to your left until a prominent cairn appears on the horizon. As you meet the cairned path which runs along the ridge, turn L along it to approach the summit stonefield and the meticulous cairn 173m surrounded by its shabby little satellites.

In clear weather the views are splendid. To the south, Lord's Seat, the highest point of the plateau can be seen.

To the north a squat triangular cairn is visible. This is the next point on our walk and is slightly higher at 175m. At this cairn the path is little more than a sheep track and does not go in our direction. Make your way north keeping along the plateau top, heading for the shallow valley of the Township Allotment to two large boulders. On closer examination they prove to be one boulder of Scottish origin, split when abandoned by the glacier which bore it from its parent rock.

Begin to descend towards a stand of birches and the stone wall which guards the western escarpment. A path gradually materialises and follows the wall to a stile. Cross this to

Erratic boulder

gain the escarpment edge. There are fine views into the Winster valley to be enjoyed in the shelter of the high wall. Cowmire Hall, in the valley below, is a seventeenth-century pele tower now incorporated into a house.

Go straight ahead where the narrow path descends through bracken then falls steeply, yet easily, down the rocky edge with the aid of a few cut steps and zigzags into the woods. The angle soon eases and the path is watered and widened by a merry spring. On reaching the end of the woodland the path follows the line of a wire fence above Fell Edge Farm. The fence is now replaced by a wall and widens to a green lane. Just past a gate the opening on the left leads down to the limekiln and car park.

WALK 55: Whitbarrow East and Lord's Seat

Windswept yew on Lord's Seat

SUMMARY: A varied walk with an interesting woodland approach on a network of sheltered tracks, to the bare summit plateau of Whitbarrow. The return along the length of the undulating plateau, edged by a wooded scarp, gives scintillating views across the Kent Estuary. A surprisingly impressive finish below a gruesome quarry completes the circuit.

HOW TO GET THERE AND PARKING: Take the A590, pass the A5074 turn to Bowness and Windermere then take the next indicated unnamed turning on the R opposite the obvious steep slopes of White Scar. After a left bend turn R in 500m to Raven's Lodge Farm. Bear R behind the farmhouse and park just beyond on the left.

Distance:	5¾ miles 9¼km
Grade:	Moderate
Terrain:	Woodland, forest, low fell
Summit:	Lord's Seat - 706ft (215m)
Map:	PF627

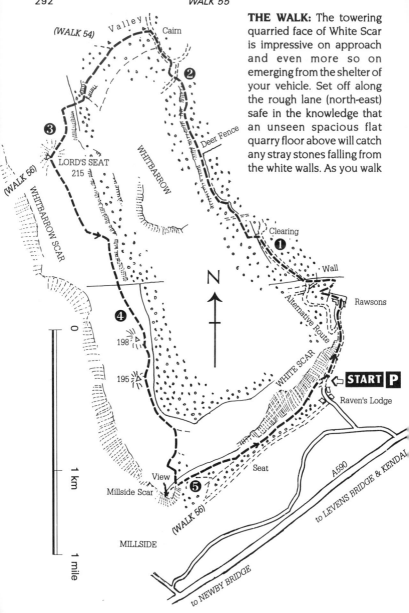

THE WALK: The towering quarried face of White Scar is impressive on approach and even more so on emerging from the shelter of your vehicle. Set off along the rough lane (north-east) safe in the knowledge that an unseen spacious flat quarry floor above will catch any stray stones falling from the white walls. As you walk

(WALK 54)

Valley

Cairn

❷

Deer Fence

WHITBARROW

❸

LORD'S SEAT
215

(WALK 56)

WHITBARROW SCAR

Clearing

❶

Wall

Alternative Route

Rawsons

N

❹

198

195

WHITE SCAR

START **P**

Raven's Lodge

0

1 km

1 mile

View

Millside Scar

❺

Seat

A590

to LEVENS BRIDGE & KENDAL

(WALK 56)

MILLSIDE

to NEWBY BRIDGE

towards Rawson's Farm a natural limestone cliff with its ash trees draped with wild honeysuckle donates a more friendly atmosphere. Pass a barn right. Rawson's Farm can be seen ahead, making an attractive picture, its buildings set at the foot of a small valley, its shape sheltered by the woodland shawl. (In the field to the left is an open gateway and a track which bends back up the hillside to enter the forest. This track is joined by our footpath further on *.) Go between the buildings and turn L behind to reach a footpath leading past the farm spring and up a narrow valley.

A zigzag path rises up the valley floor, then R up the side to a wall and L along the wall to join the forest track * at a yellow waymark. Turn R through a gap in the ageing wall and into Watson's Wood. The woodland is most attractive with a generous mixture of varieties including the delicate cypress, its dark foliage and red bark adding colour to winter's scene. At a Y-junction take the L fork, waymark. (The right fork opens onto the Forestry Commission's work area, where fragrant logs are often piled.) The track is now followed for one mile. It is muddy in places but this provides a medium to see the slot of the deer. At a cross track keep straight on, waymark. The track narrows to a path and begins to rise to a gap in an old deer fence which runs along on the right and a small scar appears up on the left. Pass by an area of limestone pavement on the right and then a slope of scree on the left. The screes dwindle and the deer fence takes a 90° turn away to the right. The character of the wood changes and tall stiff birches look down on young beech and cypress at their feet. Pass by two overgrown, barely visible cross-paths after which bend L and immediately come across a junction and clearing. Go straight across, continue for 60 yards down the clearing to meet a U-bend. Turn L and go up a slight rise to a Y-junction by two large oaks. Take the R fork down towards the valley of Gillbirks for 150m. Turn L at a Y-junction (cairn and waymark). The path now rises gradually then more steeply to a Y-junction with a cairn and yellow waymark arrow. Keep straight ahead still climbing steadily, passing a stand of young pines, the rearguard of the plateau forest. The path now levels and narrows, edged on the left by a low outcrop. Continue up through a rock gateway passing a small cair, to a T-junction. Turn R, and rise to an open glade and the boundary wall of the Lake District Naturalists Trust Conservation area. Cross the substantial stone stile and turn L.

The summit plateau is a sudden and elevating contrast to the woodlands, which still retain their gentle swathe within sight. The path runs alongside a low scar then rises right to the prominent cairn on Lord's Seat. A *plaque commemorates G.A.K.Hervey founder of the Lake District Naturalists Trust. The views are wonderful spinning the eye on a carousel of hill and vale, tree and sky and returning to the white limestones of the summit.*

Lord's Seat

Set off in a south south-east direction along the lowering ridge. Keep to the crest from which the wooded scars of Yewbarrow can be seen across the valley to the west. Pass two marker cairns on the ridge and at its end pass between two small cairns to descend and bend L to another marker cairn. Continue along the foot of a crag. *A yew springs from a crack in the crag wall and streams its branches like smoke in the wind. To the right ash trees host flocks of jostling starlings and blackbirds launch from the crag diving across the path to the pavement beyond.* Continue below the dwindling crag to reach a wall which marks the southern boundary of the LDNT Area. (By moving R a few metres to the edge of the scar there is a fine view down into the Beck Head valley.) Pass an area of gorse and stone then rise up to a huge cairn. Pass cairn 198m and before descending note the next cairn ahead. The path narrows as it goes into a depression moving close to the forest fence. At the lowest point angle slightly R and climb the stony slope to the noted cairn which quickly comes into view. Pass on and continue along the grassy path to the next cairn 195m.

Please note from this point the route instructions cover shorter distances than you have become accustomed to along the open felltop. We are about to descend White Scar and it is important that the right path is located. Continue on the grassy path leading over the rise close ahead. The pine forest is now further away to the L. Ignore small cross paths right and left. Pass a cairn and boulders. (The forest edge now turns away L.) Keep ahead passing a pair of small cairns set off to the R and continue on the broad green way. The path now bends right (ignore a small path leading left in the direction of the forest) to descend and cross an open expanse of heather and bracken to a cairn on its L and a junction of small

trods. Go straight ahead and downhill to the L of a fortress of gorse. The path is now clearer. Pass a flattened cairn and go by a slope scattered with silver birches then plunge into the wood. In 100 yards meet a wall with a gap.

Caution: Beyond this wall is the top of Mill Side Scar, a place to take close control of children. (Through the gap and 50 yards to the right is a large grassy eyrie with a wonderful bird's eye view of Mill Side and the Kent Estuary.)

The route continues. Go through the gap, turn to the L for 10 yards then L again through another gap in the wall to a narrow path by an iron fence. Keep on the path which traverses the wooded slope. (Ignore an obvious path which zigzags down right by a tree with a carved heart.) Pass an area of scree where an opening in the trees gives a glimpse up to the left of the scar above. Keep on descending, now more steeply, to join a wider level path. Turn L and pass a seat, where you can collect yourself for the sudden arresting sight which awaits a little way ahead. Emerge from the woodland onto the bedding plane of the old quarry floor. I will not try to describe the scene other than to say you will be impressed. Keep to the R-hand edge of the floor. Go carefully down its gradual incline as the limestone is slippery in places and the eye is continually drawn away from its task to the awesome fascination of the rock.

Keep on the track past semi ruined buildings to Raven's Lodge and the start.

WALK 56: Whitbarrow West (Lord's Seat) and Witherslack

The restored water-wheel at Millside

SUMMARY: A popular circuit from Millside gains the Whitbarrow plateau by a steep ascent through woods, to culminate in the fine summit viewpoint of Lord's Seat. A descent of the western scarp is followed by a woodland stroll along its base.

HOW TO GET THERE AND PARKING: Leave the A590 2 miles south-west of the A5074 junction. Turn R to Mill Side. Parking 100 yards on where the old road crosses the Mill Side lane.

THE WALK: Walk up the lane towards Mill Side - notice the dark Silurian rock by the roadside, a complete contrast to the light carboniferous limestone towering above. *At a junction by the telephone box the stream is dammed into an attractive pond forming a head of water for the mill on the left. The*

Distance:	5¼ miles 8½km
Grade:	Moderate
Terrain:	Woodland, low fell
Summit:	Lord's Seat - 706ft (215m)
Map:	PF627

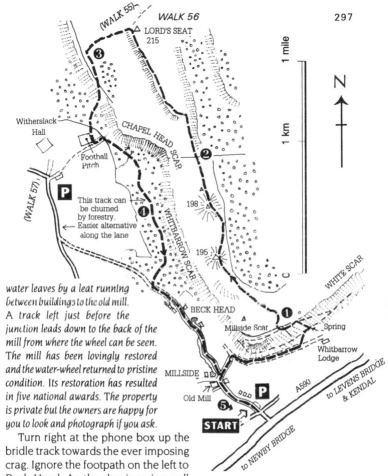

water leaves by a leat running
between buildings to the old mill.
A track left just before the
junction leads down to the back of the
mill from where the wheel can be seen.
The mill has been lovingly restored
and the water-wheel returned to pristine
condition. Its restoration has resulted
in five national awards. The property
is private but the owners are happy for
you to look and photograph if you ask.

Turn right at the phone box up the
bridle track towards the ever imposing
crag. Ignore the footpath on the left to
Beck Head. As the domineering wall
recedes behind a plantation of larches the track levels. Look along the
track and stop as soon as a pair of gateposts (Whitbarrow Lodge) appear
on the right about 300 yards away. Take a signed permissive path slanting
L up the hill. (If you reach the gateway on the right you have gone too far,
go back and try again.)

The path rises steeply along a line of mature yews, their fluid trunks
upright in the sheltered haven of the scar. The path levels and is man-made
for a while. At the junction with an upper path turn R for 25 yards. Here a

spring gurgles from the rock, dives under the path, then slips down a pretty shy cascade into the wood. At the spring turn sharp L above it and continue on the rising path to join an upper traversing path. Turn L to an old wall. Go through the gap, turn R along the wall for 10 yards then turn R through the next gap. (The path continuing along the wallside leads to a splendid viewpoint at the top of Millside Scar.)

The path now continues clearly through the diminishing woodland to a cairn (cairn 1) on the birch and bracken clad expanse. From here the eye can travel south over the Kent Estuary to Arnside, Morecambe Bay and on a clear day beyond. Continue straight on to the next level shelf and cairn 2, the views expanding with the extra height gained. The next cairn can be seen but the path heads towards the forest belt then swings back leftwards onto the ridge to pass the cairn 3. The hard work is now over and the full impact of this secluded limestone plateau can be enjoyed to the full. Pass the two little guiding cairns and with the forest line to your right the trigangulation pillar on Lord's Seat can be seen in the distance.

Keep on the path passing large boulders to a large cairn 4 at summit 195m.

Descend passing cairn 4a into a depression where the path snuggles up to the forest then branches away left to summit 198m cairn 5. Continue past an area of exposed limestone beds, not quite a pavement, and a more mature forest of shapely pines to the right. At the crosswall the area of the Cumbria Trust for Nature Conservation is entered. Cross the stile and please do not stray from the path. The route now passes a line of crag and a bleached no-mans-land scattered with ash and birch relieved only by the evergreen of the bent and stunted yew and gorse. The cairned path swings away left from the crag to pass between two cairns on the ridge top. As the waymarking cairns guide the elevated way to the summit a panorama of

View north along Whitbarrow Scar ridge to Lord's Seat

interlocking folds reach eastwards to the distant Pennines.

Pass cairn 5, which is actually the end view of a fragile windbreak, to the monolithic cairn on the summit of Lord's Seat 215m. *This was built, as the plaque relates, to the memory of Canon G.A.K.Hervey, Founder of the Lake District Naturalists Trust. And the views are extensive, yet the hills and far mountains do not steal the scene. The valleys - flat floored and patterned - draw the eye and the imagination into history. To the north-east lies the Lyth; the Kent to the south and to the west the Winster, these valleys have attracted man from pre-Viking times as local archaeological finds testify.*

Turn 90° L, south-west, to a big cairn and descend a series of small scars on a wide stony path. The path winds about but is multi-cairned, holds its general direction and is easy to follow to the grassy edge of the main escarpment. Turn L on the narrowing path. The wall on the right marks the edge of the crag where the updraught of the wind becomes visible in the styled tresses of the undaunted yews. The path now loses height gradually, passing through a glade of silver birches still running parallel to the wall then a steeper descent begins. At a small cairn ignore a narrow trod branching left and keep on the main path right and down to approach the wall. Care is needed from this point as any moisture on the limestone renders it very slippery. Go through the gap in the wall and down the steeper zigzag. A short rocky section is encountered but the stone is sound and this is negotiated easily with care. It is one of those little steps in a path that is hardly noticed when going up, yet can appear strangely formidable when coming down. The angle becomes easier as the path enters the wood and there are only occasional roots to trip the unwary. Pass an arrowed signpost placed to indicate the route in the reverse direction. At a wall go through the gap into the football field and follow the yellow arrows left to a stile.* **

WOODLAND ROUTE TO BECK HEAD*

Turn L and over the ladder stile into the wood. Turn R on the rising forest track. After passing a spring look out for a notice board set apart on a path to the left. *The board indicates the climbing area of Chapel Head Scar and you may be fortunate enough to see some daring antics on the steep white walls above.* From the board you will see that the way on using the forest track is not a right of way, the owners of Witherslack Hall Estate are happy for it to remain open as a permissive right of

way. If you use it please give the owners no reason to take offence. The track leads straight with a few bends, springs and puddles to join the bridle track just before Beck Head 1½km.*

ALTERNATIVE ROUTE TO BECK HEAD**

Turn R along the track to Witherslack Hall. The next gate leads into the car park.

Go through the parking area and turn L at the road. In 700m turn L into the bridleway to Beck Head 1km. The way leads pleasantly across the flat valley floor before entering woodland. A forest track joins from the left (*) and the buildings of Beck Head are seen.

The track now becomes a surfaced lane. After a bend the resurgence of The Beck is on the left. A spring gurgles from a wall of limestone and flows hastily through a garden of watercress. Cross the bridge and continue along the lane over a little rise to the telephone box junction at Mill Side on the outward route. Keep L on the wider road and along to the start.

WALK 57:   Yewbarrow and Beck Head

The walk over Yewbarrow as seen from the descent of Whitbarrow Scar

SUMMARY: Yewbarrow is an insignificant hill only just emerging from its cloak of woodland, yet it has great charm and gives good views of the length of Whitbarrow's escarpment and the neighbouring Winster valley. Much of the walk is on pleasing paths through woodland, an excellent choice for a windy day. Beck Head is an idyllic spot, its ever-clear spring pouring from the base of a verdant limestone scar.

HOW TO GET THERE AND PARKING: From the A590 turn R, signed to Witherslack and proceed for 2 miles to a small car parking area down the track R of the gate of Witherslack Hall.

Before setting off it is of interest to consult the notice board. The diagram shows the face of Whitbarrow and the climbing area of Chapel Head Scar, where rock climbers can sometimes be seen pitting their skills against one of the most severe limestone walls in England. The permeable limestone sits on top of the impervious Silurian rock giving a line of springs and vegetation contrast which is intrinsic to the pleasure of this walk.

Distance:	7½ miles 12km
Grade:	Moderate
Terrain:	Valley, woodland, low fell
Summit:	Yewbarrow - 420ft (120m)
Map:	PF627

THE WALK: From the car park turn R up the road for 100 yards then turn L along the public bridleway to Knot Wood and Halecat. Before the bend look back and the

NEWTON FELLS

WITHERSLACK HALL

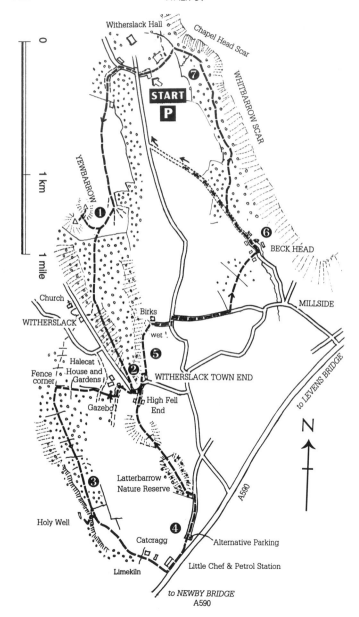

Witherslack Hall

Chapel Head Scar

WHITBARROW SCAR

❼

START
P

YEWBARROW

0

1 km

1 mile

❶

❻
BECK HEAD

MILLSIDE

Church

Birks

WITHERSLACK

wet

❺

❷

WITHERSLACK TOWN END

Halecat
House and
Gardens

Fence
corner

Gazebo

High Fell
End

to LEVENS BRIDGE

N

❸

Latterbarrow
Nature Reserve

Holy Well

A590

❹

Catcragg

Alternative Parking

Limekiln

Little Chef & Petrol Station

to NEWBY BRIDGE
A590

screened Witherslack Hall (now a school) can be seen through winter branches. The walled ivy-clad bridleway rises gently then descends to a gate at Lawns House. Take the R fork across the field to a gate giving access to a wood. The bridleway continues through an array of grey coppiced poles springing in concord from a greenery of dog's mercury. Soon the left-hand woodland gives way to pasture and on the right the slopes of Yewbarrow rise as open short-turfed grassland dotted with silver birch - so typical of limestone uplands.

Pass a gate on the left (private) and up a short rise by a wall. Where the wall bends away left the path diverges into a fan of four tracks. Take the R-hand one and head across the open hillside towards the right edge of a thick cushion of trees on the horizon.

At an oak tree the path forks. (The L fork takes a direct line to a gate in the forest wall. Our route will return to go through this gate so note its position.) Go on the R fork and from its green path a view opens south to the Kent Estuary, and beyond, where the gentle skyline of Arnside Knott and its neighbouring tree-clad hills are scarred by the great orange-coloured limestone quarry at Haverbrack. Pass a group of delicate silver birches and continue on the rising path to bend right between the two heights of Yewbarrow. Mount the grassy slope to the left (west) for a superb panorama of the Winster valley. Return across the path and climb the slope on the R (east) to the cairn. The protruding white stones of Yewbarrow make a fine flat seat from which to admire the complete length of Whitbarrow Scar.

Return down to the path, or retain the view a little longer by strolling along the lowering ridge, to the group of silver birches then fork R to reach the aforementioned forest gate.

Go through the gate into an area of open woodland. The path is narrower but straight and clear, passing through a blend of deciduous and evergreen trees offering a charm unchanged by the seasons. Ignore any lesser paths to left or right until the path descends beneath yew trees to a small cairn at a fork. Keep straight on along the level path. (The R path descends to the Winster valley.)

The path now adds a lilt to the stride as it begins to lose height almost imperceptibly and runs on a shelf between a screebank and a small vegetated outcrop. Pass through a gap in the remains of an old wall and carry on to join the road near Halecat House. Turn L for 25 yards along the road.

SHORT RETURN:* Continue round the corner on the road for 100 yards to a sharp right bend at Merlin Cottage where a signed path branches L to Birks.

TO CONTINUE: There is a signed footpath on the R to Slate Hill. Go over the stile and enter an enclosed footpath which descends steeply giving a view of Halecat House. Pass between ruined buildings and turn L along a bridle track. To the right is a stand of yews - not normally so stiff and upright and just beyond them look R for a small footpath crossing the field. *In this field is an elegant gazebo crowned with a gleaming weather-cock, stealing prominence from the drab façade of Halecat House.*

Cross the field to the end of an old wall and carry on into the woodland. In high summer the path may be lost in the grass but it passes to the L of the gazebo between damson trees. Turn L along a track by the wall bounding the Halecat Nursery gardens. Then go R on a wide woodland path still beside the wall. Pass a cross wall. The path, now fenced, rises gently over Halecat Hill, a mere undulation in the forest, and on to meet a crosspath at the R-hand fence corner.

Turn L on a wide path which gradually narrows, the plants and grasses grasping intimately as you pass. After passing a gap in a crosswall a gentle descent begins, then a second crosswall brings a change in the woodland where signs of coppicing remain. Go straight on at a signpost to a gate. *The woodland is now more open with aged elderberries staggering to hold their yearling shoots aloft.* Go straight over a crosspath, the narrow trod winding through high grasses yet it is smooth underfoot, and following the tapering hill crest. Cross a wall stile and approach another stile into a field.

DIVERSION TO THE HOLY WELL AND NICHOLL'S MOSS

It is worth spending a few minutes to visit the secret dell of the Holy Well. Before the stile turn down R into the dell avoiding a small crag. *The site of the well is elusive but the situation is charming. There are a few small caves in the rather shattered rock, but the spring and pool hosts reflections despite being incorporated into the drainage channel of the moss.*

Return to the main path keeping parallel to the wall and as you go over the rise refreshing views back to Yewbarrow appear. Keep on down the pasture, through a gate in the fence and straight on to another gate. Pass a limekiln in an excellent state of preservation, and carry on past Cat Crag Farm to the main road (A590). Turn L across the front of the garage and cafe and at the P sign fork L onto the old road, (where there is alternative parking).

After 100 yards or so on the L is the entrance to the Latterbarrow Nature Reserve. The way to High Fell End is signed by blue waymark arrows.

Go into the reserve, turn R and follow the waymarks, passing a memorial to Dr F.H.Day 'Geologist & Naturalist'. After crossing the reserve at a fork by a high wall to the R, do not branch down left to the spring but keep ahead to enter a field by an iron gate. Keep parallel to the L edge of the field to the gate by High Fell End Farm. Pass between the buildings to the road (junction with short return)*.

Turn R to the next bend and Merlin Cottage where the route turns L on the public footpath to Birks.

Follow the instructions on the notice keeping to the fenced walk, turn R behind the shed, go into the field and turn L keeping by the fence. The scar over the fence is busy with tiny coal tits and as you go over the rise, Birks Farm can be seen ahead. Cross the field to the farmyard gate (muddy in wet weather) go between the buildings and in front of the house into the access lane and the road (retrospective footpath sign to High Fell End).

Turn L then almost immediately R at the junction. As you walk along the road for a third of a mile, notice the walls which are built from the Silurian rock of the valley, note the change in colour and the heath-type vegetation. Look out for the footpath L to Beck Head. Go over the stile and enter a pathway through bramble, bracken and gorse. After passing the ends of an old wall the path narrows but nowhere do you get trapped in its tentacles or sink in its clammy springs. Hold to the line of travel ignoring the odd sidepaths of the fruit hunters and after a patch of particularly equatorial gorse the reassuring chimneys of Beck Head are seen ahead. Go through gates and turn R at the cottages to join the road at Beck Head. Turn L to the spring where the beck comes welling from its limestone dungeon to a paradise of pines, meadow and watercress. *This is a spot to sit and be entertained by the two frogs on the roof of the little building before continuing up the road.* At the last cottage the road becomes a bridleway. Keep ahead past an old barn and into the woodland. **Return A**. Keep on the main track between stone gateposts. The track now runs for three-quarters of a mile along the edge of the wood then through fields yielding views up the valley. At the road turn R for half a mile to Witherslack Hall and the start.

Return B. Branch R on the woodland path below Chapel Head Scar then L to Witherslack Hall and start.

The Holy Well and Nicholl's Moss
The Holy Well lies on the eastern side of Nicholl's Moss, an important remnant of estuarine raised bog which is 2 to 3 metres higher than the neighbouring farmland. It is now richly wooded and hosts many species of butterflies and moths.

Halecat Garden Nurseries
These are open all year to the public. Monday to Friday and Sunday afternoons. Closed Saturdays.

Witherslack Hall
Built as a hunting lodge in 1874 by Lord Derby it is now a special school for boys.

Witherslack Village

The village which is just up the road from Halecat is worth seeing. The church was built in 1664 by the bequest of John Barwick who became a dean of St Paul's. Other notable buildings are the Old School Masters' House, The Dean Barwick School and the Old Coach House.

WALK 58:   Hampsfell

The Hospice on Hampsfell

SUMMARY: The modest hill of Hampsfell makes a lovely short walk typical of the best South Lakeland limestone can offer - beautiful woods, interesting natural rock sculpture, a curious summit and sparkling views over the estuary.

Distance:	3³/₄ miles 6km
Grade:	Easy
Terrain:	Woodland, low fell
Summit:	Hampsfell - 727ft (222m)
Map:	PF636

The Victorian seaside resort of Grange has always been genteel. As a seaside hot-spot it has little going for it. Cut off from the estuary by the railway its sands are not the sort you could happily let your children play

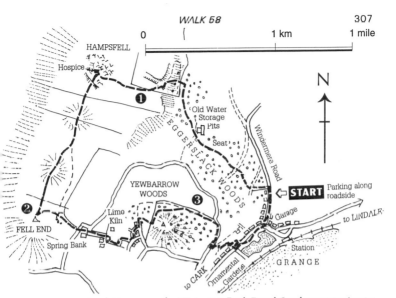

on unsupervised. However, the Victorian Park Road Gardens are a joy to visit and an air of tranquility and pleasure pervades.

This walk could be easily combined with a visit to Humphrey Head (Walk 60), or a look round the historical village of Cartmel, to make an excellent day out.

HOW TO GET THERE AND PARKING: At Grange-over-Sands. If approaching from Lindale (from A590) pass the Shell garage and turn immediately R into Windermere Road. Parking allowed for cars on the right. *Toilets at the station.*

THE WALK: Continue along Windermere Road and turn L on the public footpath signed 'Routon Well and Hampsfield'. This is part of the Cistercian Way and carries an attractive descriptive waymark. Climb up through woodland, once coppiced and set on limestone. Cross a surfaced lane, then continue to meet and cross another lane. Continue up the path left into Eggerslack Wood signed to Hampsfell (yellow waymark). *The woods are noted for its purple hair-streaked butterflies and red squirrels.* Keep straight on at a bench by a path junction. A little further, on the right, is a wall which proves to be a dam. Behind it are two concrete tanks in a state of disrepair. *These acted as an emergency water supply for Grange, fed by Routon Well and were last used in World War II.*

Continue up the path more steeply now, and when it levels you are near a seat, sign and stile at the fell wall.

The woodland is left behind exchanged for flower-flecked short turf with protruding slabs of limestone, weather-worn into karren grooves. Keep straight on under the electricity line towards a low band of crag. Looking back right a view of Whitbarrow and the Howgill Fells gradually sneaks over the tree-tops as you gain height. Pass the end of the crag then continue for 50 yards to a cutting and cairn on a fine piece of limestone pavement. Keep straight on to go over a stile in the wall on the left. Keep along the wallside R and where it turns away look well ahead for a yellow arrow on a short post to guide you over the rise where the hospice together with a mighty stone summit cairn cannot be missed. *The large cairn is reputed to be a burial cairn made after a battle between Dunmail, King of Cumbria and Edmund, King of the Saxons.*

Read the message inside the Hospice and enjoy the splendid view from the rooftop over the Estuary. *The view indicator was built by a retired railway man. The Hospice was built in 1835 by George Remington, a former pastor of Cartmel parish, for the shelter and entertainment of wanderers over the fell. His verses around the inside walls are in the form of a puzzle.*

Leave by turning L from your approach direction (south). Go through a nick in the limestone and along the broad green ridge top to a large cairn. Keep on to a stile in a crosswall, pass another broken wall and begin to descend into the dip beyond. At a Y-junction branch R (arrow waymark). The path now runs along the western side of the ridge giving a view of Cartmel village huddled round its priory amid rich green pastures. Away to the SW are the gas rigs in the Irish sea.

At the top of the rise you will see ahead the cairn on Fell End and the promontory of Humphrey Head pointing over Morecambe Bay to Heysham Power Station. Pass another crosswall. Our way now turns L (SE) down the hill but before leaving the ridge carry on ahead the short distance to the cairn on Fell End. The reward is a fine seascape which catches the light and blends a glow into the banks and channels of the Bay. Return towards the wall then branch down R (SE) to gain the path as it enters a hollow with a collection of stones crowned by blackthorn. Keep down the depression towards Springbank Farm and a gate in a wall. Cross a lane and follow the public footpath sign to Ashmont Road and Chaney Road. This cuts a corner to the left of the farmhouse. Ahead is a limekiln.

At the farmhouse turn R down the lane and go over a stile on the L into the field with the limekiln. Keep to the R up the wall side and through a slit stile into a walled pathway going left. Keep on round the bend to a road by some houses. Turn L, then take the second left where a track leads by an electricity sub-station into Yewbarrow Woods. The path bends R then next turn right at a Norweb EHT stone. Go on over a slight rise and keep

R to descend to a wall. Go through the gap and turn L through a stand of mature larches. Pass the end of a broken wall as the path now circles Eden Mount. When you reach the wall at the edge of the wood turn R. Follow the wallside path to a stile in a fence and continue until it joins a drive then the surfaced road. Turn R for 200 yards then enter the public footpath to Main Street on the left. In 20 yards fork sharply R (do not enter the iron fenced area where the broader path leads), then L to descend a zigzag path through a ranson-carpeted wood to the main road. Go R a few yards then cross over into the lovely promenade gardens and turn L along the lakeside. The lake is home to a collection of ornamental wildfowl. An information board will aid identification. The gardens end opposite the start, the shops, cafe, the station and toilets. *The Clock Tower built in 1912 is a distinctive landmark and there are many fine Victorian buildings.*

Castle Head

On the way into Grange from Lindale you pass an 'almost' island! This was the site of Atterpile Castle, a Romano-British fort. A mansion, now a field study centre, was once the home of John Wilkinson, the ironmaster (see the notes on Backbarrow, page 200).

The Victorian Park Road Gardens at Grange are a haven for wildlife

WALK 59:   Humphrey Head

Humphrey Head viewed from The Point

SUMMARY: The Humphrey Head area of open access is a whaleback promontory of limestone forming the western seaward boundary of the Kent estuary. Gentle slopes to the east contrast with the vertical white crags on the west which present a playground for rock climbers. The walking is easy but care must be taken if the rock is wet. A pleasant spot for a short afternoon stroll or picnic.

Many rare plants grow in the headland, particularly the goldilocks aster and rock samphire.

Humphrey Head was a popular spa in the eighteenth and nineteenth centuries, used by lead miners from the North Pennines who came to take the well waters. For more details read 'Lost Lancashire' by A.L.Evans.

HOW TO GET THERE AND PARKING: Go through Grange-over-Sands on the Cark road to Allithwaite where a lane branches left to Humphrey Head. This twists and turns, passing Wrayholme Tower, an old pele tower.

Car Park at the end of Holy Well Lane on the beach below the Humphrey Head cliffs.

Distance:	3 miles 5km
Grade:	Easy, but the shore can be a rough scramble
Terrain:	Woodland, low fell
Summit:	Humphrey Head - 172ft (52m)
Map:	PF636

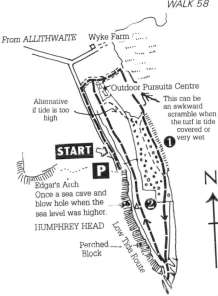

From ALLITHWAITE   Wyke Farm

Outdoor Pursuits Centre

Alternative
if tide is too
high

This can be
an awkward
scramble when
the turf is tide
covered or
very wet

START

P

Edgar's Arch
Once a sea cave and
blow hole when the
sea level was higher.

HUMPHREY HEAD

Perched
Block

Low Tide Route

N

HUMPHREY HEAD POINT

THE WALK: From the car park return inland along Holy Well Lane, passing the entrance to the North Yorkshire Outdoor Centre on the right. In about 20m turn R into a walled green lane. This is Pigeon Cote Lane which rises over the narrow isthmus with no sign of the cote and descends to the eastern shore by a small pebble beach. An old finger post points left but we turn R along the fringe of the shore (take care, the rocks are slippery if wet), until a sloping path to the right enters the wood. This stretch can be awkward when the marsh is covered by the tide but is short and it is worth persevering.

A stone stoop, with a half red/half blue oblong sign, is partly hidden in a dog rose bush but it serves to confirm the spot where we leave the shore and take a higher parallel path in the wood.

This is a delightful part of the walk. *Gnarled oak trees make a perfect frame for views of the estuary's silken sands and the misty wooded slopes of Arnside Knott reflected in the lingering tide.*

At the edge of the wood cross a stile and continue in the same direction across the field. The seaward fence has three stiles but unless you have a special reason to venture onto the cliff edge pass them by. As progress is made along the field, height is gradually gained and the vista expands until suddenly Humphrey Head Point is reached. A stile allows access onto a spiny extremity of the headland which stretches into the sea. The inshore sand is firm and a short excursion to the end of the point is rewarded with fine retrospective views of the cliffs, but beware, **it is dangerous to venture further out onto the sands or into the channels**.

From the stile go up the slope to the triangulation point 172 feet. From here a fine 360° view can be enjoyed. Continue northwards heading for the L-hand edge of the wood (ignore a gate on the left in the cliff edge fence). The path descends gently to the NCC Outdoor Centre. Keep to the L of its fence and at the road bear L down to Holy Well lane. Turn L to return to the car park.

At low tide it is possible to walk from the car parking along the sands at the base of the cliffs to the Point. Note the fine natural arch high in the cliffs. Where the shallow water channel comes close to the rocks it is possible to remain dry shod by scrambling over the rocks. There is a steep 12-foot scramble to a shelf with a perched block and another traverse of a steep slab beyond. Carved into the rocks near the base of the crags is this warning verse.

> 'Beware how you these rocks ascend
> Here WILLIAM PEDDER met his end
> August 22nd 1857, aged 10 years'

Note: *Do not be tempted to extend the circuit of Humphrey Head by beginning the walk at Kents Bank station. Whilst the walk begins pleasantly enough along the sea wall with magnificent views, it is soon necessary to traverse the shore below the railway embankment which hides the sewage works. The mud underfoot, if disturbed, releases foul odours which linger longer in the mind than on the boots and spoil the pleasure of an otherwise beautiful area.*

The sands between Humphrey Head and Kents Bank are being taken over by Spartina Angelica grass. In winter oystercatchers come to roost in thousands, together with grey lag geese, wigeon and teal.

Humphrey Head with Edgar's Arch on the left

WALK 60: Cartmel and the Ellerside Ridge

The historic village of Cartmel

SUMMARY: This walk should really be classed as 'beyond the limestone fringe' for it traverses a long ridge of Silurian slate, between the Leven Estuary and the shallow valley of Cartmel. There were problems here for a while, particularly with the linking path to Speel Bank which is on the Council's Definitive Map as a Right-of-Way but not on the OS map. The steps of the stile were smashed to deter walkers, do not let this put you off. The walk traverses some lovely country, an attractive mix of woodland, rough fell, ancient bridleways, and outstanding views from the Ellerside ridge.

The village of Cartmel, justly famed for its historic priory and horse race meeting, is a tourist honey pot, with pubs, cafes, book and gift shops.

HOW TO GET THERE AND PARKING: Reach Cartmel from the A590 either through Grange or by a signed road which leaves the A590 north west of Lindale. Go through the centre of the village to park by the race course.

Distance:	9 miles 14¹/₂ km
	2¹/₂ miles extension to Bigland Barrow
	6³/₄ miles by Short Return
Grade:	Moderate
Terrain:	Valley and Low Fell
Maps:	PF 626 PF 636

THE WALK: Go through the car park and along the unmade road which continues into parkland. At once tracks branch left and right but keep straight ahead through smooth meadow fringed with mature woodland. *It is difficult to imagine the annual eruption when this mellow, tranquil scene is suddenly transformed into the vibrant, vivid throng of the race meeting.* Cross the racecourse, go through a gate and ahead passing the rather derelict buildings of Seven Acres Farm. The next gate carries a warning of adders. Do not freeze on the spot but turn R along the fieldside on the remains of an old track. On reaching the woods the track becomes walled and in use. Go straight on through a gate and over the bridge spanning Burns Beck, a noisy little stream rushing on its way to join the River Eea.

Pause and look around for we have now entered a secluded vale with Walton Hall Farm in a picturesque setting. *Walk slowly along for the hedgerows are a delight. Pink campions and wine coloured foxgloves are a few of the seasonal flowers tempting a wealth of summer butterflies.* The track crosses the stream and continues to the farmyard where an old pump occupies pride of place. Go between the house and the barn winding R then L to reach the surfaced road. (Footpath sign pointing back to Mere Beck.)

Turn L up the quiet road for a short distance then branch L on the Cistercian Way (a long distance footpath from Grange to Ulverston and Furness Abbey), also signed Public Bridleway Mount Barnard ½. Cross the stream and proceed up the rise past Hill Mill House. From here look at the view down the valley and out to sea before we enter the wood at an "adder" gate and in 20yds take the R branch. *Do not be worried, we have never seen any adders and if there are any, they will retreat in haste at the vibration of your footfall. You will however see bluebells in spring, be enchanted by the sunlight dancing through the branches and surrounded by birdsong.* At the top of a rise keep ahead ignoring a path joining from the right. Continue to the edge of the wood then go through the exit gate and turn R along a walled track. *The track is edged with gorse and has an open view over the fields to Morecambe Bay and the square shape of the nuclear power station at Heysham.* Soon the track is enclosed by forest and has a damp atmosphere. Make straight for the gate at the far end. (Sign CCW) You are now on the fell pasture having gained height, almost imperceptibly, with the hump of Howbarrow, its triangulation point among its summit rocks, rising just ahead.

Aim diagonally across the fell towards the electricity pole striking a path coming from the gate in the wall on the left. *There is a rock to sit on and look west to the Leven Estuary spanned by the railway embankment carrying the line to Ulverston. The little island in the estuary is Chapel Island*

Bend R on the path then left along the wallside. (Do not follow the Public Footpath sign to Burns Farm.) Go gently uphill through the gate in the fence. In 50 yards ignore the fork R waymarked CCW which keeps by the

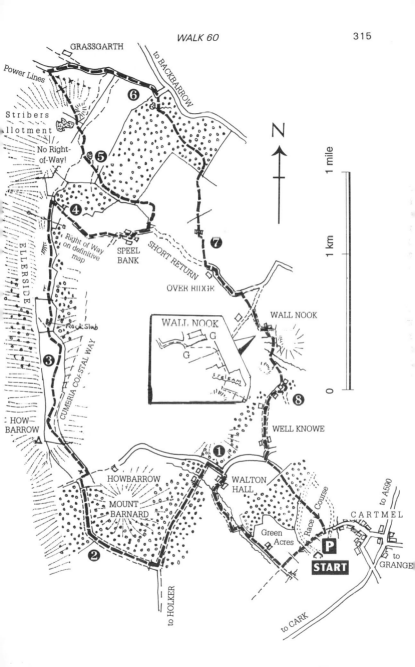

View from the Ellerside Ridge to the Coniston mountains

wall. and follow the main track up to the gate in the wall. (Unfortunately there is no right of way to Howbarrow summit 170m which is through the gate and off to the left.) Turn R along the wall for 100yds then gradually veer right away from the wall, there are a variety of wheeltracks around, to arrive at a gate in the right-hand corner of the next cross wall. *As you go do not miss the extensive vistas of southern Lakeland and on a clear day, the distinctive plateau of Ingleborough on the eastern horizon.* You are now on the Ellerside Ridge. Go through the gate bend L of an intermittent reedy pool then on a slight descent by a long, low, scarred rockbar. (Ignore the prominent vehicle track leading left over the brow.) The path becomes clearer and runs parallel to a wall and we can pick out the shapes of the Coniston mountains on the skyline ahead. (Over the wall at a distance and to the right is the farm of Speel Bank which we visit later.) Keep by the wall to a gate in a crosswall Straight on again past a larger scarred rockface with rowan trees to a col where you are halted by the view. *The woodland below on the left is the nature reserve of Roudsea Wood.* Continue by the wall under the electricity wire to the next gate near a yellow topped gas pole . The line of the obvious route we have been following continues through the next field and up the rise beyond. Due to some quirk in the map making the right of way ends here, then carries on at the top of the rise, so the next two gates were barred and we must make a detour passing Speel Bank Farm on another footpath to regain the onward route.

The old stile on the right has been vandalised on our side of the wall so go through the gate and turn R through the adjacent gate to gain the field Proceed down the field past the remains of a broken cross-wall. Keep parallel to a broken wall through two pastures then beside the fence to gates into the farm lane. This section can be rather spongy. Turn L by the stables and barn. *You may see a herd of red deer in the fields.* Join the surfaced road for 100yds or so then branch L on a track through a gate.

SHORT RETURN Carry on along the surfaced lane to meet the longer route at Over Ridge.

TO CONTINUE At first the surface is rather bovine but quickly improves as it climbs in a circle back on itself above the farmhouse and deer enclosure to a forest gate. Onward now between the wall and the fence on a path which climbs steadily to emerge on the open fell.

There are many tracks and paths around but the route has now been waymarked. Straight ahead to join another track then bend R between a boulder and a rock sprouting an oak tree. Go up the rise (ignore track on right parallel to the wood) and keep L of a small tarn. Continue up the rise and meet the non-right of way ridge path again. Turn R then on to a wall where we bend R to walk beside it to a gate. Go through into Stribers Allotment, another short-turfed enclosed area on the same wide ridge. Keep ahead now until meeting a cross path above a tarn. Turn right and on to go through a gate in a fence. Now we meet an abandoned bulldozer. Do not be drawn to its funereal path but bear L towards a shapely tree, also a skeleton but a signal that the climb is done. Stay to the right of the tree and freewheel down the path to a gate in a fence and on to the surfaced road. Turn R and a few yards down the road is the cottage of Grassgarth.

EXTENSION TO BIGLAND BARROW From this point Walk 37 can be followed in reverse to Bigland Hall, Bigland Barrow and Black Beck Tarn. An additional distance of 2½ miles (see map page 202)

TO CONTINUE Keep on the road for ½ml. *The road is quiet and the Outley Mosses provide a complete change of scene. Orchids and cotton grass provide a bright contrast to the black water reflecting the primeval shapes of the mare's tails.* When the road begins to rise look for a Public Bridleway sign into a plantation on the right.

Extension from Bigland Barrow rejoins here.

Go into the dark archway and on across Great Allotment. Pass through a clearing with a little tarn then through the trees once more. At a waymarked junction keep L and eventually the path leaves the trees to run between the edge of the forest and the fell wall to a gate with a wooden stile. There is not much indication of a path but just go ahead across the pasture and look for a gate with a waymark in the wall on the left. Keep ahead through the mud to a fine, new, waymarked gate between farm buildings. Exit the yard by the gate ahead/left and through the pasture to a metal gate giving access to an unmade road. Plain sailing now for a while passing clumps of gorse to meet a surfaced road where we turn L and, with the ridge of Hampsfell and its hospice providing an interesting skyline, descend the steep bend of Over Ridge.

SHORT RETURN joins here.

Pass by four old pines then look for a footpath sign hidden in the right hand hedgerow pointing to Wall Nook. Clamber through the stile into the field. The next stile to locate is in the far wall and is so thin that it is almost invisible to the naked eye. Look diagonally left for a set of pink chimneys peeping above the trees and home in towards them. Pinpoint the stile and squeeze through, then take the far track right by gas sign 21/22 to a gate giving access to a walled track. Bend R at Wall Nook cottages and go through the gate ahead (not the gate beyond the cottages) into a field. Trek diagonally up the field to the top corner and a stile. Keep straight across the pasture to the next stile, go over and look at the way ahead. There is a little depression with a tiny stream. Go diagonally R to cross the stream and through a broken down gateway with a redundant stile in the wall to

its left. Now turn L by the wall and cross a stile over the wire fence. Go straight ahead towards the chimneys of a cottage. The gate is on the left of the house. Go between the house and the stable then R

*Narrow
stile near
Cartmel*

across the front of the garden. Discover a narrow enclosed path leading R to a gate behind a cottage. Carry on between the escaped raspberries and straight down the access track passing a graveyard of abandoned vehicles and Well Knowe to the road.

The character of the land changes again as we turn R along the road and round the bend to a Public Footpath sign to Cartmel. This directs the way into a cultivated field. Tread close by the left edge of the crop and up a grass bank to a stile into the wood. There are paths everywhere in this popular woodland so go straight ahead on the main path through the trees which eventually winds steeply down to a kissing gate at the racetrack. Cross the track and bear slightly right across the park to the start. Now you can have that welcome drink in the village.

Cartmel

A picturesque village which contains a wealth of interesting buildings, a square, several small art galleries and bookshops, a gatehouse, and dominating all, the Priory founded in 1188. Don't miss seeing the wonderful carvings of faces on the oak misericords, which display both skill and humour.

✳   ✳   ✳

SELECTED BIBLIOGRAPHY OF USEFUL REFERENCE BOOKS

Coniston Copper - A History - Eric G. Holland *Cicerone*

Coniston Copper, A Field Guide - Eric G. Holland *Cicerone*

The Cumbria Village Book - Cumbria Federation of Women's Institutes
    CFWI & Countryside Books

The Industrial Archaeology of The Lake Counties - J.D. Marshall &
    M. Davies-Shiel *David & Charles*

The Lake Counties - W.G. Collingwood *J.M. Dent & Sons Ltd.*

The Lake District - Michael Dunn *David & Charles*

The Lake District - R. Millward & A. Robinson *Eyre Methuen*

The Lake District - W.H.Pearsall and W.Pennington *Collins New Naturalist
    Series*

Lakeland Villages - Jim Watson *Cicerone*

Lost Lancashire - A.L.Evans *Cicerone*

The Naturalist in Lakeland - Eric Hardy *David & Charles*

The Priory of Cartmel - Dr. J.C.Dickinson *Cicerone*

Three Westmorland Rivers - A Wainwright *Westmorland Gazette*

PRINTED BY CARNMOR PRINT & DESIGN, PRESTON, UK